Better Homes and Gardens®

Herbs
Gardening Made Easy

Meredith Consumer Marketing
Des Moines, Iowa

CHAPTER ONE

All About Herbs

Herbs have been used for centuries to bring health, beauty, fragrance, and other benefits to homes and gardens.

6

The World of Herbs

Herbs have it all—interesting foliage, attractive flowers, and heady scents. Most thrive happily in a sunny spot, in the garden, or in containers.

Herbs come in many shapes, sizes, colors, and flavors. They vary in form from towering trees and spreading shrubs to climbing vines and creeping plants. This diverse plant category has one common trait: Herbs are the workhorses of the plant world. They play roles in the garden, kitchen, crafts room, and spa as well as having a long history of medicinal use.

Herbs are also easy to grow. Regardless of your climate and herbal interests, you'll find a wide range of species and varieties that complement your garden, excel in containers, and add edible beauty to your landscape. This book will help you discover the ancient and modern secrets of herbs. In the following pages, you'll find everything you need to grow and use these versatile plants.

Herb plant life cycles

Plants are categorized by their life cycle, and herbs fill all three categories: annual, biennial, and perennial.

Annual herbs, such as basil and cilantro, sprout, bloom, produce seed, and die—all in one season. These fast-growing plants are perfect for containers and window boxes, as well as for landscape edgings or flower borders. The more you clip and harvest, the more annual herbs continue to produce—a very profitable arrangement for the gardener and the plant.

Biennial herbs live and grow for two years. The first year the plant produces foliage; it overwinters and comes back the second year to flower and fruit, after which it dies. Biennial herbs include parsley, angelica, and caraway.

Perennial herbs last the longest—some for many years. They are ideal additions to landscapes, garden beds, borders, and containers. Perennial herbs include hardy species, such as oregano and chives, that can survive winters in cold climates. Tender perennials include rosemary and lavender, which return year after year in temperate regions. In general, perennials get bigger and better every year, making them economical as well as low-maintenance planting choices.

Using herb plants

Herb plants are useful from top to bottom. For most species, the leafy green parts can be used in preparing food or making tea. Dill, rosemary, and thyme are a few examples of leafy herbs commonly used fresh or dried in cooking. Some plants, such as lavender, borage, and bee balm, produce edible or usable flowers. Herbs that produce edible seeds include coriander, caraway, and dill. Herb stems are also employed: Rosemary stems are useful as grilling sticks, and sage stems release their fragrance when burned in a fireplace. Chicory and Florence fennel are grown for their flavorful roots.

Adding herbs to the garden

Most herb gardeners appreciate the plants for their versatility. There are herbs to suit any garden, whatever its size and style. Many herbs adapt to a wide range of climates. Most herbs require a sunny location, but some species thrive in partial shade. While they come in a wide palette of leaf shapes and textures, most herbs are leafy plants (herbaceous), and they grow in an array of hues, from gray to green to blue. Many herbs offer colorful blooming displays, including the showy flowers of lavender, anise hyssop, and bee balm.

opposite left A well-positioned herb garden allows you to snip and use herbs every day. A circular herb garden in a sunny spot outside a back door allows easy access. **opposite, top right** Feverfew is a perennial herb that grows about 2 feet tall and produces large quantities of small white daisylike flowers with yellow centers. **opposite, middle right** Lavender is one of the most popular herbs. Used in aromatic sachets, the leaves and flowers keep clothes smelling fresh and also help deter insects. **opposite, bottom right** Basil produces leaves that make flavorful pesto. Harvesting leaves from annual herbs such as this makes them produce more growth.

Herbal Roles

Herbs do more than flavor food. They have been used for centuries for medicinal and aromatherapy applications, as well as for clothing dyes.

Most of us are introduced to herbs through food. What would Italian cuisine be without the flavor of oregano? Can you imagine French dishes sans tarragon or rosemary? And would Thai and Vietnamese specialties taste the same without lemongrass or holy basil? Herbs have a long history of other uses, too. Consider their multitude of talents:

Culinary herbs

Ethnic cuisines and a revived interest in locally grown whole foods have introduced a wide variety of herbs to cooks and food fans. Fresh and dried herbs offer distinctive flavors that enhance foods in healthful ways. Herbs often top lists of healthful foods because they add flavor without adding empty calories, fat grams, or scads of sodium. That's why people who love natural flavors, as well as those on restricted diets, turn to herbs to add great taste to their food.

Raising herbs for culinary use allows gardeners and chefs to experience herbs at their peak of freshness and to experiment with seasonings that may not be readily available otherwise. Growing culinary herbs provides you with a source of delicacies as well as essentials that can be preserved for year-round staples. Many herb species include varieties that produce different flavors and aromas within the herb's spectrum. For example, thyme comes in many varieties with different flavors; lemon thyme tastes and smells distinctively different from common thyme. Growing herbs in a kitchen garden or containers allows you to enjoy their freshness and flavors while keeping them within easy reach.

Dying herbs

For centuries herbs colored our world through yarn and fabric dyes. Natural dyes can be made from various herbs—and from different parts of the plants: leaves, flowers, stems, and roots. Yellow dye is made from chamomile and yarrow. Brown hues come from comfrey, fennel, and juniper berries. Green dye can be made from rosemary and hyssop. Russets and reds, harder to produce, come from St. John's wort and dandelion root. The most difficult dye colors to create—blue and purple—can be made from hibiscus and violet flowers.

Crafting herbs

Fresh herbs make edible floral arrangements; just set them in the center of a table, and clip off tasty leaves and flowers. Dried herbs can be fashioned into wreaths and swags. Sachets blended with the fragrant charms of lavender, scented geranium, and rosemary add fragrance to drawers and closets while keeping insects at bay. Crafters of soaps, lotions, and skin- and hair-care concoctions use herbal essential oils.

SAFETY FIRST!

The science of phytotherapy involves treating illnesses with plants or materials derived from plants. Herbalists have been doing this for centuries. But the knowledge needed to use herbs medicinally is complex. Consequently, it is not recommended that you make your own medicines from herbs. Any references to the historical use of a plant in this book should not be construed as medical advice. You can, however, use herbs in a variety of healthful and restorative ways. Always take care to test a new herb by using a small quantity, whether in food or applied to skin. Understanding what herbs do, how they work, and how you react to them is the commonsense way to use them safely.

Aromatherapy herbs

Herbalists use herbal scents in a form of alternative medicine called aromatherapy. Essential oils, or pure essences extracted from herbs, are used to alter a person's moods, alleviate physical symptoms, and provide healthful side effects. Essential oils are made from herbs using various methods, including steam distillation. There are many practical uses for these essences: in the environment, in products such as room sprays or sachets for clothing; for inhalation, such as steeping herbs in hot water and breathing the steam to alleviate chest congestion; and for direct application, in products such as bath salts, compresses, and massage oils.

The scents of some herbs also have repelling qualities. Plants containing phenols, naphthalene, pyrethrum, and citronella are natural insect repellents, keeping flying and crawling pests away from people and possessions. It's no surprise that these same chemical components are part of the pest repellents used today, whether replicated synthetically or derived naturally. Our ancestors used wormwood to deter moths and flies, rue to control Japanese beetles, and tansy to repel moths and ants.

Medicinal herbs

Herb gardens have long been nature's pharmacy. Ancient physicians turned to native plants to remedy illness and improve health. For almost every illness, there was an herbal remedy: Insomnia was treated with chamomile; migraine headache sufferers were prescribed feverfew; asthma was assuaged with mullein; and nausea was eased with a dose of basil. Plant parts were brewed into teas and ingested internally or mashed into poultices and applied externally. No doubt, this trial-and-error method of treatment resulted in a wide range of effects.

But herbal medicine wasn't a precise science, and some herbs historically used have now been proven ineffective, baseless, toxic, or even deadly.

right It was common practice in ancient times to use flowers, stems, leaves, and roots of plants to treat the body.

America's Herbal History

Modern herbs are steeped in ancient history. But if you step into a health food store or the pharmacy section of your local grocery, you see their modern use.

As the saying goes, "What's old is new again." It is also said that St. John's wort lifts your spirits, chamomile helps you sleep, and ginkgo improves your memory. Herbs, it seems, are a hot new health trend, even though many of today's remedies have been used for centuries.

Colonial herbal history

Modern herb use started centuries ago. America's herbal pioneers, like their ancient predecessors, gained plant-use knowledge from many sources. The herbs used in the Colonial United States had roots in two cultures: Europe's and America's. The settlers brought knowledge of herbs with them from England, and Native Americans introduced them to their native herbs.

Native Americans shared indigenous herbs such as sage, sassafras, and tobacco with the colonists. In 1672, John Josselyn published *New England's Rarities Discovered*, a book that resulted from eight years of herbal research into Native Americans' use of plants. Throughout New England, housewives kept kitchen gardens that fed their families and produced herbs for seasonings, food processing, medicines, and household chores, such as cleaning and dying fibers. A kitchen garden was a way to be self-sufficient in a new land.

America's oldest botanical garden

America's oldest living botanical garden, in Philadelphia, was created by John Bartram in 1728. Bartram, a Quaker farmer, included varieties from old-world apothecary gardens as well as new plants native to North America. New-world herbs included bee balm (*Monarda didyma*), black snakeroot (*Cimicifuga racemosa*), and American ginseng (*Panax quinquefolius*). Today Bartram's Garden is a living museum and garden where you can follow the steps of famous visitors such as Thomas Jefferson and Benjamin Franklin. It features various theme gardens, including a kitchen garden with raised beds of herbs and vegetables. Like the kitchen gardens of its time, the herbs grown in Bartram's Garden have culinary, medicinal, and household uses.

The science of herbs

In the early 19th century, scientists became able to chemically analyze plants. Understanding herbs and extracting their properties led to the discovery of plants' active ingredients. Eventually scientists learned to modify plant ingredients, making their own versions of plant compounds. Thus, modern drugs replaced herbal remedies—at least in the United States. According to the World Health Organization, 80 percent of the worldwide population still uses herbal medicines. The high cost of prescription drugs, coupled with a renewed interest in natural remedies, has increased medicinal herb use in the United States.

WHAT'S IN A NAME?

Many herbs still bear common names that tell the stories of their past use: Lungwort was used to treat pulmonary infections; feverfew treated fevers or head ailments; and soapwort was used to clean household items.

The Latin name also reveals a plant's story The botanical name of an herb consists of two parts: a genus and a species. This naming system was invented by Carl Linnaeus, a Swedish botanist and zoologist known as the father of modern taxonomy. The naming system is the same for all living things. For example, the genus and species for humans is *Homo sapiens*.

Here's how it works: The genus is a closely related group. The name always begins with a capital letter and is written in italics. The second part of a plant name, the species, is written after the genus and is also italicized. For example, *Lavandula* is the genus of lavender. *Lavandula* has dozens of species. *Lavandula angustifolia* is English lavender, *Lavandula stoechas* is Spanish lavender, and *Lavandula dentata* is French lavender. These species reflect similarities to the genus *Lavandula* but bear distinct differences—enough to make each an identifiably different plant.

A species can be further divided into varieties (also called cultivars or cultivated varieties). These are plants created through natural mutation, plant selection by breeders, or hybridization. Cultivars of lavender include 'Provence', 'Hidcote', and 'Silver Cross'.

top Bartram's Garden in Philadelphia is the oldest botanical garden in the United States. The living museum of plants includes a kitchen garden with medicinal and culinary herbs cultivated in the 18th century and growing there now. **right** An especially fragrant English lavender hybrid is *Lavandula* × *intermedia* 'Provence'. **far right** Bee balm, also known as bergamot, is an herb that's an American native.

Traditional Gardens

As far back as medieval times, herb gardens provided plants for medicines, restoratives, and cooking.

Today anyone with a spot of ground or a container and bag of potting soil can have an herb garden. But herb gardens didn't used to be so egalitarian. In medieval times, traditional herb gardens were cultivated by the educated and the wealthy. The study of herbs and their powers became a science.

Cloister gardens

In medieval times, herb gardens were tended by monks and called cloister gardens. These gardens were an integral part of the monastery and served as a way to feed the brothers and provide a place of work, solitude, and prayer. Cloister gardens sometimes also provided an income for the monastery. Herbs played a role in making spirit-base drinks that were used as medicines and restoratives.

Benedictine monks in France created the liqueur Benedictine in 1510. This cognac-base drink, originally formulated to treat malaria, is made with fruit peels and more than 25 herbs that include angelica, coriander, fennel, hyssop, tansy, mint, and thyme. Chartreuse, another French herb-base liqueur, has been made by Carthusian monks since the 1740s. This light green liqueur continues to be made using a secret recipe of more than 130 herbal extracts.

Physic gardens

Gardens cultivated for their healing and restorative powers were called physic gardens. They were, in practice, the first pharmacies. The Chelsea Physic Garden in London, the oldest surviving garden of its type, was founded in 1673. First called the Apothecaries' Garden, it was a training ground and laboratory for medical apprentices.

Physic gardens weren't created to be pretty. Their aesthetics were driven by practicality and use. Beds were labeled by botanical classification and arranged by area of specialization. For instance, the Chelsea Physic Garden has a pharmaceutical garden that displays plants by specific cures. The oncology bed features numerous anticancer plants including Madagascar periwinkle (*Catharanthus roseus*), a plant that contains alkaloids used in anticancer drugs.

Potager gardens

Kitchen gardens, called *jardins potagers* or potager gardens by the French, were an aesthetic way to raise vegetables, fruits, and flowers. Herbs had their own place in the potager. The Renaissance-era potager could be large or small. The design, as one might see on a large estate, could be elaborate, laid out in geometric patterns with shrubs, flowers, and trees amid the vegetables and herbs.

BHG TEST GARDEN TIP — REDEFINING WEEDS

There were no weeds in original herb gardens. All plants had value, even those now considered weeds. Some of the modern weeds gardeners grapple with today, such as thistles, which have medicinal value, were welcome participants in herb gardens of the past. When planning and planting your herb garden, you might find yourself more liberal in selecting plants, perhaps including ones you once considered weeds.

left A knot garden can include herbs and flowers. Here, agastache, tricolor sage, basil, and ornamental cabbage surround a bougainvillea standard (tree form). **above** Anise hyssop was used traditionally to relieve coughing. Native Americans used it as a breath freshener. **below** A potager garden often features walls that protect the garden from weather and grazing animals. The walls also create microclimates that allow more tender plants to grow.

GARDENING MADE EASY **HERB GARDENING**

Classic Gardens

The shape and form of traditional herb gardens were dictated by how they were used. Knots, circles, and squares were common designs.

Most herb gardens of the past followed a formal design. Physic, cloister, potager, and knot gardens were designed for specific uses so the people harvesting the plants would not confuse them. The gardens could be viewed overall as a patterned, symmetrical whole, while individual beds contained herbs designated for specific purposes, such as foods, medicines, or dyes. Squares, rectangles, and circles were standard shapes within the formal gardens' designs.

Paths were part of traditional herb garden design—for both utility and symmetry. Pathway materials included small pebbles or gravel, crushed shells, mulched plant material, or low-growing, treadable groundcovers, such as thyme.

Knot gardens

This formal garden concept was established in England during the reign of Queen Elizabeth I, coming into vogue at the time Shakespeare was penning plays. The framework of a knot garden is square or circular. It can be edged with boxwood, germander, lavender, santolina, or other shrubby herbs pruned into neat shapes, such as squared edges, pyramids, or rounded mounds. A knot garden may feature multiple beds or compartments within the outer framework.

A knot garden depends on the patterned combination of plants in repeated forms. Plants are set out to follow lines and fill in areas, giving the garden a sense of movement and continuity. The shapes intertwine, which is how the knot garden gets its name.

opposite The pleasing symmetry of this knot garden comes from the patterned plantings of lavender, boxwood, germander, and red barberry.

PLANT A KNOT GARDEN

Plants used in a knot garden may include aromatic, culinary, and ornamental herbs; for example: germander, marjoram, winter savory, thyme, southernwood, purple basil, globe basil, rosemary, and santolina.

1 DRAW THE OUTLINE
Measure and mark off the area for a square in a sunny area. Remove sod, if present. Use a can of spray paint to mark the outline of the square garden edges. Within the square, outline a circle.

2 PLANT THE EDGES
Using plants of your choice (contrasting colors work best), plant the inner circle outline. Then plant the edges of the square. Position the plants close together to make the garden look more full. The spacing of plants depends on the species you use. Check plant tags for mature widths.

3 FILL IN THE BEDS
Plant the interior of the herb bed circle. Then plant the triangular beds created by the circle in a contrasting color. (There will be four triangles.) Water each plant deeply after planting. Spread a 2-inch layer of mulch among plants; mulching means you'll need to water less. Choose a mulch color that complements the plant colors. As a final touch, create a focal point by placing a potted herb, such as a topiary rosemary, in the center of the bed.

4 NIP AND TUCK
Herbs such as lavender and sage grow quickly in hot weather. Trim plants regularly to keep their shapes as they grow.

BHG TEST GARDEN TIP — EDIBLE EDGING
Use alpine strawberries, curlyleaf parsley, or fast-growing, shrubby 'Spicy Globe' basil for edible edging plants in a knot garden.

ALL ABOUT HERBS

left Modern herb gardens can feature traditional elements such as topiary and organized raised beds. **above** Add herbs to your garden for their textural and color appeal. Gray-leaf lavender, two-tone sage, and small-leaf thyme add three levels of texture as well as subtle color variations. Planting herbs en masse heightens the appeal. **below** Lavender, rose, mint, and rosemary begin the list of fragrant plants most useful for homemade bath salts and other delightful concoctions.

Modern Gardens

Modern herb gardens can take whatever shape that is pleasing to the gardener. Let use guide the design.

Modern herb gardening is all about you as a gardener and a lover (and user) of herbs. Unlike herb gardeners of the past, you can grow herbs as a supplement to a natural lifestyle and not depend on them for medicines and household products. Herbs can enhance your life rather than sustain it. Nothing says you have to plant every herb in this book. Instead, create an herb garden that reflects your lifestyle, your penchant for flowers, and your hobbies that include any of herbs' many facets, from preserving food to crafting.

Go formal or casual

An herb garden can be aesthetic, utilitarian, or both. You can follow a traditional herb garden plan that is highly organized, symmetrical, and even historical, including plants from a specific era or theme (such as a Shakespearean or biblical herb garden). You can adopt a more utilitarian approach and plant a kitchen garden where herbs rub shoulders with vegetables and fruits. Herbs can easily be grown in containers—alone or in combination with other plants. By all means, add herbs to flower gardens as planting partners with perennials and annuals. Tuck them into rock gardens or crevices in walls, or amid the paving stones or bricks in a pathway. Attract butterflies, bees, and hummingbirds to your yard with an herb garden made to sustain them. That's the beauty of modern herb gardening: There's no right or wrong way to do it. Whatever your goal—fresh herbs, dried herbs, herbs for cocktails or creative projects—you can plan and plant an herb garden that will fulfill your needs.

Personalize your herb garden design

Think about size. Although herbs are a fairly easy-care group of plants, you should avoid committing yourself to a garden you can't maintain—one that is too large or too complicated. Choose herbs that appeal to you based on their appearance and how you will use them. Fit planting, maintenance, and harvesting into your daily life.

Let your palate guide you

If you love Italian cuisine, pack your herb garden with the traditional herbs essential to the recipes: basil, oregano, rosemary, and fennel. If your family likes to spice it up with south-of-the-border dishes, plant hot peppers, cilantro, and Mexican oregano. If you want to raise fresh, organic herbs for teas, plant chamomile, bee balm, and mint. And if crafting is your hobby, plant herbs you can use dried or fresh to make wreaths and sachets—lavender, artemisia, and roses.

BHG TEST GARDEN TIP

YOUR NOSE KNOWS

Fragrance is a big draw for herb fanciers. Herbs that release their perfume with a simple touch include scented geraniums, mint, and rosemary. Even if you never harvest a leaf, flower, or stem, a scented herb garden can be a place of peace for you at the end of a long day. Just sitting amid the fragrances of an herb garden provides powerful relief from stress.

Grow Your Garden

Most herbs are easy to grow, and they'll thrive without much attention. But they do have preferences for light, water, and soil.

Plant in sun

Most herbs are sun lovers, requiring about six to eight hours of light a day. This allows them to grow vigorously and produce ample leaves, flowers, and seeds for harvest. Some herbs, however, such as mint and sweet woodruff, thrive in shady locations.

Soil options

Site your herb beds in an area with well-draining soil. If the soil doesn't drain well, work in organic material such as compost, chopped leaves, and other natural amendments. Herbs that sit in soggy soil may succumb to root rot and fail to thrive. If your soil is too difficult to amend (such as heavy clay), build raised beds and add custom-blended soil (a mix of organic topsoil and compost works well). Or plant your herbs in containers.

Annual herbs generally like richer soil with lots of moisture to help in leaf development. Leafy annuals such as basil and cilantro are perfect planting companions for vegetables, which are also annuals and need plenty of moisture for fruit development. That's why you'll find basil and tomatoes planted together or summer savory paired with green beans.

above left New materials offer herb gardeners a variety of options. A raised bed made with commercially available interlocking wall stones makes for easy and long-lasting construction. **left** Most herbs do best in well-drained soil. If your soil is too sandy, add organic matter. Clay soil is dense and drains slowly; amend it with coarse sand, perlite, and organic matter.

Pests and disease

Keeping any plant healthy is one of the best ways to protect it from pests and disease. Even so, most herbs aren't bugged by insects. This is because herbs have a natural immunity against insect infestations. The concentration of essential oils that makes the plants flavorful and fragrant also protects herbs from most insect attacks. Those same qualities are also why many herbal compounds are used as insect repellents.

The presence of herbs in the garden also helps repel insects that may be interested in other plants. This is why herbs make excellent companion plants in vegetable and flower gardens. Herbs can benefit the garden in several ways: They can deter bad insects, attract good insects, and enhance the flavors of the plants growing around them. For example, dill helps repel squash bugs while attracting important pollinating insects such as honeybees. Garlic, leeks, and onions stave off aphids from attaching to surrounding plants.

Some apparent pests are, on closer examination, insects you might want to welcome. For example, parsley and fennel are host plants for the larvae of butterflies such as Monarchs and Swallowtails. If you want to encourage a healthy, wildlife-friendly garden, plant extras of these plants so these caterpillars can make themselves at home.

THE EASIEST OF THE EASY

These herbs require little upkeep. Just plant them and wait for an abundance at harvesttime.

Annuals

1. BASIL Plants produce aromatic, flavorful leaves. Pinch back flower heads to produce more leaves.
2. PARSLEY Curly or flat-leaf varieties are delicious used fresh or in cooking.
3. DILL Thin, ferny leaves add fresh flavor to soups, salads, and fish.
4. CILANTRO Harvest early and often before hot weather makes this annual bolt (develop seeds).
5. SCENTED GERANIUMS Grown as annuals in cold climates, the aromatic plants suit Zone 8–11 gardens as perennials.

Perennials

6. SAGE The broad gray-green leaves of this drought-tolerant plant enhance almost any garden.
7. CHIVES Clip the young tender stems for use in cooking. The spring blooms are edible, too.
8. THYME The upright or creeping plants feature tiny, aromatic leaves and flowers.
9. MINT Available in a range of flavors—spearmint, peppermint, apple mint—it's great for summer drinks.
10. FEVERFEW Two-foot-tall plants offer finely cut foliage and daisylike flowers.

ALL ABOUT HERBS

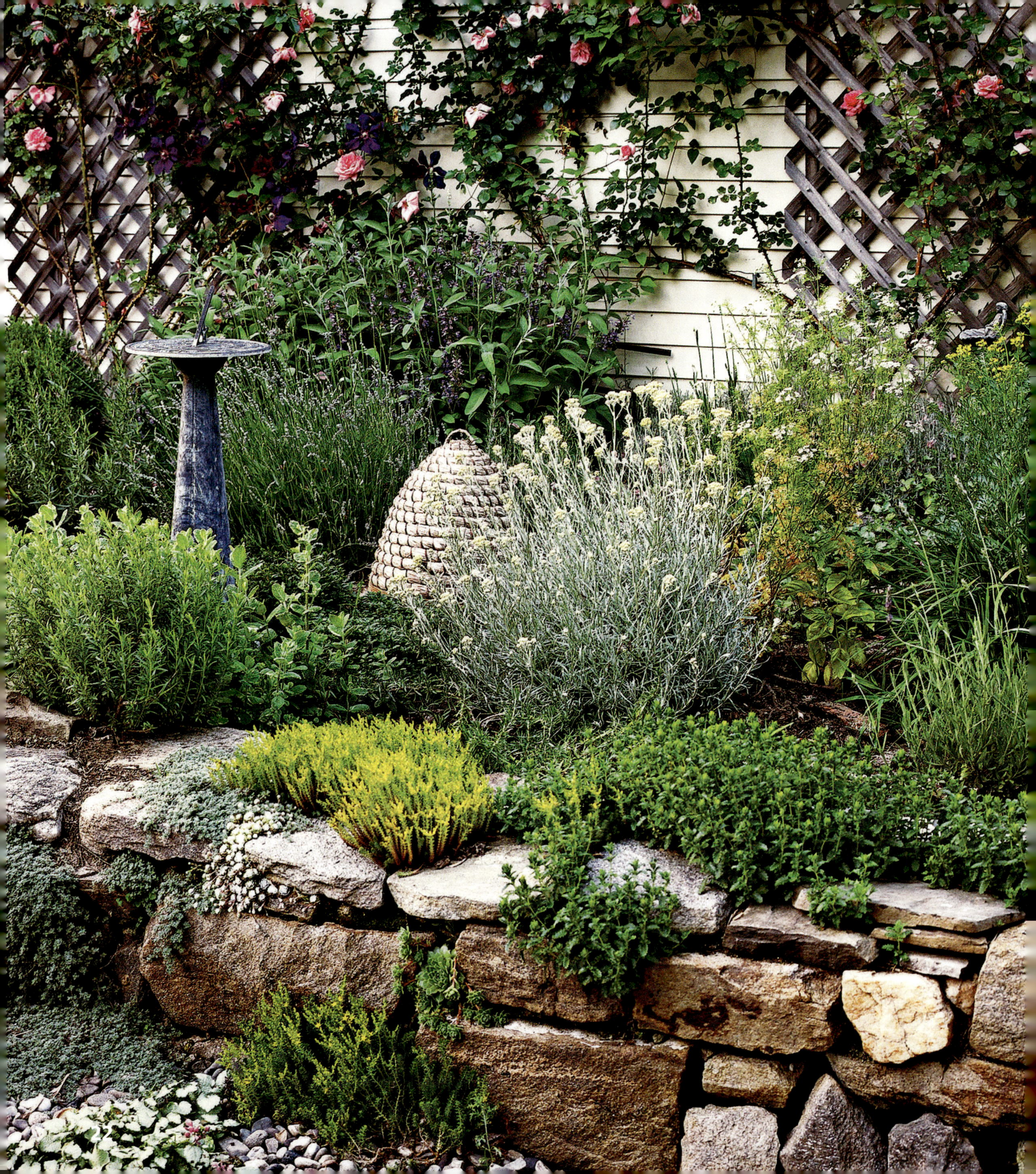

Herbs in the Landscape

Tuck herbs into beds, borders, and landscapes so you can enjoy their scents everywhere in the yard and garden.

When it comes to herb gardening, think outside the bed. While it's tempting to put all your herbs together in one garden bed, they do nicely in other spots in the landscape. Herbs are versatile plants that can enhance a variety of landscape options.

Rock gardens

A rock garden is a handsome solution to several challenging landscape problems, such as eroding slopes, difficult-to-mow areas, and awkward grade changes. And because most herbs love hot, sunny locations and well-draining soil, they are good candidates for sunny-sited rock gardens. If you have a rocky slope in your yard, you can create a low-maintenance, natural-looking garden by adding herbs. (If you don't have a rocky area, you can create one by terracing with stone or making an outcropping of large and small rocks.) The nature of rock gardens—and the associated rocky and sandy soil that surround them—creates exactly the venue in which herbs excel. Lean-soil lovers include marjoram, rosemary, and winter savory. Ground-hugging forms of herbs suit rock gardens. Try prostrate rosemary or creeping varieties of thyme, oregano, and chamomile.

Adding herbs to a rock garden is easy. Using a narrow trowel, dig into a crevice between stones and, if there is enough soil, tuck in an herb. If no soil exists for a plant to get a roothold (even the scrappiest herbs need soil), add a couple trowelfuls of topsoil to create a planting pocket.

The stones in an herb garden can help spotlight a singular herb; a backdrop of rock helps define the plant's shape, leaf texture, or flower in the way a stage highlights a performer. Rock gardens can also accentuate and show off a plant's growth habit. Rock gardens provide a microclimate for plants, with stone heating the ground around plants as well as protecting them from weather extremes such as wind.

Vertical gardens

Herb gardens can go vertical when you add planting pockets to stone, brick, or concrete walls. Soften a retaining wall by inserting low-growing herbs into the wall, along the top (and cascading over), and as a frilly skirt at the base. In stone or paver walls, leave planting pockets for herbs such as thyme, rosemary, catmint, or chamomile.

opposite A stacked-stone wall provides nooks and crannies for water to drain from the soil, as well as planting pockets for herbs including thyme, lavender, and rue.

PLANT AN HERB-PACKED PATH

Create a fragrant path with creeping varieties of thyme, mint, pennyroyal, and chamomile.

1 WEED THE CRACKS
Instead of allowing weeds or turfgrass to creep into the cracks of a stone pathway, plant scented herbs instead. First, dig out weeds from the path using a trowel. (Hint: Make weed removal easier by watering the area first.)

2 ADD COMPOST
Amend the soil with compost to give the newly planted herbs a nutritious start. Herbs need well-drained soil, so add sand if the soil feels wet. Fill in any low spots between the stones with topsoil.

3 PLANT HERBS
Dig a planting hole around the edges of the stepping-stones. Remove an herb from its nursery pot, and tuck the root balls into the planting area. Make sure the plant's roots are entirely covered. (Hint: You may need to cut the herb in half or fourths to fit into small holes.) After planting, add additional soil if needed. Water newly planted herbs, and keep the soil damp (but not wet) until they are well-rooted. After that, water regularly when soil begins to dry to help plants become established.

4 TREAD LIGHTLY
Allow the herbs to take root and grow before walking on them. Within a few months, the plants will fill in between the stepping-stones. Clip them into shape when necessary.

ALL ABOUT HERBS

Edible Landscaping

Adding herbs to your yard lets you partake of a delicious trend: edible landscaping. Use herbs to replace turfgrass in lawn areas, and add them to flowerbeds.

Go green with an herbal lawn

Low-maintenance herbs can fill in large open areas or hard-to-mow places, and they can even serve as a lawn replacement. Creeping herbs quickly create a carpet of green foliage that has the added benefit of seasonal blooms. Thyme is a favorite landscaping plant because it's hardy and treadable, and it grows into a thick mat of foliage. Available in various foliage and flower colors, thyme is often planted along pathways or between stepping-stones. Creeping mint offers a vigorous and fragrant groundcover option. Mint even grows in partially shaded locations; this herb is so ambitious that it becomes invasive, so plant it in a contained area. Rosemary, especially a prostrate variety, is an excellent groundcover that bears blue flowers and gray-green foliage. Chamomile is a hardy perennial that excels in any location—from neutral to alkaline soil and full sun to part shade. It has pretty white, fragrant flowers that bloom from late spring until midsummer. The leaves of Roman chamomile are fragrant, too; this low-growing herb is an excellent option for turf replacement. Both economical and eco-friendly, an established herbal lawn reduces the need for fertilizer, watering, and mowing.

left Fill a front yard landscape with a mix of creeping and shrubby herbs. Choose hardy perennial herbs for low maintenance.

Mix herbs with flowers

Herbs with colored or textured leaves make excellent companions in flower gardens. Purple-leaf basil such as 'Red Rubin', variegated sage, and purple-flowering chives are as pretty as any ornamental annual or perennial. The colorful leaves of shiso (*Perilla*) can be used as an edible addition to pots or window boxes. Statuesque and ferny fennel, dill, and angelica add structure to a garden, rubbing shoulders with other tall perennials such as delphiniums, baptisia, and roses. Herbs can also be used as foils in a bed, highlighting other plants. For example, tansy offers ferny, dark green leaves that complement roses. Herbs and their interesting foliage can also be used in bouquets. Parsley, sage, and lemon balm offer beautiful foliage to enhance flowers in arrangements, and they have a long vase life.

Choose colorful herbal blooms

One of the tenets of good garden design is using color effectively. Although many herbs are predominantly leafy and green, they also come in hues of green, gray, blue, and yellow. Grow herbs for their flowers, too. For example, anise hyssop offers spires of pink, purple, or blue blooms that can be used in perennial gardens regardless of their herbal status. 'Golden Jubilee' offers lavender flowers and chartreuse foliage. Varieties of yarrow also feature colorful flower clusters.

Choose a color theme for your garden beds, and select herbs that flower in those hues. Plant herbal blooms in cool hues: blue, purple, and green; these flowers create a calming effect and make a garden feel larger. Warm colors—red, orange, and yellow—are dramatic and exciting and make the space feel smaller and more intimate. Repeat color themes throughout the garden to create a unified look. Aim for two or three colors; too many colors make the plantings feel busy.

HERB FLOWERS

Herbs can play an important and colorful role in your landscape. Color your garden with bright-blooming perennial and annual herbs.

Reds/Blues/Purples

1. BEE BALM This prairie native has frilly flowers that bloom in jewel tones of red, pink, and purple, as well as white. Zones 3–10
2. LAVENDER Beautiful purple-tone blooms top foliage that exudes fragrance on a sunny afternoon. Zones 5–10
3. BORAGE Sparkling periwinkle blue blooms dance at the tips of borage's fuzzy stems and leaves. Annual
4. CHIVES Chives grace the garden with bright green stems and pinkish-purple pom-pom blooms. Zones 3–10
5. CATMINT Sky blue flowers and silvery foliage look great most of the season. Shear plants for repeat blooms. Zones 3–8

Yellows/Oranges

6. CALENDULA Cool-season blooms come in cream, yellow, apricot, and orange. Flowers are edible. Annual
7. TANSY Bright yellow, buttonlike flowers appear throughout summer. Zones 3–9
8. CHAMOMILE Dainty daisylike blooms with yellow centers and white petals make a fragrant groundcover. Zones 4–9
9. DILL Producing yellow, airy umbels, dill's flower heads beckon butterflies, bees, and other beneficial bugs. Annual
10. MARIGOLD Frilly, tightly packed flowers top sturdy plants with elegant dark green foliage. Annual

ALL ABOUT HERBS

Adaptable Herbs

Herbs can add their fragrant charms to many places in your yard and garden, as long as you site them in a sunny spot.

Create surprising herbal delights everywhere in your yard: Creeping low, growing overhead, and everywhere in between, herbs boast an exuberance that's hard to contain.

Groundcovers

Herbs are superstars when used as groundcovers; left to their own devices they grow quickly and fill in open spaces. But many low-growing herbs can also be tapped for their landscape design talents. Inspired by checkerboards, a gridlike garden design uses commercially available paving stones mixed with herbs such as chamomile, thyme, or oregano. An herb checkerboard garden is ideal for a courtyard, entryway, or pathway. It can even be installed in a children's play area (you could adapt it to a hopscotch design), using some of the more treadable herbal options. To add color to the mix, use paving stones with alternating types of thyme, such as green- and gray-leaf varieties or thymes that bloom in different colors.

Overhead

Within the category of climbing plants, hops are most notable. Some varieties are grown especially for their flowering cones. A golden vining form is especially ornamental.

Green roofs featuring gardens planted with herbs and other plants are an eco-friendly gardening concept being adopted worldwide. These roofs absorb rainwater, prevent runoff, and control erosion. They also provide habitats for birds, butterflies, and bees, especially in urban areas. Many herbs are ideal for green roofs. Either sow herb seeds or plant small seedlings.

Herb-filled hanging baskets provide other ways to enjoy herbs in places where you'll use them the most: on patios and decks or near the kitchen. Many herbs, especially dwarf and creeping varieties, suit container culture. Plant hanging baskets with herbs that meet a specific culinary use: a taste of lemon (lemon thyme, lemon balm, and lemon basil), a salsa container (hot pepper, cilantro, and lime basil), or a pesto basket (small varieties of basil, cilantro, and parsley—all of which make lovely pestos).

Containers

Whether you are short on space or just like to have herbs close at hand, containers allow you to grow any kind of herb regardless of your soil conditions or climate. Even if you lack a sunny spot in your yard, you most likely have one on a porch or patio where sun-loving herbs can excel.

Tender and tropical plants, such as citrus and pineapple sage, can be grown in pots and taken indoors when the weather turns chilly. Any herb that you can grow in a garden can be grown in a pot. And a container may be the best place to grow invasive herbs such as mint.

Grow herbs in any type of container—terra-cotta, concrete, plastic, wood, or iron, for instance. You can even use found objects, such as old teakettles, vintage tins, or wooden dresser drawers. Just make sure there is a drainage hole in the bottom of the container, because herbs don't like wet feet.

opposite left A checkerboard of dense thyme plants interspersed with concrete stepping-stones makes an unexpected garden entrance. **opposite, top right** Curly parsley, an ideal leafy and lush edger, can be clipped for salads and other recipes. Another compact, edible edger is 'Spicy Globe' basil. **opposite, middle right** Herbs in containers, set right into the landscape, allow you to grow tender perennials such as large rosemaries even if you live in colder climates. You can whisk the plants indoors before frost. **opposite, bottom right** Although you might not think of herbs as candidates for baskets, hanging the plants overhead on porches and patios—near the kitchen and outdoor dining areas—makes delicious sense.

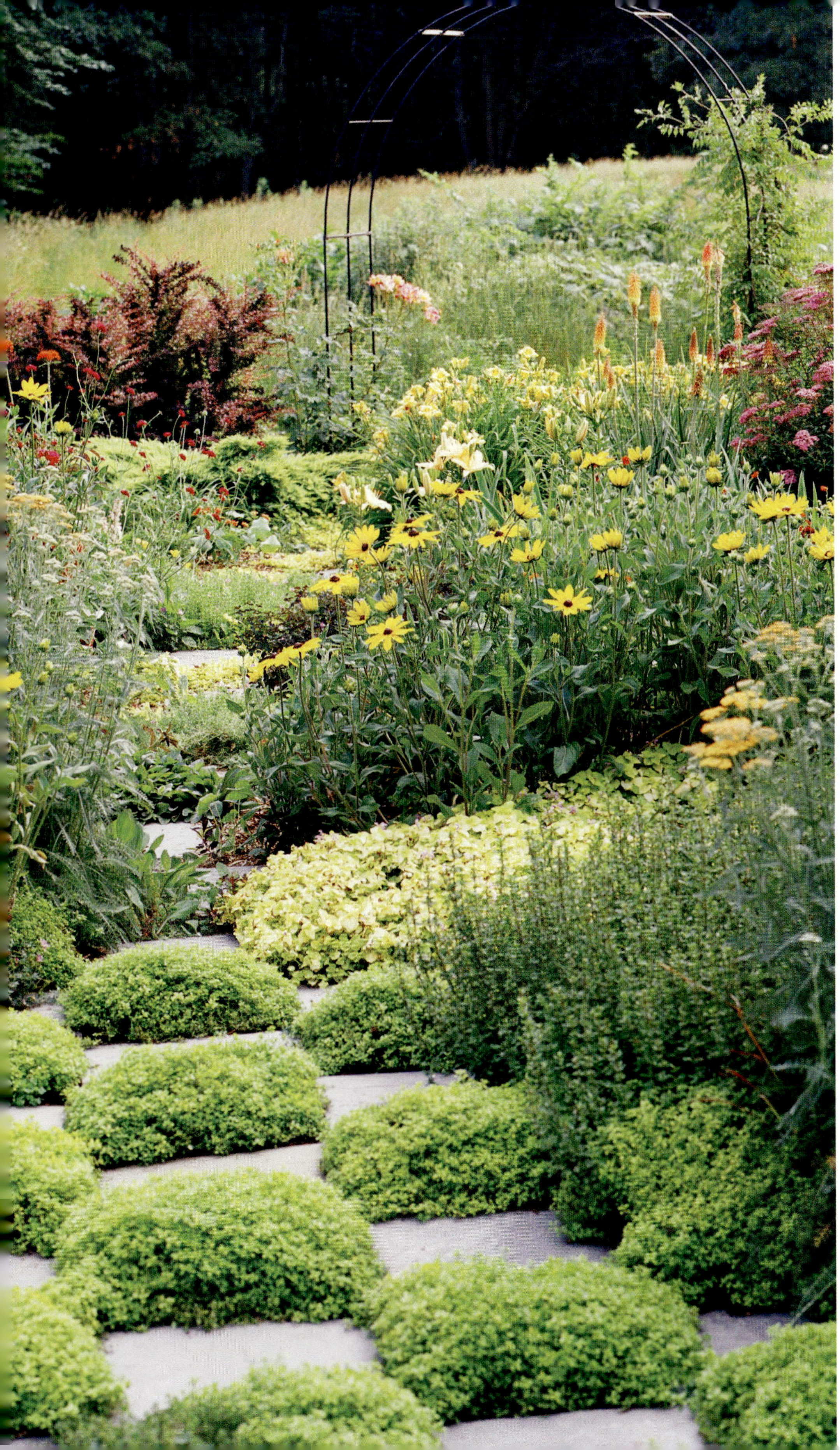
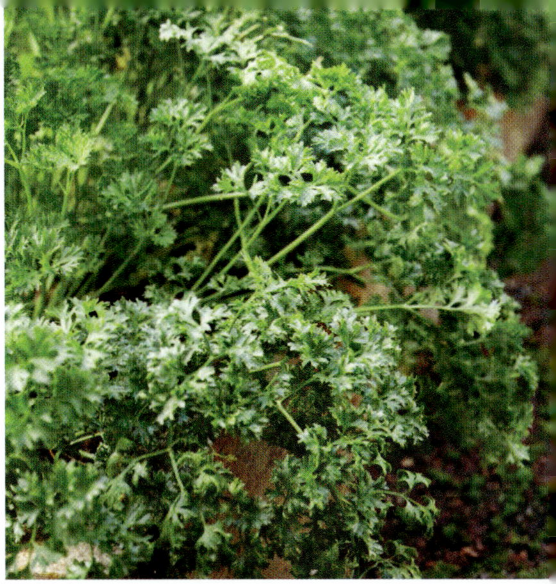
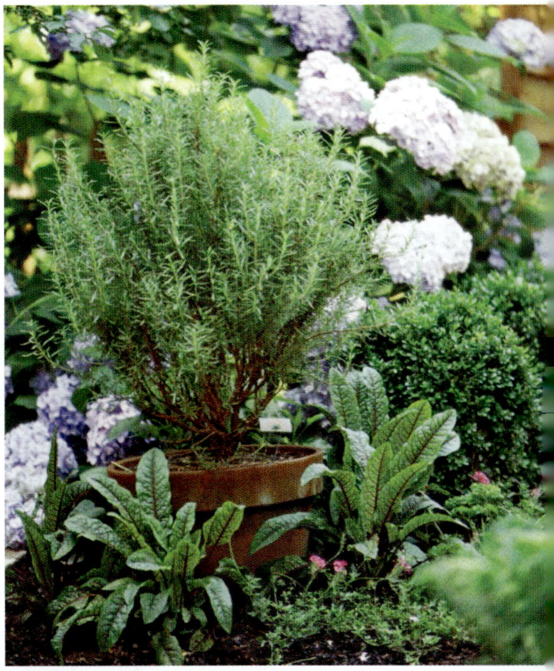
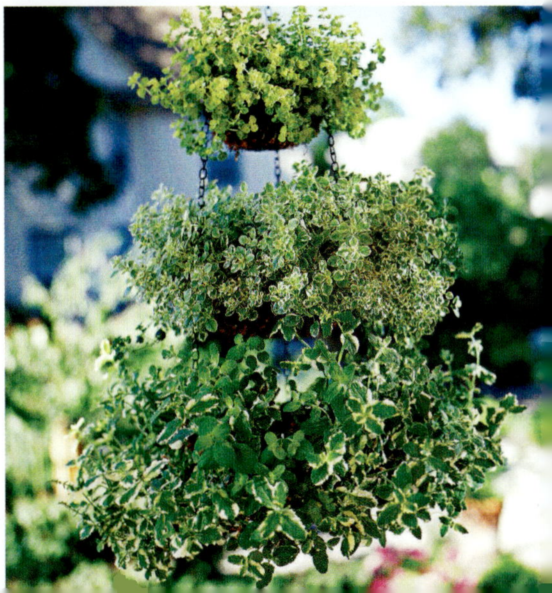

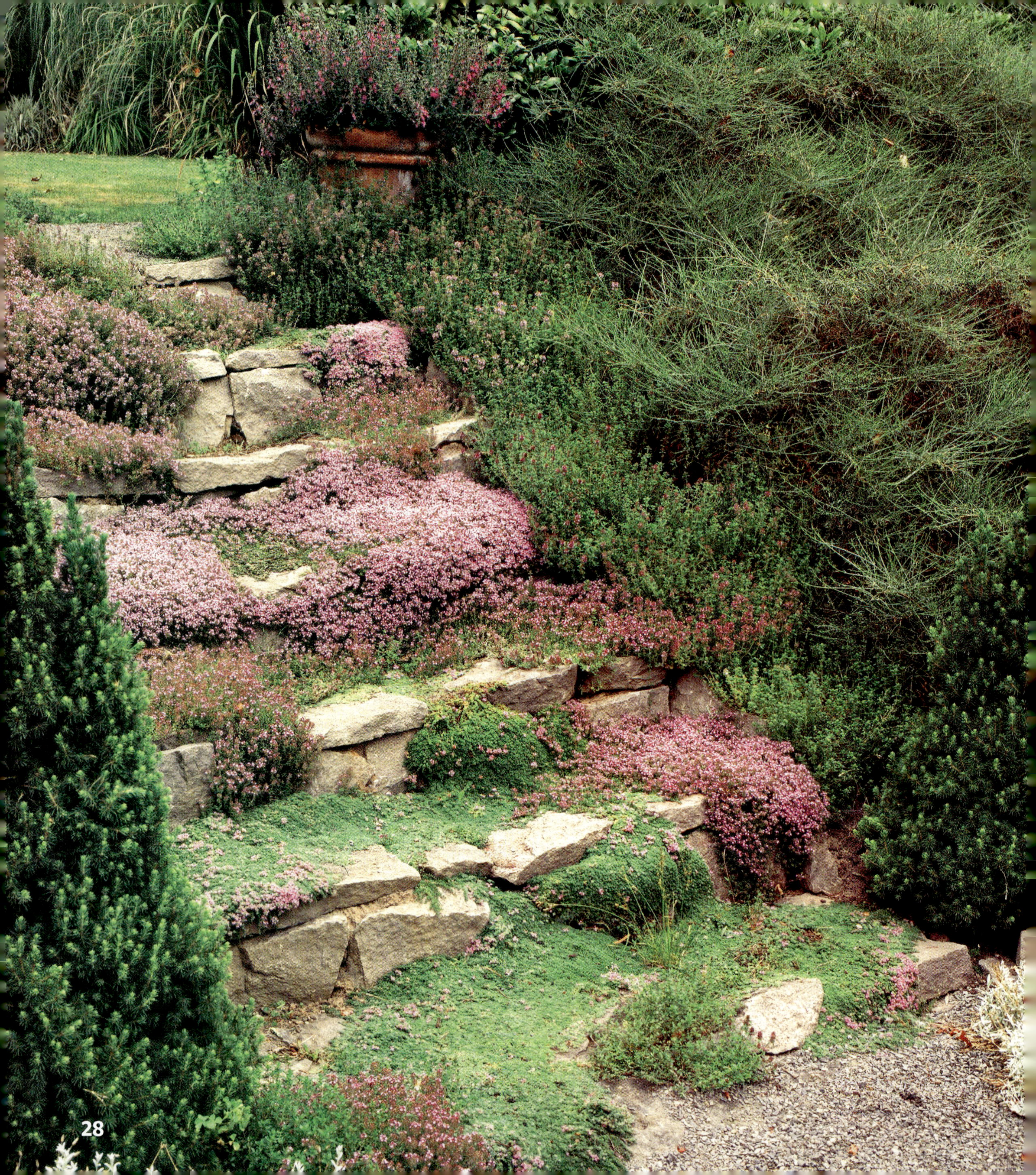

Artful Uses

Herbs can be used in amazing and artistic ways. Known for their culinary, aromatherapy, and medicinal uses, herbs also have an artful side.

Dress up objects

Landscape designers and creative gardeners have long tapped the talents of herbs to add drama or whimsy to a landscape. For example, creeping herb varieties, such as thyme, mint, oregano, and marjoram, can be used to drape structures. Benches, chairs, and bed frames can be planted with a blanket of herbs to create the soft, tufted look of textural and luxurious fabrics. A bench clad with herbs is not a modern idea, however. Medieval paintings show plant-covered garden benches. And herbs such as thyme—because of the many varieties' low-growing, matting growth habits—make excellent upholstery for outdoor benches.

Topiary

Traditional topiary is the art of shaping plants to take on different forms. Famous topiaries include shrubs pruned into animal shapes or sculpted into undulating patterns. Some herbs, however, are quick-change artists that can be transformed from potted plants into formal sculptures or topiary ducks, chickens, and rabbits.

A popular topiary technique is to prune plants to resemble lollipops or miniature trees: a small round or square topknot of leaves on a thin trunk. The exposed stem grows a thick, woody layer with a barklike appearance. Topiaries of this type are best done with woody, shrubby herbs, such as lavender, rosemary, or santolina. But you can use your imagination and pruning skills to transform other leafy herbs, such as scented geranium or basil, into elegant formal topiaries.

Herbs can also be used to create intricate shapes that are grown through and around a wire frame. Herbs that are easy to train into forms include myrtle and germander. Animal topiaries look great in cottage gardens. Kids also love topiaries because of their fun shapes and hands-on qualities. Topiaries make decorative tabletop accessories in outdoor rooms or sunny indoor spaces.

opposite Low-growing and blooming herbs are excellent choices for rock gardens, stone walls, or, in this case, a dramatic stairway. Blooming thyme is inviting, colorful, and fragrant.

CREATIVE HERBS

Herbs are elevated to higher art when added to structures or containers, or clipped into exotic shapes.

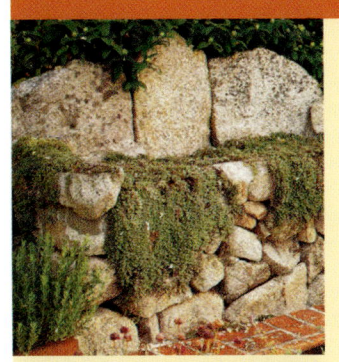

HERBAL BENCH Decorate a bench or old chair with herbs, creating a living cushion. For example, stacked stone forms the base for a bench, and crevices filled with soil hold plantings of creeping herbs. Thyme and chamomile take root easily, covering the seat and spilling over the sides.

TABLETOP HERBS A formal herb garden in miniature, swirling mini labyrinth, or tiny checkerboard—all these tabletop marvels can be made using small herb plants. Start with a low bowl with adequate drainage. You can draw a design ahead of time, incorporating stones, creeping herbs, and focal points.

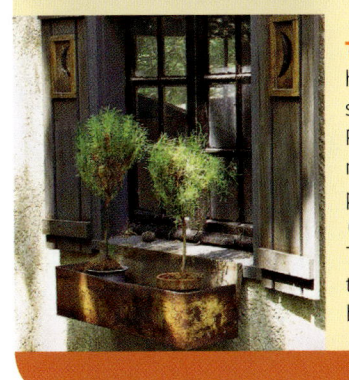

TERRIFIC TOPIARIES Some herbs can be clipped and sculpted into topiary forms. Rosemary, thyme, oregano, myrtle, and lavender can be pruned into geometric shapes (circles, squares, triangles). These whimsical plant forms take on another life in window boxes as growing sculptures.

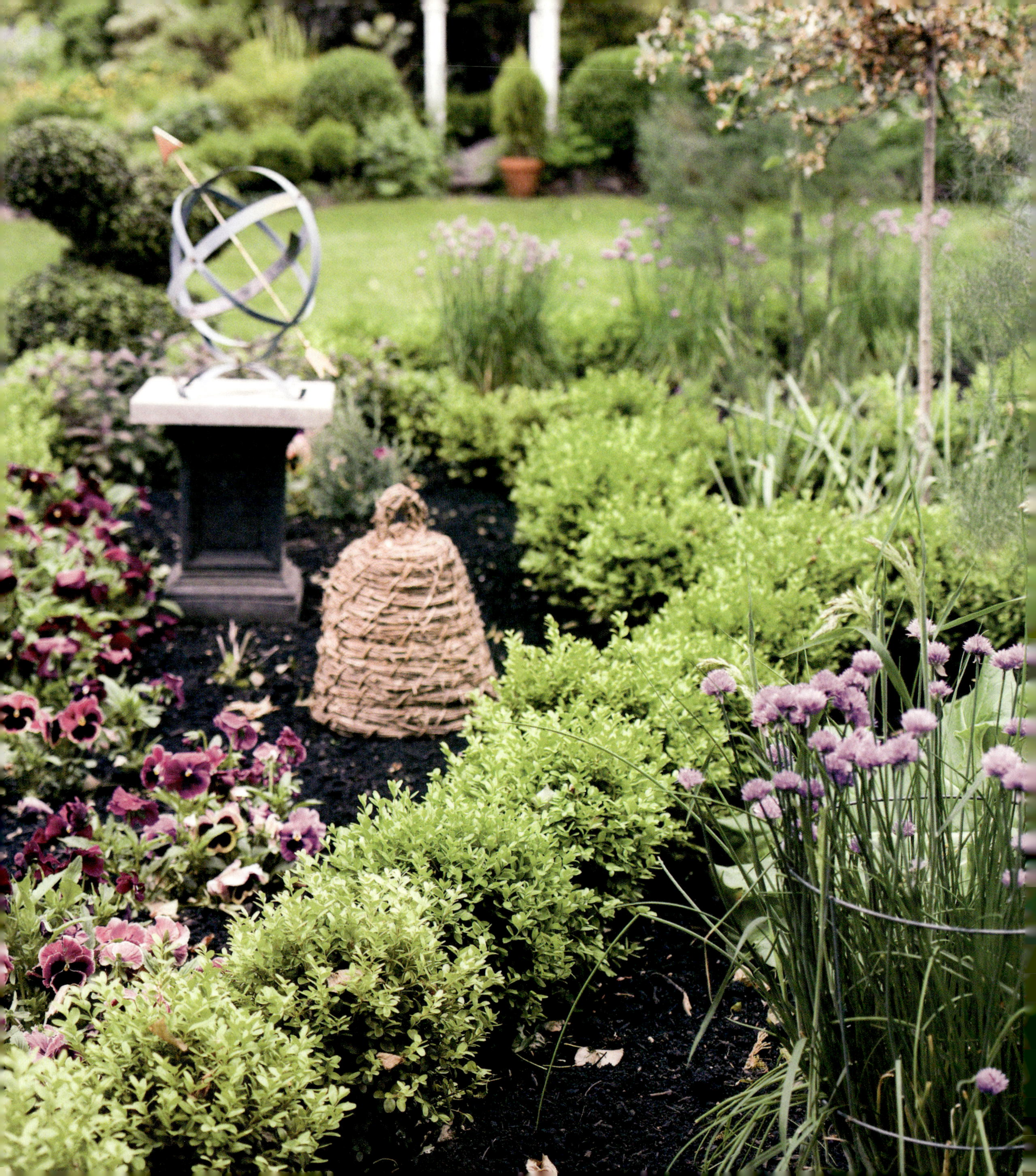

CHAPTER TWO

Herb Garden Plans

Regardless of your garden space, you can grow herbs. Choose from our plans for gardens from large formal plots to mini container gardens.

Celtic Cross Garden

Inspired by the iconography of ancient Celts, this herb garden is easy to plant and harvest. Include a mix of savory and scented herbs in the formal plan.

Ancient Celts populated today's Great Britain and Ireland. Mysterious and magical, the Celts are associated with ancient romantic myths, brave and fierce warriors, cunning wizards, and a connection with otherworldly beings such as fairies.

Although ancient Celts may not have been dedicated herb gardeners, they used herbs for savory and medicinal purposes. Druids were skilled in the study of plants and employed herbs to make teas, salves, and tinctures, as well as potions and poisons. Herbs that were commonly used in Celtic times include some of the same herbs planted today: dill, juniper, lavender, mint, yarrow, valerian, and caraway.

A Celtic-style garden features a series of curved shapes and circles. A bird's-eye view of this garden shows a Celtic cross, an iconic shape that combines a cross with a ring. In the modern world, this symbol, used throughout the British Isles, denotes an association with all things Celtic; it's also a popular motif used in garden decor.

Traditional Celtic gardens are symmetrical and in many cases employ a central focal point. In this plan, a container planted with pineapple guava sits at the center of the garden. Although this garden is a picture of symmetry, the plantings do not mirror one another.

left Fragrant and culinary herbs, interplanted with flowers such as roses and cosmos, create a bountiful garden that's beautiful from spring through autumn.

GARDENING MADE EASY **HERB GARDENING**

Plant List

A. 72 Alpine strawberries (*Fragaria vesca*) Zones 4–9

B. 16 Calendulas (*Calendula officinalis*) Annual

C. 2 Rosemaries (*Rosmarinus officinalis*) Zones 7–10

D. 10 Lavenders (*Lavandula angustifolia*) Zones 5–10

E. 1 French tarragon (*Artemisia dracunculus*) Zones 5–9

F. 3 Borages (*Borago officinalis*) Annual

G. 4 Italian basils (*Ocimum basilicum* 'Genovese') Annual

H. 5 Lemon basils (*Ocimum × citriodorum*) Annual

I. 3 Sunflowers (*Helianthus annuus*) Annual

J. 19 Musk strawberries (*Fragaria moschata*) Zones 6–9

K. 1 Chives (*Allium schoenoprasum*) Zones 3–10

L. 1 Lovage (*Levisticum officinale*) Zones 3–9

M. 7 Dills (*Anethum graveolens*) Annual

N. 4 Sages (*Salvia officinalis*) Zones 4–10

O. 63 Tall cosmos (*Cosmos bipinnatus*) Annual

P. 3 Bay laurels (*Laurus nobilis*) Zones 8–11

Q. 12 Woolly thymes (*Thymus pseudolanuginosus*) Zones 4–9

HERB GARDEN PLANS

Knot Garden

Elegant and organized, a knot garden is an easy way to grow herbs in a formal bed design. Boxwoods form the edges with herbs planted within.

Since medieval times, knot gardens have been prized in landscapes for their elegant lines and trim appearance. And in modern times they can be an oasis of order in the landscape.

Knot gardens can be quite elaborate, with low edges of different-color foliage creating an interwoven pattern. Or they can be simple, like the knot garden here. Its straightforward design makes it easy to achieve, lay out, and maintain.

Follow this pattern exactly, or alter it to better fit your own yard and personal style. The planting plan includes excellent suggestions for filling the shapes, but you may substitute freely. Include more colorful annuals, herbs, or perennials to avoid replanting each year. Just be sure to use small plants that have a tidy growing habit to keep the neat, sharp appearance crucial to a well-tended knot garden.

Also select plants that contrast with the emerald green foliage of the boxwood hedges so the design stands out. Choose brightly colored flowers or plants with contrasting foliage in silvery grays, yellow-greens, or deep purples.

above Weave a classic knot garden with low boxwood edging, and then fill it with assorted herbs and flowers.

Plant List

- **A.** 136 **Dwarf boxwoods** (*Buxus* 'Green Gem') Zones 4–9*
- **B.** 10 **Lantanas** (*Lantana*) Zones 9–11, annual elsewhere
- **C.** 38 **Zinnias** (*Zinnia*) Annual
- **D.** 15 **Vincas** (*Catharanthus roseus*) Zones 9–11, annual elsewhere
- **E.** 14 **Santolinas** (*Santolina chamaecyparissus*) Zones 6–10
- **F.** 12 **Golden sages** (*Salvia officinalis* 'Icterina') Zones 5–11
- **G.** 16 **Common sages** (*Salvia officinalis*) Zones 4–10
- **H.** 6 **Petunias** (*Petunia* × *hybrida*) Annual
- **I.** 3 **Chives** (*Allium schoenoprasum*) Zones 3–10
- **J.** 8 **Sorrels** (*Rumex acetosa*) Zones 3–8
- **K.** 10 **Mixed sweet and purple basils** (*Ocimum basilicum*) Annual
- **L.** 3 **Thymes** (*Thymus*) Zones 5–9
- **M.** 12 **Purple variegated sages** (*Salvia officinalis* 'Tricolor') Zones 6–9

* In Zones 4 and 5, wrap in burlap for winter protection.

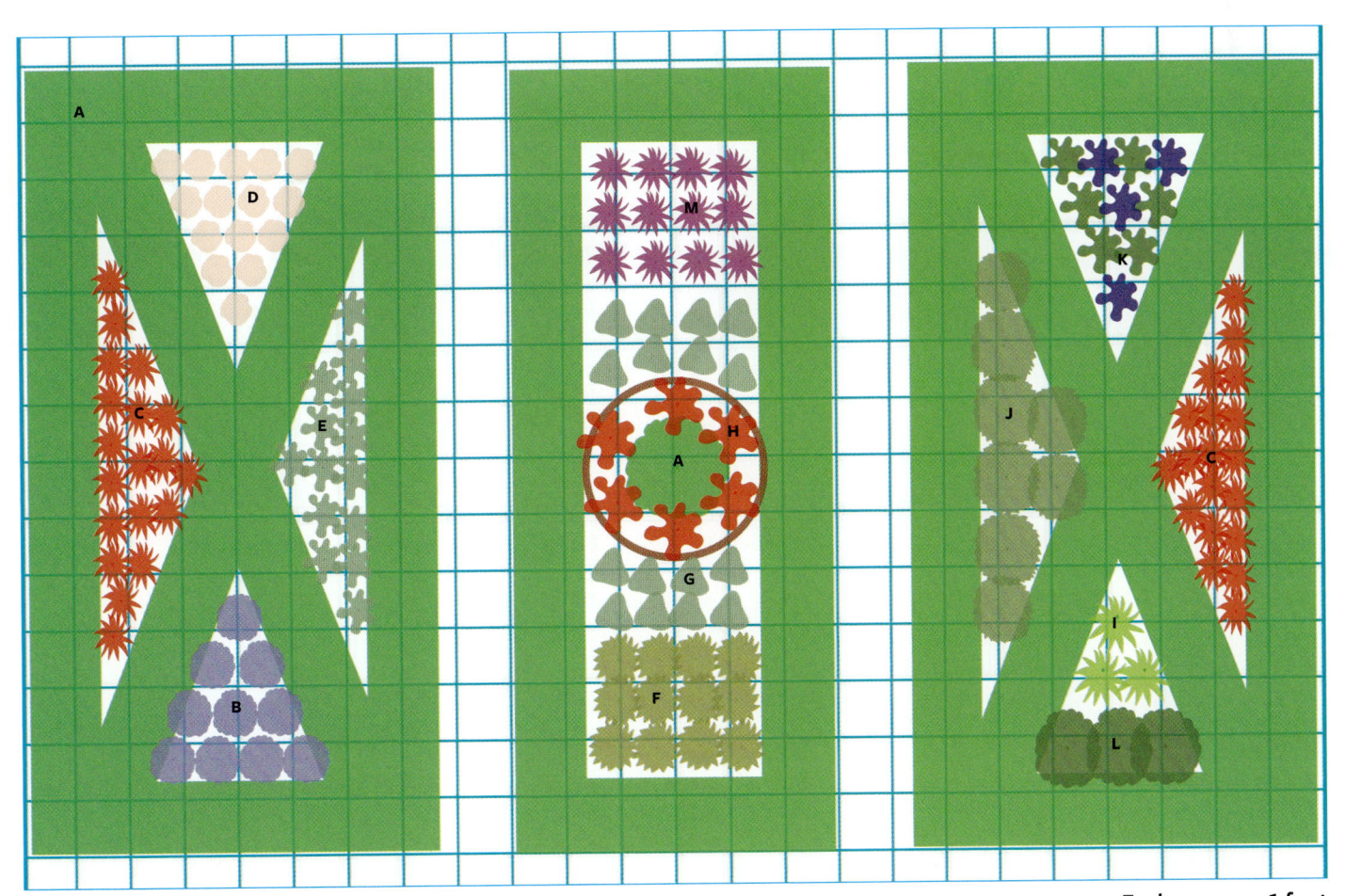

Each square = 1 foot

HERB GARDEN PLANS 35

Wagon Wheel Garden

A circular bed is a classic herb garden design. Each 'spoke' of the wheel is an herb garden in miniature.

Whether you have a large planting space or a small one, a circular shape is ideal for an herb garden. This multisection bed offers enough space to grow ample amounts of your favorite herbs. Plus, a mix of annual and perennial flowers keeps the bed beautiful all summer long.

This raised bed can sit just steps from your back door and supply you with herbs for spring, summer, and autumn meals. If you plant perennial herbs, such as thyme, oregano, and chives, you won't have to replant every spring—which makes this garden both economical and low-maintenance.

Round herb beds are easy to make. Choose a site that receives at least six to eight hours of sun a day. Figure out approximately where the center of the bed will be, and pound a stake into the ground there, creating a pivot point. Measure a length of string a foot longer than half the size of the bed (for example, if you want a 6-foot circle, measure a 4-foot length of string). Tie one end of the string to the post. With a can of spray paint in hand, pull the string taut and walk around the stake at the end of the string, painting a circle on the ground.

Each bed in this radial design has a few plant species in common, which helps to unify the beds. Repeating a dominant color, such as chartreuse, or a broader texture emphasizes the effect and makes the garden feel more cohesive. The rigid geometric shapes and construction of the bed provide a satisfying visual contrast to the loose, relaxed planting.

Adding a brick walkway gives permanent infrastructure to the bed so it looks beautiful in all seasons. The triangular beds are accessible for planting from both the path and perimeter.

above This easy-to-plant herb garden gets its great structure from a classic circle—with a round water feature as a focal point.

Plant List

A. 5 Magnus purple coneflowers (*Echinacea purpurea* 'Magnus') Zones 2–9

B. 1 Silver Mound artemisia (*Artemisia schmidtiana* 'Silver Mound') Zones 3–9

C. 4 Becky Shasta daisies (*Leucanthemum* 'Becky') Zones 4–10

D. 9 Soapworts (*Saponaria ocymoides*) Zones 3–7

E. 9 Hidcote lavenders (*Lavandula angustifolia* 'Hidcote') Zones 5–9

F. 3 Mountain bluets (*Centaurea montana*) Zones 3–8

G. 7 Georgia Blue speedwells (*Veronica umbrosa* 'Georgia Blue') Zones 4–9

H. 6 Bertram Anderson sedums (*Sedum* 'Bertram Anderson') Zones 3–9

I. 4 Woodland forget-me-nots (*Myosotis sylvatica*) Zones 3–8

J. 2 Olympic mulleins (*Verbascum olympicum*) Zones 8–10

K. 3 Lady's mantles (*Alchemilla mollis*) Zones 4–8

L. 1 Palace Purple coralbells (*Heuchera* 'Palace Purple') Zones 4–8

M. 3 Cambridge geraniums (*Geranium × cantabrigiense* 'Cambridge') Zones 4–8

N. 5 Lemon thymes (*Thymus × citriodorus*) Zones 5–9

O. 2 Woolly thymes (*Thymus pseudolanuginosus*) Zones 4–9

P. 4 Plum Pudding coralbells (*Heuchera* 'Plum Pudding') Zones 4–8

Q. 1 Berggarten sage (*Salvia officinalis* 'Berggarten') Zones 6–9

R. 1 Tricolor sage (*Salvia officinalis* 'Tricolor') Zones 6–9

S. 3 Spike gayfeathers (*Liatris spicata*) Zones 3–10

T. 1 Southern Charm mullein (*Verbascum* 'Southern Charm') Zones 6–8

U. 3 Chives (*Allium schoenoprasum*) Zones 3–10

V. 1 Russian sage (*Perovskia atriplicifolia*) Zones 4–10

W. 6 Marguerite daisies (*Argyranthemum frutescens*) Zones 7–11

X. 4 Fringed bleeding hearts (*Dicentra eximia*) Zones 3–10

Y. 12 Ageratums (*Ageratum houstonianum*) Annual

Z. 4 Rues (*Ruta graveolens*) Zones 4–9

AA. 3 Oreganos (*Origanum vulgare*) Zones 5–10

BB. 4 Marguerite sweet potato vines (*Ipomoea batatas* 'Marguerite') Annual

CC. 2 Lamb's-ears (*Stachys byzantina*) Zones 4–10

DD. 16 Blue salvias (*Salvia farinacea*) Annual

EE. 5 Blackie sweet potato vines (*Ipomoea batatas* 'Blackie') Annual

Each square = 1 foot

HERB GARDEN PLANS

Tea Garden

Herbal teas are so healthful. And what's better than growing your own organic mix of tea ingredients?

An undulating border packed with tea herbs is a beautiful landscape element as well as a great way to enjoy the restorative benefits of infused herbs. This border fits into a relatively small area and can be adapted to any sunny spot in your yard.

The scented geraniums are grown in lightweight pots, making it easy to move the tender perennials indoors over winter. Lavender, bee balm, and a rose hip-producing rugosa rose (try 'Frau Dagmar Hartopp' with single-petal pink flowers) stand along the back of the border. Two-foot-tall, easy-care lemon balm makes a delicious and soothing pot of tea. The brewed leaves yield a lemony taste similar to that of lemon verbena. This hardy herb tolerates temperatures to −20°F. Lemon balm also withstands partial shade.

Low-growing alpine strawberries are grouped in front, where you can easily harvest the delicious fruit as well as the leaves, which you can infuse in hot water. Another tea favorite, Roman chamomile, bears flowers that taste and smell like apples when infused. Chamomile is an age-old sedative and sleep enhancer.

Lavender's gray-green, sweet-smelling leaves make a flavorful and aromatic tea. Pick and dry lavender buds before the flowers open and add to hot water. You can also use these edible blooms in tea cakes and shortbread, or as a fragrant addition to a brewed pot of tea.

above The leaves of just-picked herbs such as chamomile and lemon balm can be used fresh to make tea.

GARDENING MADE EASY **HERB GARDENING**

Plant List

A. 2 **Scented geraniums** (*Pelargonium*)
Zones 8–11

B. 1 **Sunset hyssop** (*Agastache rupestris*)
Zones 4–9

C. 2 **Lavenders** (*Lavandula angustifolia*)
Zones 5–10

D. 1 **Bee balm** (*Monarda didyma*)
Zones 3–10

E. 1 **Lemon balm** (*Melissa officinalis*)
Zones 4–10

F. 1 **Rugosa rose** (*Rosa rugosa*) Zones 2–9

G. 6 **Roman chamomiles** (*Chamaemelum nobile*) Zones 4–8

H. 3 **Lemon thymes** (*Thymus × citriodorus*)
Zones 5–9

I. 14 **Alpine strawberries** (*Fragaria vesca*)
Zones 4–9

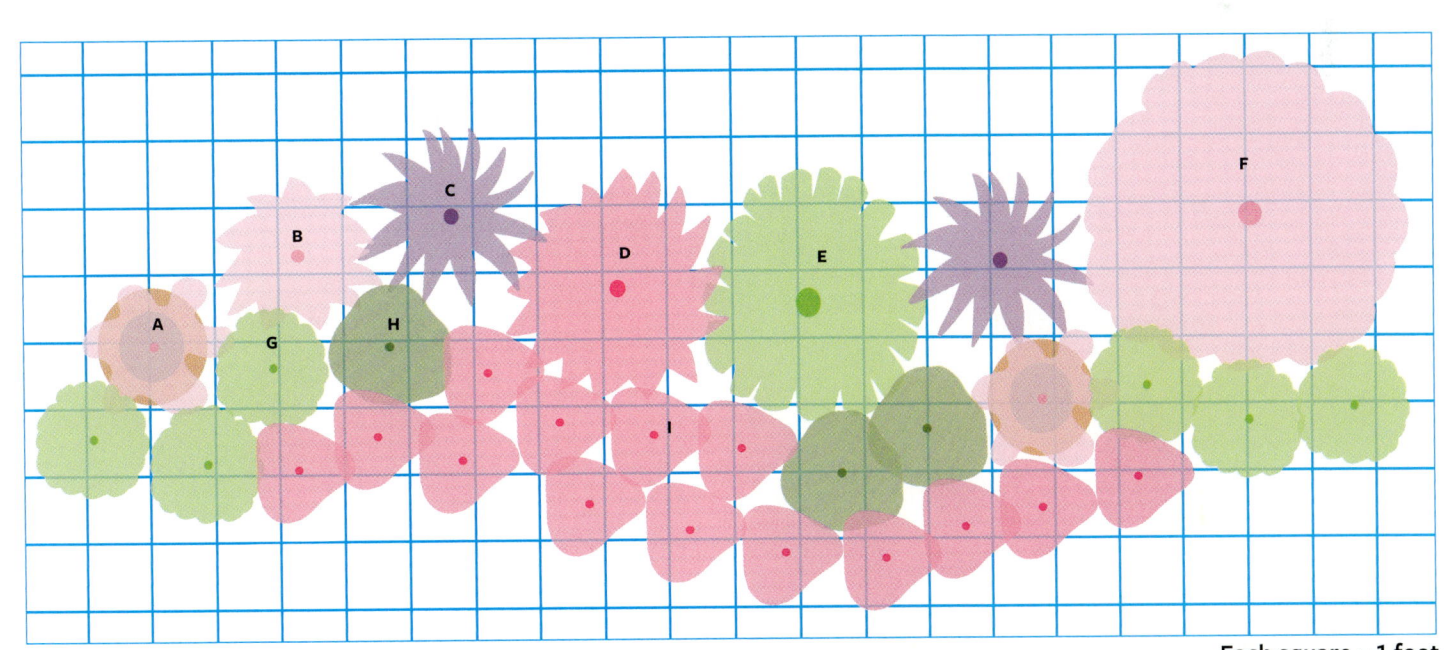

Scented geranium

Sunset hyssop

Lavender

Bee balm

Lemon balm

Rugosa rose

Roman chamomile

Lemon thyme

Alpine strawberry

Each square = 1 foot

HERB GARDEN PLANS **39**

Raised Bed Garden

Colorful and easy-care, a raised bed garden allows you to pack herbs and vegetables shoulder to shoulder to maximize space.

A raised bed is an herb gardener's dream space. You assemble a bed, then fill it, ideally with amended soil. The soil in a raised bed warms earlier in spring and drains faster in wet weather. A 4×4-foot square ensures an easy distance for reaching the middle from all sides, making it simple to plant, weed, or harvest. Removing weeds is a snap, because the soil remains soft and workable from year to year as long as you don't walk on it.

Locate your herb-and-vegetable garden in a sunny spot. Remove any turf, then rake and level the ground. Dress up a pressure-treated wood frame with a coat of exterior-type stain or primer and paint. (Here, a coat of teal stain gives the beds a bright, contemporary look.) Beds go together quickly with precut lumber (most lumber suppliers will cut to your specifications) and aluminum corner connectors.

Position the bed frame, and drill in screws to attach the corner connectors. Use an angle square to make sure the sides line up at right angles. Measure diagonally in both directions across the planter bed to make sure the diagonals are of equal length and the frame is square. A few easy connections later, you have a two-tier bed ready to be filled with soil.

Fill your raised bed with topsoil; the back tier is twice as deep as the front one. Add organic matter, such as compost, to improve the soil and help ensure the plants' success. Mulch to conserve soil moisture and minimize watering.

left Growing herbs and vegetables together in the same bed is a modern spin on the dooryard herb garden of the past.

Plant List

A. **2 Ginger mints** (*Mentha × gracilis*) Zones 6–9

B. **1 Chives** (*Allium schoenopraesum*) Zones 3–9

C. **2 Stevias** (*Stevia rebaudiana*) Zones 8–11

D. **1 Thai basil** (*Ocimum basilicum* 'Siam Queen') Annual

E. **1 Cinnamon basil** (*Ocimum basilicum* 'Cinnamon') Annual

F. **1 Lemongrass** (*Cymbopogon citratus*) Zones 9–11

G. **1 Broccoli** (*Brassica oleracea*) Annual

H. **2 Hot peppers** (*Capsicum annuum*) Annual

I. **6 Purple basils** (*Ocimum basilicum*) Annual

J. **1 Pineapple sage** (*Salvia elegans*) Zones 8–11

K. **1 Summer squash** (*Cucurbita pepo*) Annual

L. **2 Tomatoes** (*Lycopersicon esculentum*) Annual

BHG TEST GARDEN TIP — RISE ABOVE SOIL PROBLEMS

If you have rocky or clay soil, or your herb bed is too close to a black walnut tree (the leaves and nuts cause toxicity in the soil), rise above the challenge with a raised bed. Fill the bed with a mixture of organic topsoil and compost, then plant with ease.

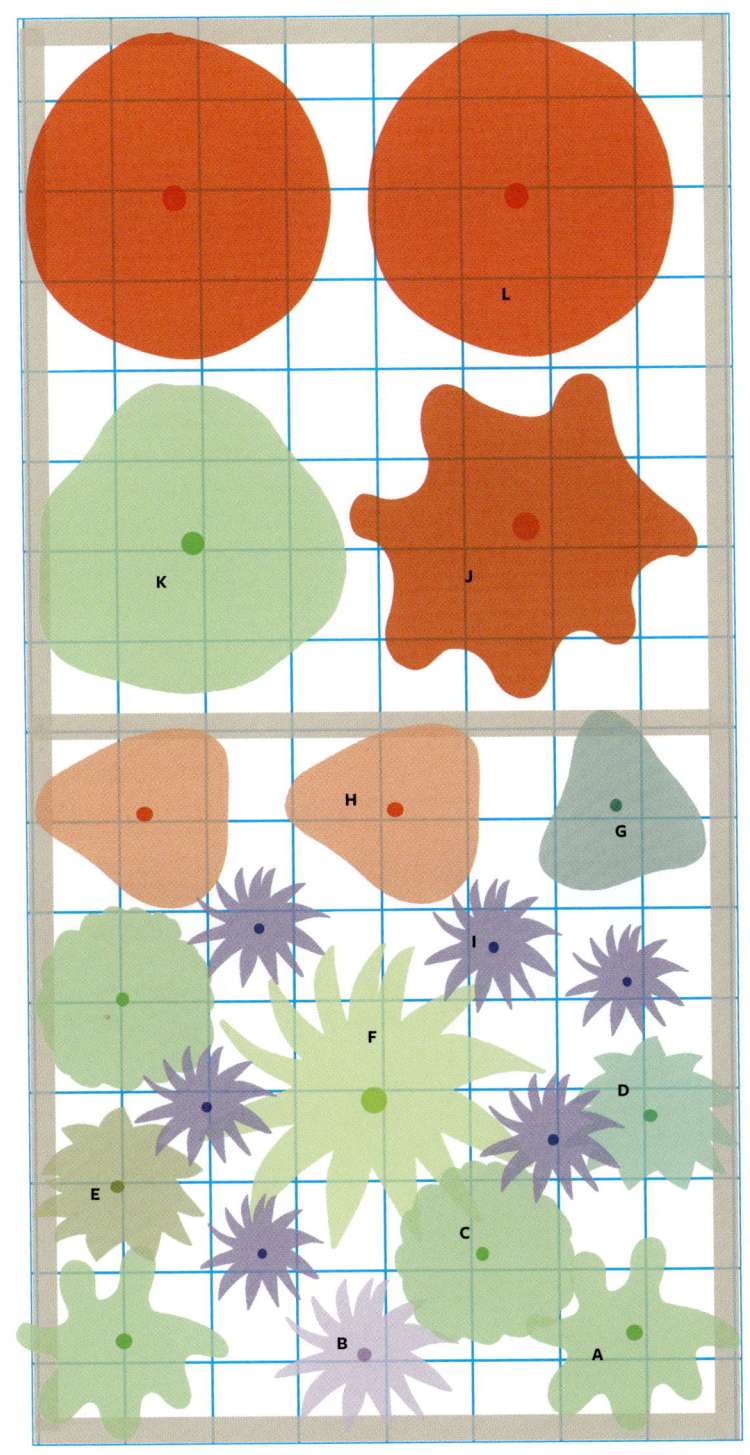

Each square = 6 inches

HERB GARDEN PLANS

Welcome Home Garden

When you arrange a cluster of containers filled with herbs, you get a double delight: Step out your door to collect herbs while the eye-catching containers garner attention from the street.

When you think curb appeal, herbs might not come to mind, in part because their charms are often enjoyed most up close. But there's a wide range of bold and colorful herbs that are nothing short of traffic-stopping—especially when planted in a cluster of colorful containers.

To create a grouped container garden resplendent with herb leaves and flowers, all you need is a collection of containers tall and small that can be displayed together or arranged along the steps of a front entryway or backyard path. Choose a similar palette of pot colors, such as those of the Provence-inspired containers at *left*, or mix it up with containers of different colors.

Amp up the color by planting showy flowering herbs such as calendula, nasturtium, and chives. Their edible flowers make ideal additions to salads and soups. Or they can be clipped for an impromptu bouquet.

Savory herbs such as thyme, oregano, basil, and rosemary are just a step away; clip container herbs often for recipes, garnishes, and herbal bouquets. Combine textural leaf combinations—such as curly and flat-leaf parsley—to make visually interesting container plantings that look good even without flower power. Add smaller-stature vegetables such as pepper, Swiss chard, and bush-variety summer squash for colorful edibles that look good with herbs.

With mixed plant combinations (solo plantings), herbs in containers make a welcoming—and appetizing—presentation.

above Containers allow you to create a temporary garden wherever you live. At the end of the growing season, empty the pots and store them until they're needed again.

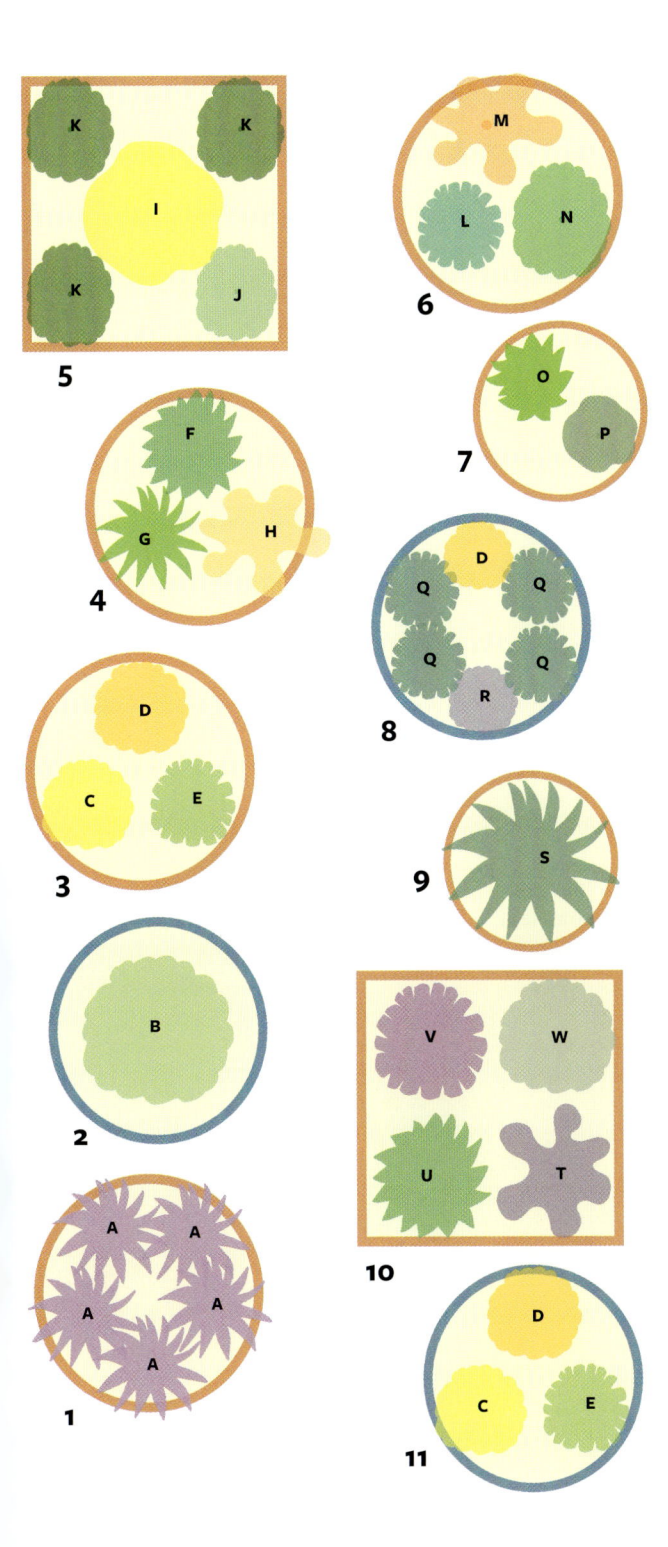

Plant List

POT 1
A. 5 Lavenders (*Lavandula angustifolia* 'Lady') Zones 5–10

POT 2
B. 1 Basil (*Ocimum basilicum*) Annual

POT 3
C. 1 Calendula (*Calendula officinalis*) Annual
D. 1 Nasturtium (*Nasturtium* 'Buttercream') Annual
E. 1 Nasturtium (*Nasturtium* 'Alaska') Annual

POT 4
F. 1 Flat-leaf parsley (*Petroselinum neapolitanum*) Zones 5–9
G. 1 Curly leaf parsley (*Petroselinum crispum*) Zones 5–9
H. 1 Pepper (*Capsicum annuum* 'Gypsy') Annual

POT 5
I. 1 Meyer lemon (*Citrus limon* 'Improved Meyer') Zones 9–11
J. 1 Silver thyme (*Thymus vulgaris* 'Argenteus') Zones 5–9
K. 3 English thymes (*Thymus vulgaris*) Zones 5–9

POT 6
L. 1 Daylily (*Hemerocallis*) Zones 3–11
M. 1 Mint (*Mentha*) Zones 3–10
N. 1 Summer squash (*Cucurbita* 'Trombetta') Annual

POT 7
O. 1 Swiss chard (*Beta vulgaris* 'Bright Lights') Annual
P. 1 Greek oregano (*Origanum vulgare hirtum*) Zones 5–10

POT 8
Q. 4 Marigolds (*Tagetes*) Annual
D. 1 Nasturtium (*Nasturtium* 'Buttercream') Annual
R. 1 Sage (*Salvia officinalis* 'Icterina') Zones 5–11

POT 9
S. 1 Rosemary (*Rosmarinus officinalis*) Zones 7–10

POT 10
T. 1 Purple sage (*Salvia officinalis* 'Purpurascens') Zones 5–9
U. 1 Lemon thyme (*Thymus × citriodorus*) Zones 5–9
V. 1 Purple basil (*Ocimum basilicum* 'Purpurascens') Annual
W. 1 English lavender (*Lavandula angustifolia*) Zones 5–10

POT 11
C. 1 Calendula (*Calendula officinalis*) Annual
D. 1 Nasturtium (*Nasturtium* 'Buttercream') Annual
E. 1 Nasturtium (*Nasturtium* 'Alaska') Annual

Set in Stone

Large cast-stone or concrete planters offer long-term homes for perennial herbs. The thick walls of these heavy-duty containers insulate herb roots from temperature extremes.

Essentials

Containers: 18×24- to 20×48-inch stone or stone-look pots
Light: Sun
Water: When the soil feels dry

Plant List

Pot 1

A. 1 Garlic chives (*Allium tuberosum*)
Zones 3–10

B. 1 Flat-leaf parsley (*Petroselinum neapolitanum*)
Zones 5–9

C. 1 Tricolor sage (*Salvia officinalis* 'Tricolor')
Zones 6–9

Pot 2

D. 1 Mint (*Mentha*) such as peppermint
Zones 3–8

Pot 3

E. 1 Lemon thyme (*Thymus* × *citriodorus*)
Zones 5–9

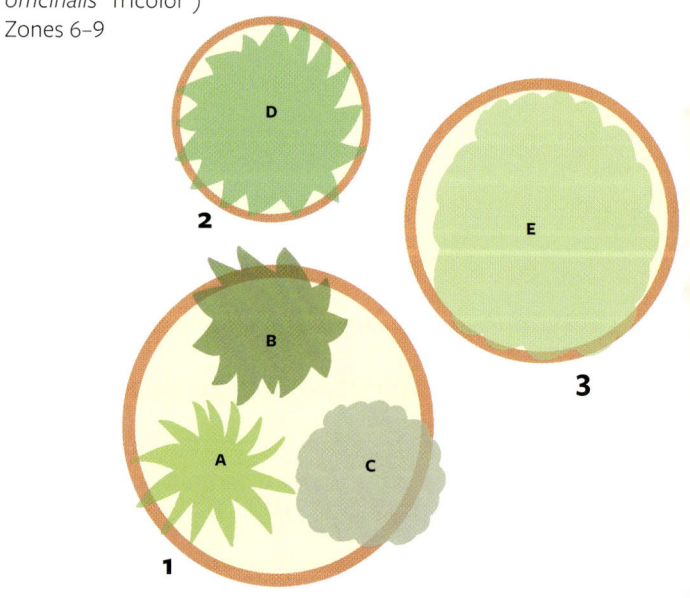

Easy Shade

Most herbs are sun lovers, but some tolerate shade. Pack these low-maintenance, unfussy herbs into a metal container that will shine on a partially shaded patio or terrace. Transplant perennial herbs into the garden by early fall.

Essentials

Container: 18-inch galvanized pot
Light: Partial sun
Water: When the soil feels dry

Plant List

A. **3 Foxgloves** (*Digitalis purpurea*)
Zones 4–9

B. **1 Lemon balm** (*Melissa officinalis*)
Zones 4–10

C. **1 Ginger mint** (*Mentha × gracilis*)
Zones 6–9

D. **2 Sweet woodruffs** (*Galium odoratum*)
Zones 4–9

HERB GARDEN PLANS

Tasteful Window Box

Enjoy the view out your window, then step outside and harvest snips of parsley, basil, and thyme. Tasty herbs make a lush green planter, and edible petals from violas and marigolds add dots and dashes of color.

Essentials

Container: 48-inch window box
Light: Sun
Water: When the soil feels dry

Plant List

A. 4 **Flat-leaf parsleys** (*Petroselinum neapolitanum*) Zones 5–9

B. 2 **Basils** (*Ocimum basilicum*) Annual

C. 1 **Marjoram** (*Origanum majorana*) Zones 8–10

D. 1 **Lemon thyme** (*Thymus × citriodorus*) Zones 5–9

E. 3 **Spearmints** (*Mentha spicata*) Zones 4–10

F. 1 **Cilantro** (*Coriandrum sativum*) Annual

G. 2 **Violas** (*Viola tricolor*) Annual

H. 2 **Marigolds** (*Tagetes*) Annual

I. 1 **Thyme** (*Thymus*) Zones 4–9

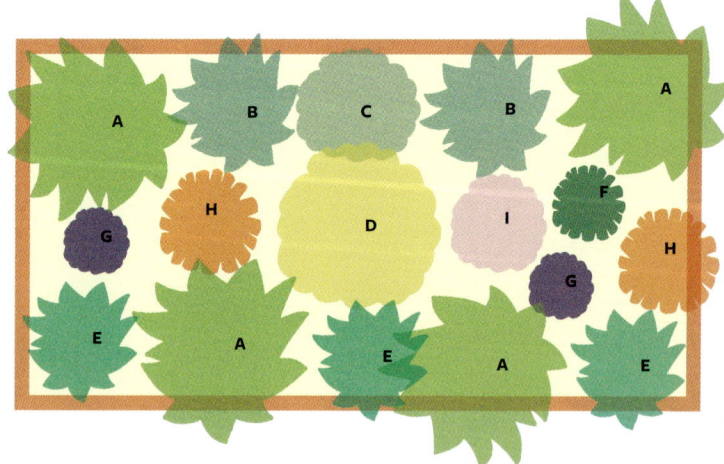

Fresh and Flavorful

Keep a basket of mint mixed with lemon balm near outdoor seating areas so you can snip garnishes for drinks or desserts. Protect the basket by lining it with a sheet of landscape fabric with added drainage holes.

Essentials

Container: 17×11×9-inch basket
Materials: Liner (sheet plastic or moisture-holding type)
Light: Partial shade
Water: Keep soil moist

Plant List

A. 1 Peppermint (*Mentha × piperata*)
Zones 3–8

B. 1 Lemon balm (*Melissa officinalis*)
Zones 4–10

C. 1 Spearmint (*Mentha spicata*)
Zones 4–10

D. 1 Pineapple mint (*Mentha suaveolens* 'Variegata')
Zones 5–10

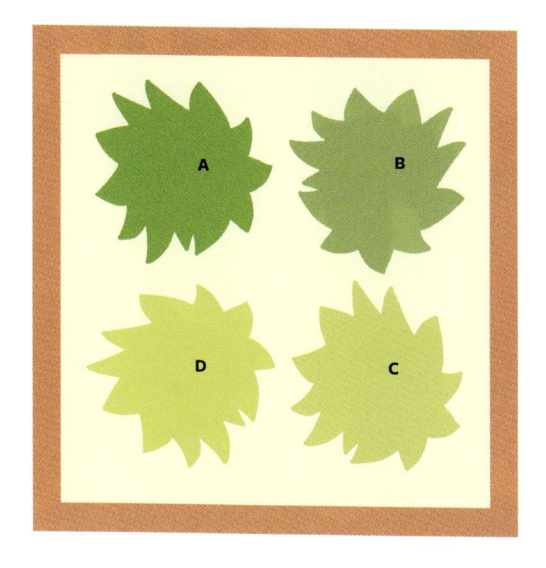

HERB GARDEN PLANS

Savory Centerpiece

A snip-and-eat centerpiece keeps savory herbs—such as chives, rosemary, sage, and basil, where they will stimulate the taste buds as well as the conversation.

Essentials

Containers: 16-inch terra-cotta bowl
Light: Sun
Water: When the soil feels dry

Plant List

A. 1 **Chives** (*Allium schoenoprasum*) Zones 3–10

B. 1 **Rosemary** (*Rosmarinus officinalis*) Zones 7–10

C. 1 **Sage** (*Salvia officinalis*) Zones 4–10

D. 1 **Marjoram** (*Origanum majorana*) Zones 8–10

E. 1 **Thyme** (*Thymus vulgaris*) Zones 5–9

F. 1 **Basil** (*Ocimum* 'Spicy Globe') Annual

Pest-Away Planter

Some herbs have seemingly magical bug-repelling qualities. Standing on a patio or deck, this fragrant garden deters mosquitoes, moths, and ants. Solar lights add practicality.

Essentials

Container: 39×16×32-inch self-watering planter
Light: Sun
Water: When the soil feels dry

Plant List

A. 1 **Rue** (*Ruta graveolens*) Zones 4–9

B. 6 **Marigolds** (*Tagetes*) Annual

C. 1 **Southernwood** (*Artemisia abrotanum*) Zones 4–10

D. 1 **Catnip** (*Nepeta cataria*) Zones 3–9

E. 1 **Tansy** (*Tanacetum vulgare*) Zones 3–9

F. 2 **Scented geraniums** (*Pelargonium*) Zones 9–11

G. 1 **Variegated plectranthus** (*Plectranthus coleoides*) Annual

H. 1 **Santolina** (*Santolina*) Zones 6–10

I. 1 **Feverfew** (*Tanacetum parthenium*) Zones 4–9

J. 1 **Variegated sage** (*Salvia* 'Tricolor') Zones 6–9

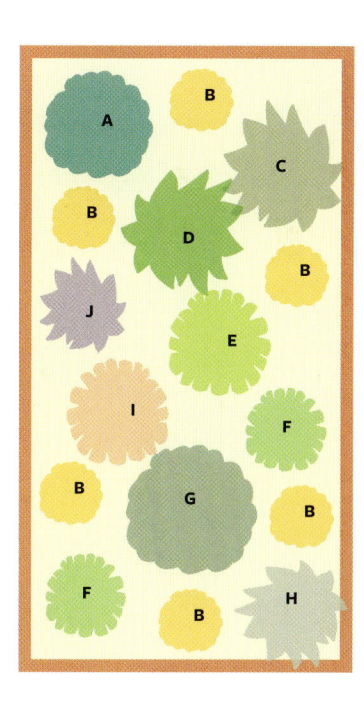

HERB GARDEN PLANS

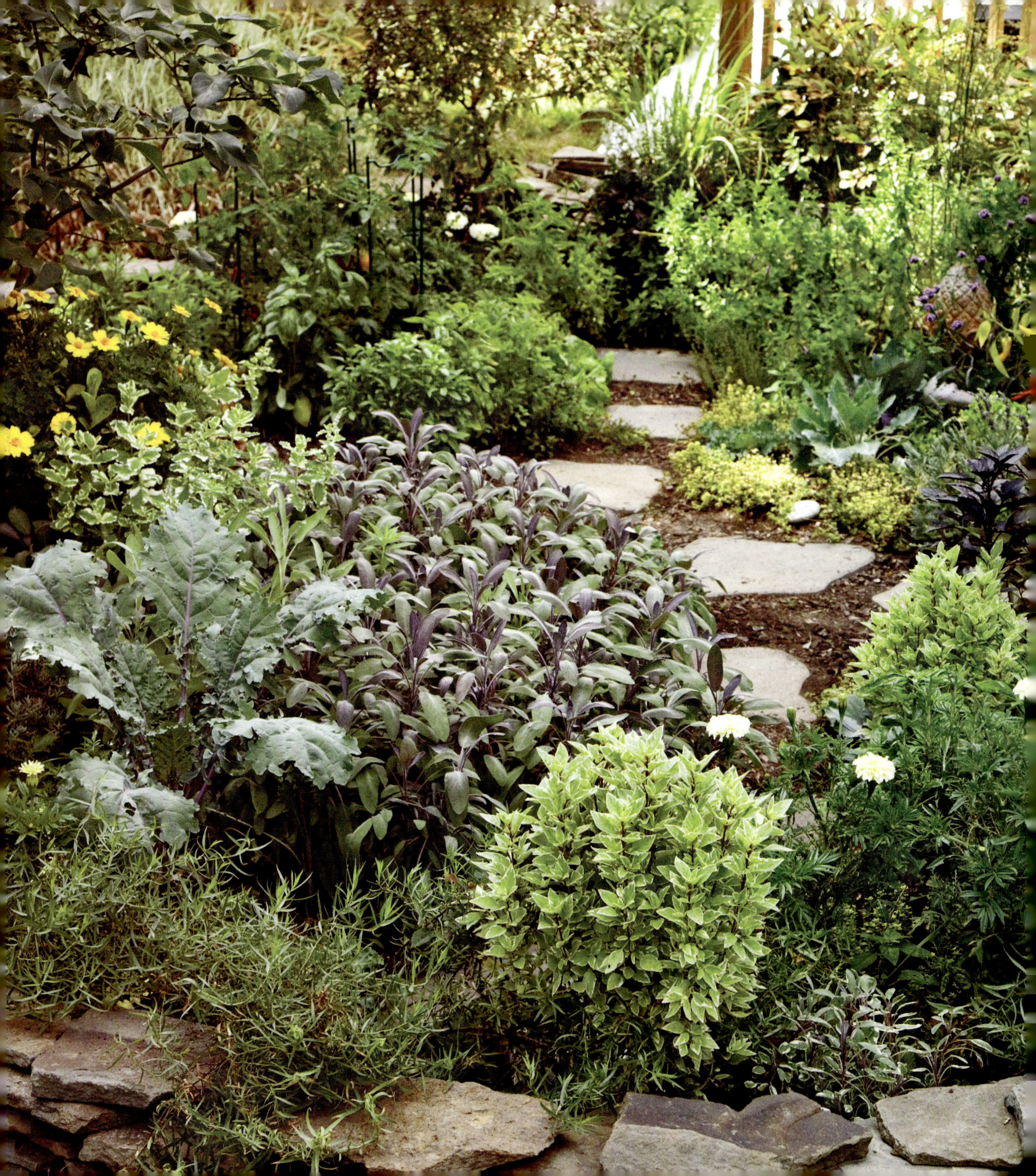

CHAPTER THREE

A Year of Herbs

Herb lovers can revel in a variety of herbal activities from spring through winter. See how you can enjoy herbs all year.

FRUGAL GARDENING: SPROUT HERBS FROM SEED
Starting herb seeds indoors is easy. You need seed-starting supplies, a warm spot, and a good light source (a south-facing window or grow-lights).

1 GATHER Get the supplies needed for starting herbs indoors, including premoistened soilless seed-starting mix, peat pots, and seeds.

2 FILL Add seed-starting mix to fill the peat pots or other multicell packs, then level the tops.

3 SOW Sprinkle several seeds per cell. Cover seeds with seed-starting mix following seed packet instructions.

4 WATER Gently sprinkle the plantings to avoid washing the seeds out of the mix. Set them in a warm, sunny place.

Spring
Selecting Herbs

Choosing herbs for your garden is easy. Just select types you like to cook with, make tea from, or use in crafts.

Which herbs to select for your garden depends on the growing conditions. Sunlight, climate (how cold your garden gets in winter and how hot it gets in summer), and soil play important roles in the success of the herbs you plant.

Seeing the light (and how to interpret it)
Most herbs are sun lovers, but a few herbs grow in shaded locations. The range from full sun to full shade is filled with varying degrees of light. Light requirements for plants are expressed in these terms:

Full sun. Herbs that require at least six to eight hours of sun per day.
Part sun. Herbs that need three to six hours of sun per day, preferably in the morning or evening.
Part shade. Herbs that thrive with three to six hours of sun per day but require shade during the afternoon—under a tree or near a building.
Full shade. Herbs that require fewer than three hours of direct sunlight. This describes planting locations that receive filtered light or light shade created by trees or other structures.

Climate considerations
Each herb has the ability to withstand cold and hot weather. Temperature ranges are expressed by a hardiness Zone. The U. S. Department of Agriculture designates 11 Zones from Canada to Mexico. Each Zone is based on a 10° F difference. Once you know your hardiness Zone (see the map on *page 211* to find your Zone), you can choose herbs that will thrive and flourish. The hardiness Zone range for all perennial herbs appears on the plant tag (when you buy live plants in nurseries) or on the websites that sell herbs online. Temperature affects the growth and life cycle of herbs—something to consider when you plant. Some herbs, such as dill and cilantro, produce lovely edible leaves in cool weather, but once the weather turns hot, these annuals quickly develop seeds. Many perennial herbs, such as oregano and rosemary, really get growing when summer weather sets in.

The right soil
For the most part, herbs are not picky when it comes to soil, except when it involves drainage. Most herbs prefer well-draining soil. If your soil is poor-draining or clay, amend it with organic matter (chopped leaves and compost). Test your soil's nutrient levels using directions from a county extension service or a nearby soil laboratory. If the soil pH factor is higher than 7.5, add sulfur; if lower than 6.5, add lime. Boost soil nutrients naturally with amendments. Find organic matter for your garden in a variety of places: Get composted manure from a dairy farm or horse stable. Compost made from collected leaves and grass clippings may be available from your municipal composting program. Purchase bagged products at your local garden center or from online or mail-order sources.

opposite top Most perennial and annual herbs do best in a sunny location. For herbs that prefer cooler, shadier spots, plant near a building for protection. Enjoy a long growing season by using cloches and cold frames to protect tender herbs in early spring and late fall.

> **BHG TEST GARDEN TIP**
> **CUT BACK LAVENDER**
> In early spring, prune lavender, sage, and other woody herbs when you see new green growth. Prune back to new growth on short varieties; prune up to one-third of taller plants. This keeps plants nicely shaped and encourages new growth.

Spring
Planting Herbs

Raising herbs is easy. You can plant them from seed or buy ready-to-transplant herbs from a variety of sources.

After you've determined what herbs grow best in your climate, the next step is buying plants and seeds. Herbs are available from various sources these days: mail order, online, garden centers, grocery stores, farm stores, plant swaps, and herb society plant sales.

Buy healthy plants
There are several things to look for when buying herbs. Take a look at the leaves. Although most herbs aren't bugged by insects or disease, damaged leaves might indicate a problem. Also inspect the root system—roots that circle the bottom of a pot are a sign that the plant might be root-bound after living in the nursery pot too long. Before planting, gently loosen compressed roots.

Easy planting: Use potting mix
If you have less than optimal soil (remember, herbs like well-draining soil), use an all-purpose potting mix, especially if you are planting in raised beds or containers. You can buy commercially prepared potting mix or make your own blend. Combine equal parts peat moss, topsoil, compost, perlite, and sand to create a soil mix that's light, retains moisture, and drains well. Because many herbs are indigenous to areas with coarse, sandy soil (think of the Mediterranean), some herbs benefit from having gravel and finely crushed limestone added to the planting hole to facilitate drainage.

Planting container-grown herbs
Herbs are sold in a variety of container sizes: 3- to 4-inch pots hold small plants; perennial herbs may come in larger quart- and gallon-size containers. Regardless of the size of the container or the plant (including your home-raised seedlings), plant herbs in the same way: Dig a hole. Remove the plant from the container by tilting it upside down (yanking the plant out of the pot by grabbing the foliage and pulling risks damaging the plant). Squeeze the pot to loosen the plant, if necessary. Place the plant in the hole and backfill with soil, tamping gently to remove any air pockets. Water deeply.

Sowing herbs by seed
You can sow many herbs directly into garden soil in spring (or fall in warmer regions). Prepare the planting area by digging in compost and loosening the soil. Use a garden rake to smooth the area. Sow herb seeds according to their packet instructions. Cover seeds with a thin layer of soil, if required. Sprinkle the area with water daily until seeds sprout.

Planting depth
Most herb seedlings or plants do best when their crowns are planted at the same depth as they were in their nursery pots. Dig a hole, then set the herb in the hole. Adjust the planting depth to raise or lower the plant so the crown is even with the top of the hole.

Mulching herbs
Add a 2- to 4-inch layer of mulch (shredded bark, chopped leaves, cocoa shells) between plants to preserve soil moisture and deter weeds. Keep mulch about 2–4 inches away from plant stems to allow water and air to reach roots. Water after applying mulch—especially dry mulch. Watering will help hold the mulch in place on windy days.

Planting tender perennial herbs
If you live in a region of the country where temperatures dip below freezing, you can still grow tender perennial herbs—but you may need to plant them in a container if you want to keep them for the next year. Tender perennial herbs such as rosemary and lemon verbena do well in containers in summer and are easily transported indoors once warm weather ends.

opposite top Starting an herb garden from scratch is easy with young herbs. Buy your favorites and combine them in a bed or container. Look for healthy plants that show new growth.

DIVIDE TO MAKE NEW PLANTS

Many herbs benefit from a spring division. It will make the mother plants healthier, and you'll have plants to share.

1 DIG
Use a trowel or spade to dig up the plant. Make a trench around the plant on all sides. Dig under the roots to loosen the plant.

2 LIFT
Gently lift the plant from the ground, detaching the roots from below with the sharp end of the trowel.

3 DIVIDE
Pull apart the plant to make several smaller plants. Divide large plants with big root balls by cutting them with a spade or large knife.

BHG TEST GARDEN TIP: IMPROVE DRAINAGE

For plants that require lots of drainage, such as Mediterranean natives lavender and rosemary, toss handfuls of coarse gravel along with crushed limestone into planting holes to improve the soil's drainability.

A YEAR OF HERBS

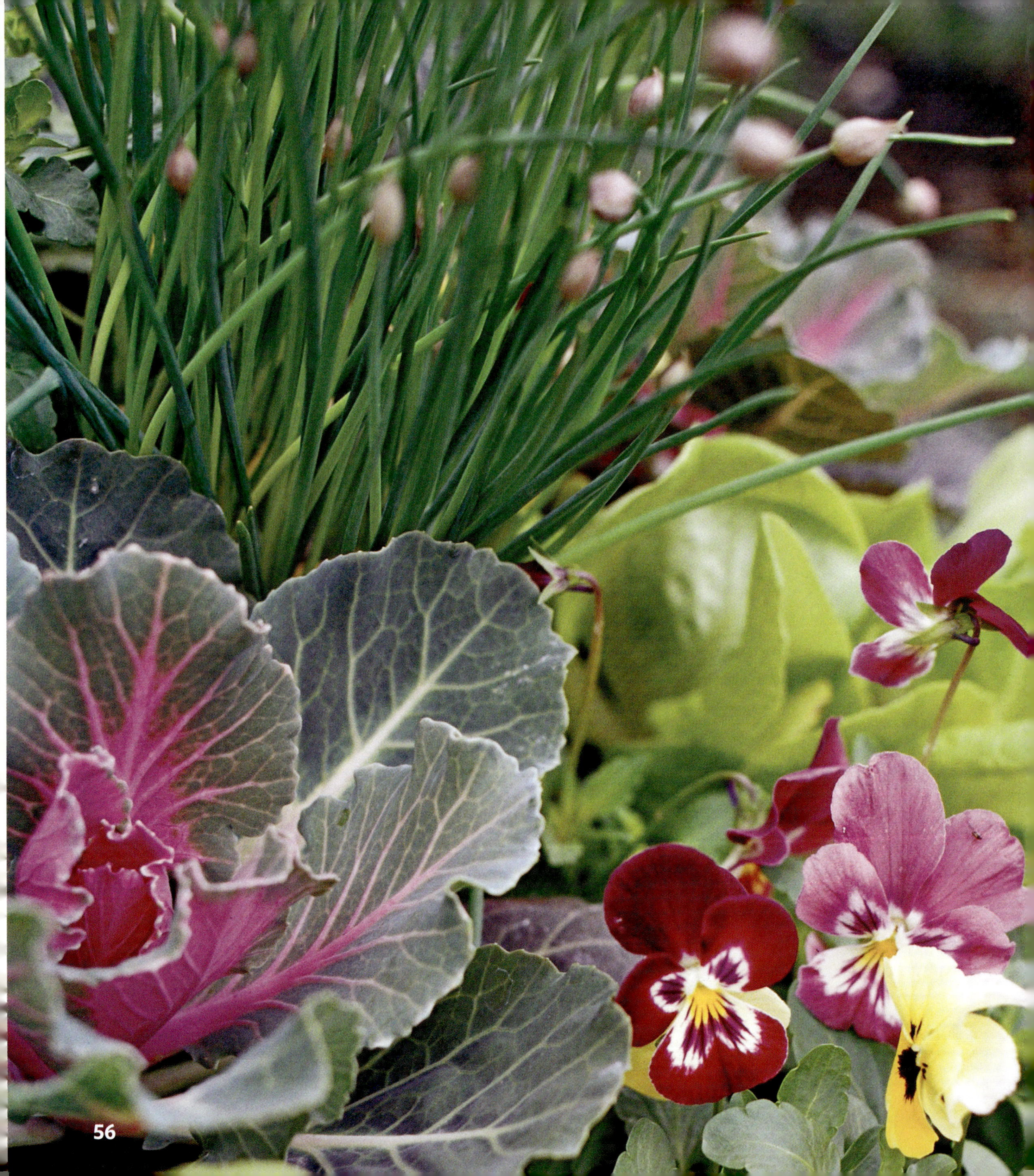

Spring
Herb Duets

Herbs make excellent bedfellows with a variety of annual and perennial flowers, as well as other herbs.

Herbs range in size from low-growing, creeping pennyroyal to magnificent 6-foot-tall angelica. So planting—both herbs and flowers—means you need to pay attention to all their attributes: size (height and width), leaves (size, texture, and color), and flowers (form and color).

Even at a distance, many herb gardens appear green and luscious. Herbs have been used for a plethora of purposes since antiquity, from medicines to seasonings and simply for their presence in a garden. Among all plants, herbs are considered beautiful in their own right. So be sure to consider the color and texture of herbs when planting your garden, and include them with other plantings in spring.

Pretty planting partners

Depending on your herb garden design, certain herbs make ideal companions. Think about creating planting combinations so paired plants can show off each other's attributes. For example, dill and chervil pair nicely: One is spiky and the other feathery. Tansy and lovage make good partners; both are tall, and tansy's intricate dark green leaves and yellow flowers contrast nicely with lovage's flat green leaves. Contrast silver thyme and creeping thyme for color interest. Both are low-growing but have dramatically different leaf colors.

Spring herbs on the rise

In the herb garden, herbs come into their own each season. In early spring, shoots of chives rise from the ground like missiles. How pretty they are when paired with equally early species of tulips. Leafy, lacy fennel comes up around the same time violas are spreading their joy throughout the garden. And perennial herbs that don't die back in winter look stunning with early-rising bulbs: Woody-stemmed lavender greens up nicely near nodding narcissus, creeping thyme, and crocus; and sage and scilla look lovely together.

opposite Flowering herbs such as chives (still in bud in this photo) look right at home in a mixed flower-and-vegetable garden.

HERB PAIRINGS

Herbs are known for their beneficial qualities, such as repelling pests in the garden. Here are some tried-and-true pairings.

SAGE WITH BROCCOLI
Pair sage with broccoli, cabbage, and cauliflower to repel cabbage moths and black flea beetles.

HYSSOP WITH CABBAGE
Plant hyssop near cabbage and kale to deter cabbage moths.

MARIGOLD WITH TOMATO
Marigolds help repel nematodes, aphids, whiteflies, and hawk moths (the parent of the tomato hornworm).

CHERVIL WITH RADISHES
Chervil planted near radishes and carrots improves the flavor of these root crops.

CHIVES WITH CARROTS
Plant chives near carrots and tomatoes to improve the flavor of the crops.

GARLIC WITH ROSES
Garlic deters the tiny bright green aphids that can infest roses.

A YEAR OF HERBS

Spring
Invasive Herbs

As with all plant groups, there are overachievers that can take over a garden. Some herbs can be invasive, so border control is important.

Some herbs are ruthless garden grabbers. One season you have a well-behaved plant, and the next spring the same plant expands in size or number and spreads into other areas of the garden. Annual herbs can spread by self-sowing. Perennial herbs can self-seed or spread via above- and underground shoots. Self-propagation and spreading can be a good thing—until it goes too far.

Defining invasive species

Opportunistic plants that become weedy by growing where they shouldn't are called invasive species. The U. S. Department of Agriculture (USDA) defines invasive plant species as those that are "characteristically adaptable, aggressive, and have a high reproductive capacity." Some of the common herbs encountered in wild meadows and rural ditches today—mullein, St. John's wort, soapwort, elderberry, chicory, and others—are species the first Europeans brought with them. They have survived and spread across the country, but that does not make them invasive.

Imposing border control

Invasive plants outcompete others, cause problems in native habitats, and resist elimination. You can keep aggressive herbs within bounds by planting them in containers or segregating them in areas of the garden where they can't spread and take over. Perennial herbs considered invasive include mints, pennyroyal, comfrey, and bee balm. Herbs that can reseed excessively include lemon balm, dill, garlic chives, and borage. If you have space in your garden and you like these plants, you may view their spreading habit as a good thing. It's up to you to decide whether a plant is a ruthless invader or a welcome colonizer.

But there are other reasons to put the brakes on invasive plants. They can spread into neighboring gardens. They can also adversely affect the use of the plants around them. For example, the unchecked intermingling of different types of mint results in the loss of the individual plants' scent and flavor: You can end up with chocolate mint that tastes very much like orange mint. Another reason to keep invasive species in check is to keep them from spreading to areas outside your garden, taking away resources from native plants.

How plants become invaders

Some annual herbs become invasive because they reseed themselves. Annual herbs do this by nature. In the case of all self-seeders, such as dill, garlic chives, catmint, and anise hyssop, you can simply cut off the seed heads as they form. Avoid allowing them to dry and produce viable seeds. If self-seeding occurs and you find a batch of seedlings growing around and beneath their parent plants, simply weed them out.

Some perennial herbs take over because they self-propagate by producing shoots that grow aboveground or rootstocks that creep belowground. These shoots are called rhizomes or underground runners. Members of the mint family produce this way. You can stop plants from spreading by runners by segregating them into their own planting pockets, creating deep edging around them so they can't spread, planting them in containers, or planting them in containers with the bottoms cut out and sunk directly into the soil.

BHG TEST GARDEN TIP — IS THIS A WEED?

Sprouting herbs (especially those that may have self-seeded) are difficult to differentiate from weeds. Let plants grow a bit before yanking them, to identify friends from foes. Thin herbs to produce healthier plants. If the plants are weeds, pull them.

KEEP MINT FROM SPREADING

Mint and other members of the mint family are notorious spreaders. You can solve the problem of invasions to other parts of your garden by corralling their roots. Here's how:

1 BURY
Cut the bottom out of a plastic grower's pot using a pair of pruners. Plant the pot into the garden so the top edge is even with the ground.

2 PLANT
Remove a mint plant from its container and plant it into the grower's pot. Add more soil if necessary. By planting this way, only the roots of the mint plant will make contact with the soil. Runners will not form, and the plant will not be able to spread. Water well after planting.

3 COVER
Add soil around the base of the plant and to cover (and disguise) the rim of the pot. This way the mint will appear as though it is planted in the garden. Add a layer of mulch to help maintain soil moisture.

right Aggressively growing mint is best sequestered in containers in the garden. Otherwise, this wandering herb may take over a garden bed.

Spring
Planning a New Bed

Adding a new herb bed to your garden is easy. Just follow simple planning and planting rules for success.

Creating a new herb garden is just like creating any other type of garden. You decide on the style of herb garden you want—cottage, traditional, historical. Then determine its size. If you've never gardened before, it's a good idea to start small. A 4×4-foot herb garden is large enough to contain lots of different types of herbs but small enough to care for easily.

Draw a plan
Use a piece of plain or graph paper to sketch a plan. You don't need to do it to scale; just make a rough drawing including overall shape and features, such as a path or fence. One way to design a garden is to borrow a classic geometric shape: square, circle, rectangle, or diamond.

Mark your herb bed
An easy way to mark your bed is to use a can of spray paint. You can spray right on the ground to mark the area where you will dig.

Make a plant list
Determine which herbs you will grow and use. Make a list of the herbs you want to grow from seed, those you want to buy as established plants, and those you can get from friends' gardens. (Spring is the ideal time to divide plants—swap herb divisions with friends or neighbors, and attend plant swaps or sales.)

left An herbs-only garden can be small but fully packed with plants. Although the footprint of this bed is petite, it features nearly a dozen different varieties of plants.

How many plants?
The plants and their space requirements will indicate how many plants you need. When you plant herbs, space them according to their mature size, leaving room for air circulation. If a plant grows 1 foot wide, place it at least 1 foot from the plant next to it. When you arrange young and small herbs in a bed, you'll see plenty of soil between plants. Overplanting or planting too tightly can increase problems with insects and diseases.

Prepare your soil
Till your soil and add appropriate amendments for your soil type. Digging in a layer of compost annually infuses the soil with organic material and nutrients, promoting healthy plants.

Water and mulch
After you plant your herbs, follow up with two more essential steps: watering and mulching. Water herbs to help them establish healthy root systems, even if they are low-maintenance and drought-tolerant varieties. Mulch helps maintain soil moisture and reduces weeding chores.

BHG TEST GARDEN TIP

MULCHING
Mulching herbs benefits them in many ways: It smothers weeds, helps maintain soil moisture, and unifies the look of an herb planting or flowerbed. Herb beds can be covered with organic mulch such as finely shredded bark. Gravel mulch looks neat and clean when used in containers.

HERB GARDEN DECOR
Many herb gardens have common decorative and utilitarian elements. Which ones to choose depends on style and need.

1. BEE SKEP Traditionally used to house bees (the honey was extracted by crushing the skep at the end of summer), these former bee abodes are purely ornamental.
2. BIRDBATH A birdbath provides water for drinking and bathing, helping to sustain birds in all seasons.
3. PATHWAY Made from bricks, stones, pavers, or gravel, a walkway is essential for access to a large herb garden.
4. CLOCHE Glass bell-shape plant covers, cloches are used in the herb garden to protect tender plants.
5. SUNDIAL A sundial is an ancient device for telling time. The classic ornament in herb gardens is often placed among thyme or lavender to enhance the presentation.

A YEAR OF HERBS **61**

Spring
Early Harvests

Herb lovers have a special place in their hearts for spring herbs. Among the season's first greens, aromatic and delectable herbs are as welcome as the season itself.

Perennial spring herbs, such as sorrel and chives, are at their most tender and tasty in early spring. In cold climates they sprout before some of the spring-blooming bulbs break ground.

Sour savory sorrel
Young leaves of tart sorrel make excellent fresh additions to salads mixed with spring greens, such as arugula and leaf lettuce. You can also make a hot or cold sorrel soup, called schav, from sorrel leaves, onion, lemon juice, and other ingredients.

Tender, strappy chives
Chive leaves are most tender in early spring. Harvest and eat the shoots before the plants mature, producing buds and blooms. Snip the long, slender leaves, then dice and sprinkle into salads, soups, or sauces. Puree chive leaves with olive oil and almonds to create a chive pesto that adds flavor to bruschetta or pasta.

Spring herb harvesting tips
Harvest herbs early in the day, after dew has evaporated from the leaves but before the sun bakes out the flavor and fragrance (essence). Herbs harvested early in the morning taste better because the plant's essential-oil concentration is at its peak. Snip off the new growth of herb plants using scissors or pruners. Inspect the leaves before eating: They should be free from insect holes or leaf spots. Turn over the leaves and make sure there are no eggs or larvae on the undersides. Wash herb leaves under cool running water to remove any soil. Shake off the water and pat dry with paper towels. Use herbs fresh, or bundle stems and hang them in a cool, dry place to air-dry.

Fall planting for spring herbs
If you live in a warm climate, you can plant some herbs in fall and harvest them in spring. Parsley can be sown in autumn; this perennial prefers cooler weather. Cilantro also prefers the lower temperatures of autumn; it will germinate and grow, reseeding itself to come up in spring. Combine spring-picked leaves of parsley and cilantro with garlic and olive oil to make chimichurri, an Argentinean sauce used as a marinade for meat.

GROW A THREE-POT HERB GARDEN
Planting a snippable garden of spring herbs is easy. Plant three pots with fast-growing annual herbs to create a mini kitchen garden. The more you clip, the more the plants will grow.

1 SOW
In a container filled with potting mix, sow your favorite herb seeds. Easy-to-sprout herb seeds include annual dill, cilantro, and chervil. Simply sprinkle them over the surface of the soil, and gently scratch them shallowly into the soil. Keep the mix moist to prompt germination.

2 SPROUT
Place the pots in direct sunlight. Keep the soil moist but not wet. The seeds of chervil, dill, and cilantro sprout quickly in warm weather. If you want to make more room in the pot, you can pull out some of the seedlings, which you can add to salads or soups.

3 CLIP
Harvest leaves as soon as they are big enough. Snip the plants regularly to keep them producing new leaves. Annual herbs will keep producing more leaves if you cut them back. Keep cutting so they don't produce seed heads.

opposite Clip herb leaves and flowers for use in recipes and bouquets.

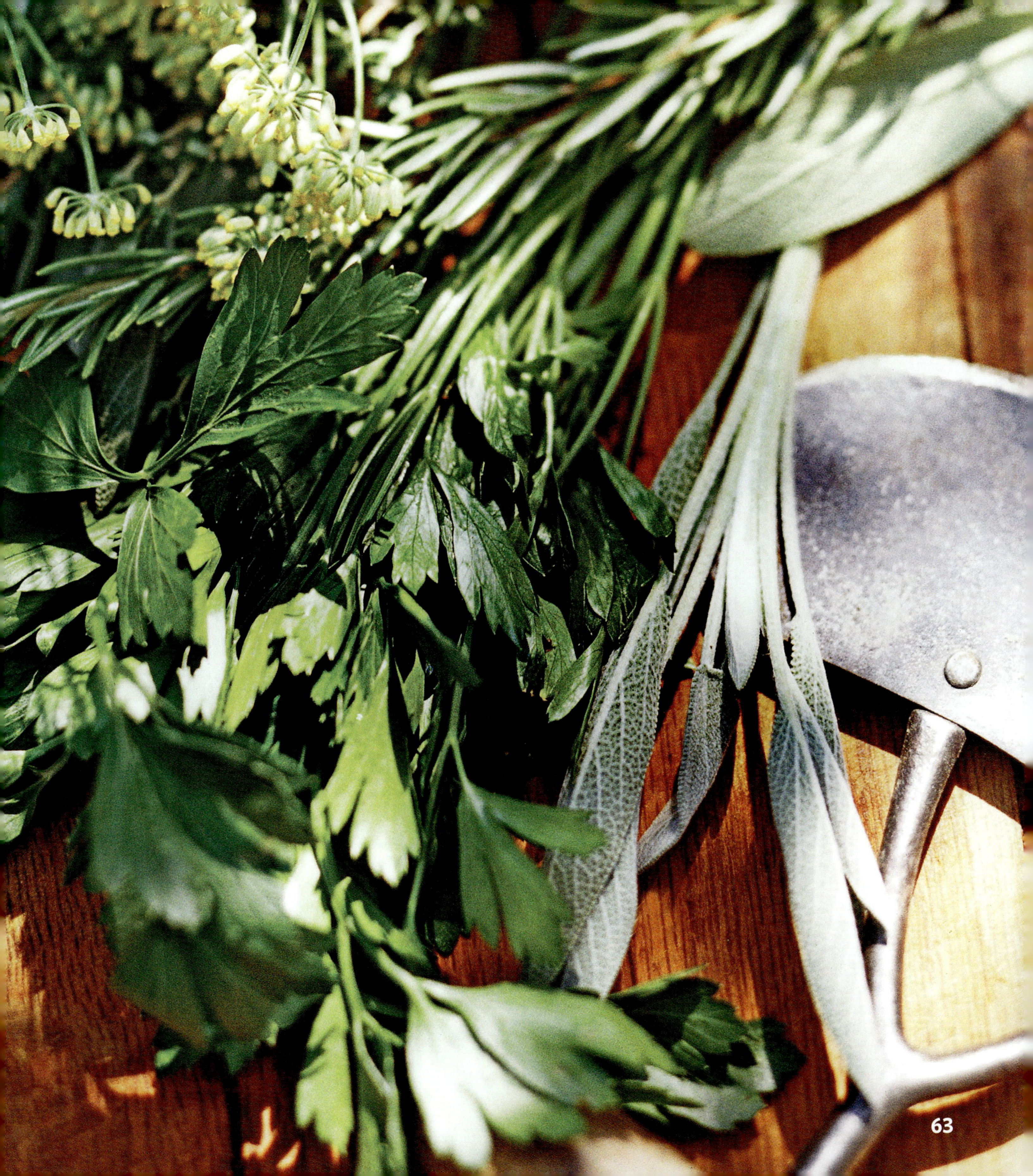

Spring
Watering

Like other types of plants, herbs require water to thrive. Most herbs aren't thirsty plants, so hit-and-miss watering works.

Water is essential to any plant's survival, but many herbs are less thirsty than other plants. That's an advantage. Yet even though you will need to water young plants until they're established, you'll also need to give established herbs supplemental moisture (other than what Mother Nature provides).

How do you know when your herbs need water? You can look for the obvious sign of wilting leaves, but wilted, droopy plants may also indicate overwatering. It's important to feel the soil before watering. Poke a finger into the soil. If the first 1–2 inches (up to your first or second knuckle) feels dry, it's time to water.

Group by needs

Some herbs, such as Mediterranean natives rosemary, lavender, and thyme, prefer dry soil. Other herbs, such as mint, prefer moister soil. By grouping your dry-loving plants—away from herbs that like wetter conditions—you can suit the plants' water needs more easily. In the process, you will make less work for yourself and keep your herbs happier, too.

Low-maintenance watering options

There are a number of ways to water herbs—almost without lifting a finger.

Soaker hoses. These permeable hoses sweat moisture, allowing small beads of water to slowly seep into the ground. You can shallowly bury these hoses under mulch, making them discreet. Attach the hose to a timer to water the garden more efficiently and on a schedule.

Drip irrigation. This watering method uses in-ground hoses or PVC tubes to deliver water directly to a plant's roots. Instead of being permeable, drip irrigation hoses have attached emitters that drip water directly onto the ground.

left Herbs in containers need more moisture than herbs planted in the ground. Water at the base of plants to keep from wetting the leaves.

Both soaker hoses and drip irrigation systems are efficient ways to water large herb gardens because moisture is delivered directly to the plants' roots without loss due to evaporation. This close-to-the-soil delivery method keeps herb foliage dry and helps prevent diseases that develop and thrive in damp conditions.

Hand-watering options

If your garden is small or you want to water specific areas (such as herbs planted in containers, which require more frequent watering than herbs in the ground), you can use the following:

Watering can. This is an old-fashioned but still-effective way of delivering water to plants. Use a can with a rosette for a fine spray (best for herb seedlings) or a thin stream (best for watering at the base of plants).

Hose and watering wand. A wand or stick waterer that attaches to a hose offers an excellent way to water herbs in hard-to-reach places, such as window boxes or hanging baskets.

BHG TEST GARDEN TIP

AVOID EXCESS WATER

Herbs are often drought-resistant, and they can suffer from overwatering or too much rain. Also watch for signs of mildew or fungal disease, which can be caused by too much moisture. Water herbs early in the morning, allowing water on leaves to dry during the day.

MULCH OPTIONS

Mulch helps conserve soil moisture so you don't need to water your herbs as often. Organic mulch breaks down, adding nutrients to soil and improving drainage. Here are some mulch options for your herb garden.

WOOD MULCH Bark dust lasts up to two years and looks neat. Shredded bark looks better around the small leaves of herb plants than small pieces of bark.

COCOA HULLS These chocolate-scented pieces last for six months. This mulch is unsafe for use if you have a dog.

PINE STRAW Regionally available and inexpensive, pine straw lasts about one year. It is not good for windy locations.

CHOPPED LEAVES Free in most places, leaves are best when used chopped and partially decomposed.

MUNICIPAL COMPOST Available locally in some areas and often free for the taking, compost lasts a few months. Reapply seasonally or annually.

A YEAR OF HERBS **65**

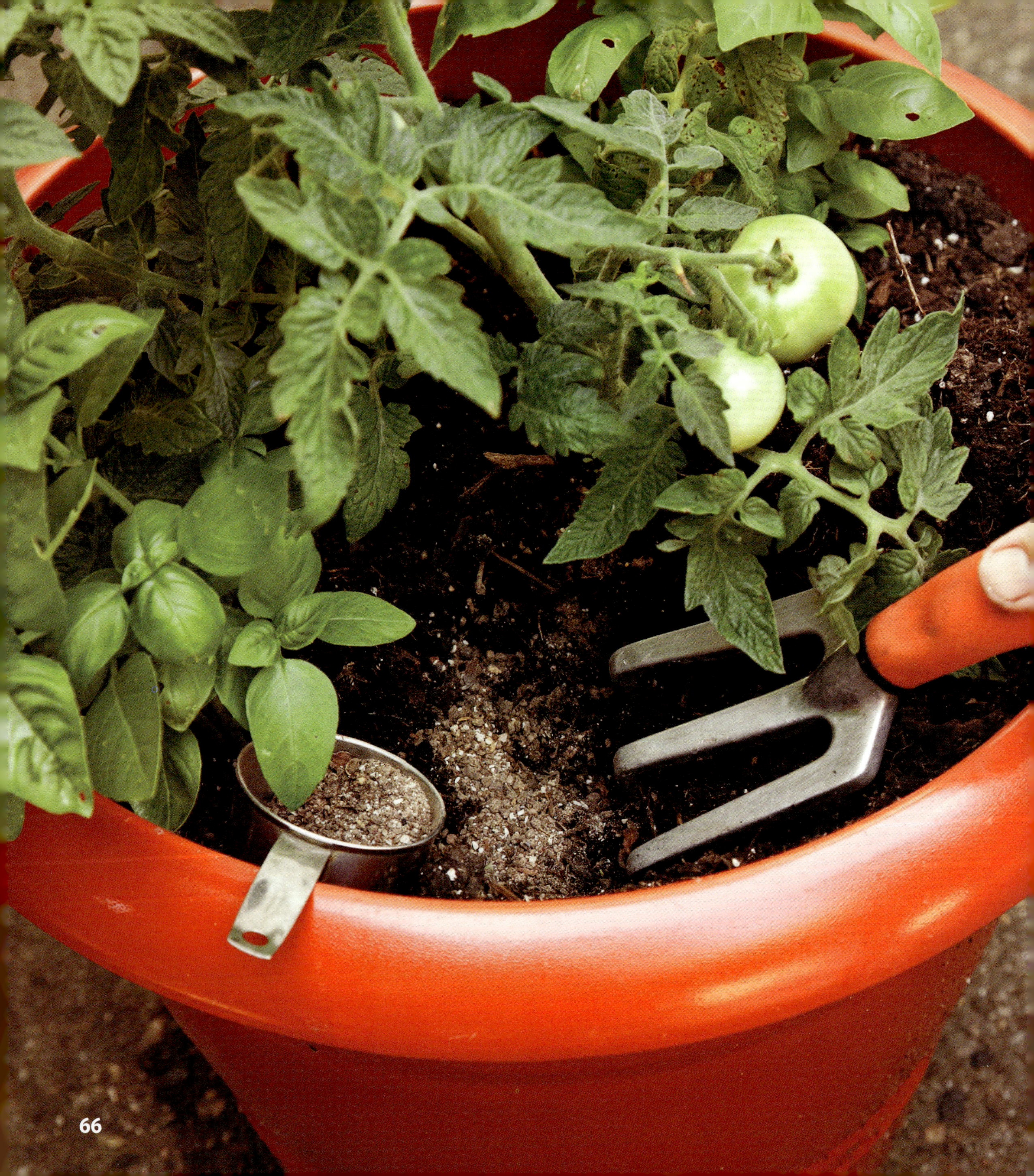

Summer Fertilizing

Herbs aren't heavy feeders, but a nip of additional nutrients will help them stay in top shape.

Here's the good news: Herbs need little fertilizer. Like other plants, herbs make their own food, using light and water in photosynthesis. They also draw essential nutrients, including nitrogen, phosphorus, and potassium, from soil. If a soil test detects nutrients are lacking, you'll need to fertilize.

Liquid fertilizer blends
Water-soluble fertilizers can be applied to herb plantings using a watering can or sprayer. You can also use a foliar fertilizer, such as kelp, fish emulsion, or comfrey tea.

Granular fertilizer
There are fast- and slow-release granular fertilizers. Uncoated granular fertilizer releases nutrients quickly; the release is triggered by moisture. Even the moisture from your hands will start the release, so wear gloves when applying. Slow-release granular fertilizer is coated and releases nutrients at a slower but constant rate. To apply granular fertilizers, scatter the product over the soil's surface around plants. Scratch the fertilizer into the soil, covering the granules. Avoid letting the fertilizer remain on leaves or fall into the crown of the plant. If you add fertilizer to a mulched bed, pull the mulch away and apply the fertilizer, then reposition the mulch. Apply fertilizer to moist soil, or water after feeding. This enables plants to use the food by taking it up through their roots.

Compost
A nutrient-rich mixture of well-rotted organic materials, compost is a great way to amend the soil in your herb garden. Use compost from commercial sources (available in bags at garden centers) or municipal sources (some towns and cities compost yard waste and give it away), or make it in your yard or a composting unit indoors.

opposite A tomato-and-basil veggie-herb combo in a container benefits from a dose of granulated organic fertilizer scratched into the soil's surface early in the season.

COMFREY TEA FERTILIZER
Brew a strong herb tea for plants using comfrey leaves. This liquid solution is rich in calcium, phosphorus, potassium, and other nutrients that will boost your plants' vitality and help your garden grow.

1 PICK
Harvest comfrey leaves anytime during the growing season. This large, leafy plant produces ample amounts of foliage by midsummer, so you can remove lots of foliage without harming the plant. Cut stems at the base of the plant, and strip off the large leaves.

2 PACK
Fill a 5-gallon bucket with comfrey leaves, packing the leaves tightly. Add water until the leaves are covered. Place a cover, such as a board or garbage-can lid, on top of the bucket.

3 STEEP
Allow the comfrey leaves to steep in water for several days. The leaves will start to disintegrate, creating a dark brown-green liquid that is quite smelly. (You may want to wear rubber gloves when handling.)

4 FERTILIZE
Strain the liquid from the leaves. Add the leaves to your compost bin. Pour the liquid into a garden sprayer. Use the spray to foliar-feed your garden plants. Or you can pour the nutrient-rich tea directly into the ground around the base of plants. Use all the comfrey tea fertilizer right away. Do not store it.

Timing and cautions
When do you need to fertilize? Before summer gets into full swing, when plants are putting on growth spurts, adding fertilizer improves growth. When using fertilizer, keep it away from water features, and sweep up spills on hard surfaces such as sidewalks and driveways. Use fertilizer according to package directions. Overfertilizing can injure plants.

Summer
Pruning and Deadheading

Pinching, pruning, and deadheading make herbs more productive. And best of all, you can use the delicious clippings.

Herbs don't need a lot of extra care, but an occasional nip and tuck will help plants stay healthy and produce more blooms.

Pinching back
When you pinch the top off an herb plant, it reacts by growing more at the bottom. Removing the growing tip stimulates the plant to produce hormones, causing the lower buds on the stems to sprout. This results in a bushier, fuller plant. You can pinch plants back in spring, when they are putting out new growth, and throughout summer to encourage lush, dense plants. Use clean, sharp pruners to snip woody or tough-stem herbs; pinch off soft stems or spent flowers between your thumb and forefinger. See the herb encyclopedia, starting on *page 128*, for advice about grooming specific herbs. For perennial herbs, stop deadheading and pruning in late summer to allow them time to prepare for winter.

Shearing back spring bloomers
Many spring-blooming perennial herbs can be revived after they have flowered by cutting them by one-third. Herbs such as chives, viola, and comfrey appear spent and tired by summer. Prune the plants after they finish flowering to shape them and to prompt new green growth. Other herbs that benefit from a revival pruning after they flower include catmint, catnip, sage, bee balm, and lavender.

Deadheading
Deadheading is the gardening term for removing faded flowers from plants. When an herb finishes blooming, some plants' flowers fade away on their own with little tending. Others linger, looking dead and brown and detracting from the plants' appearance. Clipping off spent flowers benefits plants in two ways: It neatens your garden, and it stops seed formation. The second benefit is most important for herb plants that are voracious self-seeders.

And with leafy edible herbs, removing the flower before it blooms (sort of predeadheading) is an important step in retaining the most flavor. Literally nipping the plant in the bud halts the plant's seed production, which puts more energy (and flavor!) into the leaves. In fact, if you allow some herbs to flower, you'll notice the decrease in flavor in the harvested leaves. This is especially true for annuals such as basil, whose leaves are the key element of the plant.

When not to deadhead
You may not want to remove the heads of faded flowers for many reasons. Some seed heads are beautiful, providing winter interest in your garden. For example, the waving heads of anise hyssop and the bright red hips of roses provide texture and color in the winter garden. Another reason to withhold the pruners is that if you deadhead, you cannot collect seeds at the end of the season. If you want to harvest seeds of coriander, dill, and fennel, you need to allow the flower heads to fade and set seed.

> **BHG TEST GARDEN TIP**
> **CUTTING TOOLS**
> Keep your herb garden nipped, tucked, and flavorful by removing dead foliage and spent blossoms with bypass hand pruners, small scissors, and grass shears. Keep blades of cutting tools sharpened for the cleanest and healthiest cuts. Use lubricating oil when sharpening and cleaning cutting tools.

opposite top Shearing back an herb such as garlic chives after blooming revives the plant, neatens its appearance, and stops it from reseeding.

CREATE A ROSEMARY STANDARD

Standards, or tree-shape herb plants, are elegant ways to raise potted herbs. They're usually pricier, too. You can breathe new life into a rangy, sparse rosemary by transforming it into a chic little standard. Then use your clippings in recipes. Here's how:

1 CHOOSE
Start with a sparsely growing plant that needs revitalizing or one that is newer and fuller from a local nursery or other retail store.

2 CLIP
Remove the side shoots by clipping them off with a hand pruner. Start at the bottom and work your way up.

3 SHAPE
Clip the branches close to the stem. Use the tip of the pruners to get in close. Snip and shape the top growth of the plant.

4 MAINTAIN
Keep your standard clipped into the desired shape, such as a globe or cone, by cutting off new growth every few weeks.

Summer
Ornamental Herbs

Herbs play starring roles in landscape design when mixed with flowers, shrubs, and trees.

Use herbs in your landscape the way you do other plants. Capitalize on their flower colors, textures, heights, and growth habits.

Landscaping with herbs
Perennial herbs can be used as long-term landscape participants. In warm, dry climates, rosemary flourishes as a drought-tolerant shrub. It can be shaped to fit any space while providing ample cuttings for recipes. Bay laurel and citrus trees provide structural assets to a landscape. Although these trees require warm climates, cold-weather gardeners can plant them in containers that can be brought indoors over winter.

Tall perennial herbs, such as angelica and fennel, can be planted en masse for a lovely effect or used as background plantings in flower borders. A hedge of artemisia at the edge of a property provides ghostly gray foliage that can be enjoyed even after dark. Flowering perennial herbs, such as yarrow, chives, and tansy, can be tucked into herbaceous borders, where they hold their own amid other flowering perennials.

Walkway edgers
Create a welcoming walkway with low-growing herbs. Mounded clumps of parsley make a lavish all-green border. This evergreen herb grows fast in sunny locations and maintains its good looks even after modest harvests. Shrubby, small-leaf basils such as 'Spicy Globe' or 'Boxwood' form tight, rounded mounds and look like topiaries. Add a colorful array of 'Tricolor' or 'Icterina' sage to highlight their garden companions: They attract attention and provide a colorful, leafy foil. Their variegated foliage is as flashy as it is tasty.

left Herbs are natural mixers in a landscape. In this entryway planting, potted rosemaries join a gardenia and a Japanese maple.

Shady areas

Although most herbs prefer sun, a few excel in shade. Consider planting lady's mantle, sweet cicely, lemon balm, and mint in the dappled shade of a tree. Also, sweet woodruff, pennyroyal, and Roman chamomile are groundcovers that offer flowers and fragrance in partial shade.

BHG TEST GARDEN TIP: STAKE TALL HERBS IN SPRING

When you fertilize herbs, it's also a good time to stake any tall plants, such as bronze fennel, to keep them growing upright. Use a grow-through support that hides in the plant's foliage and keeps the plant from flopping over.

HERBS BY HEIGHT

Plant herbs in your garden the same way you plant other annuals and perennials: Stagger them according to their heights so they all can be seen clearly.

Landscape Herbs: Low to Medium
(less than 3 feet)

1. LAVENDER
2. SANTOLINA
3. CATMINT
4. 'TRICOLOR' SAGE
5. 'SPICY GLOBE' BASIL

Landscape Herbs: Tall
(3 feet and taller)

6. MULLEIN
7. FENNEL
8. TANSY
9. BORAGE
10. ANGELICA

A YEAR OF HERBS 71

Butterfly

Caterpillar

Bee

Hummingbird

72

Summer
Attracting Wildlife

The leaves and flowers of many herbs draw winged wildlife to the garden.

Important garden pollinators, including hummingbirds, butterflies, and bees, find herbs both delicious and alluring. With declines in pollinator populations, it's especially important to offer a wide variety of nectar, pollen, and larvae food sources in your garden. A diverse herb collection does just that. In addition to diversity, pollinators need chemical-free dining. If you want to attract and protect the health of pollinators, refrain from using pesticides in your garden.

Butterflies
Butterflies flitting about your garden are a treat. The fluttering creatures are colorful, ephemeral, and joyful. These insects with delicate crepe-paperlike wings are attracted to a variety of flowering annuals, perennials, shrubs, and trees—including herbs. Butterflies sip the nectar from herbs including mint, catmint, marjoram, chives, and thyme.

Caterpillars
If you want to attract butterflies to your herb garden, consider the whole life cycle of the butterfly. It starts out as a larva—a caterpillar; so to enjoy butterflies, you must also welcome their larvae. Before you destroy any caterpillars, first identify them. For example, the pesky tomato hornworm can defoliate a tomato plant quickly; to control this large larva of the hawk moth pick it off the plant and drop it into a cup of soapy water. However, the nearly equally large Swallowtail or Monarch larvae should be left to munch leaves.

Bees
Bees busily buzzing from flower to flower are a sign of a healthy garden. Bees gather nectar (to make honey) and at the same time spread pollen. In honey from areas with lots of the same plants (such as lavender fields), you can taste the flavor of the flowers.

BEE GARDEN IN A POT
Create a container that will delight bees in your garden.

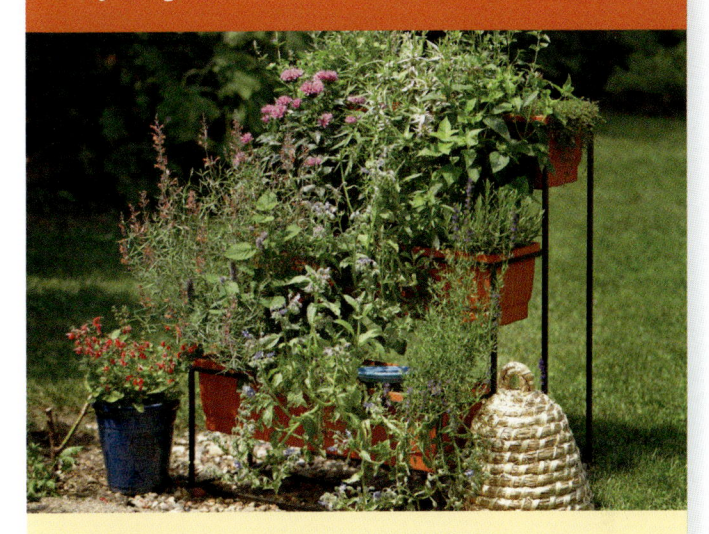

GATHER Choose nectar-rich, bee-attracting plants, such as hyssop, catmint, lavender, bee balm, thyme, borage, and salvia.

POT Use a spacious container or grouping, such as this tiered planter, to offer bees a diverse plant menu. Also include a saucer of fresh water.

POSITION Locate the plants away from entryways or dining areas; give your bees space to gather nectar and pollen away from people.

The herbs bees love most include borage, chamomile, germander, hyssop, lavender, basil, lemon balm, bee balm, anise hyssop, salvia, mints, sage, savory, rosemary, and thyme. Like butterflies, bees prefer flowers in sunny locations. They easily navigate single flowers; double-flower species are harder to sip from.

Hummingbirds
Hummingbirds dine on the nectar from many flowering herbs. The tiny birds' long beaks are best suited to tubular flowers, such as those of pineapple sage, mint, hyssop, lavender, and bee balm. Hummingbirds also prefer the color red, so offer them red-blooming varieties of bee balm as well as pineapple sage. Other herbs that attract hummingbirds include anise hyssop, catnip, comfrey, and rosemary.

Summer
Midseason Harvests

Picking herbs at their peak reveals their best flavor. Clip often to use fresh and preserve for later.

Summer's heat brings on fast growth for herbs that are hot-weather lovers, such as basil, rosemary, and thyme.

When to harvest
You can clip summer herbs anytime there is enough growth. Cut the stem ends of plants to prompt new growth. Snip herbs by midmorning, after the morning dew has dried from the leaves but before the hottest part of the day cooks out their flavor. The peak flavor of most herbs develops right before they flower. Avoid snipping herbs during or after rainy weather unless you plan on using them right away. Generally you should cut no more than one-third of the stem's length. Exceptions to this rule include chives and lavender: When they bloom, harvest only the flowering stems at ground level.

Hot-weather harvests
Perennial and annual herbs can be harvested all summer, but don't put added stress on plants by cutting them back too much during hot weather. Cut as many herbs as you want to use fresh. Allow them to stay on the plant until you want to use them. If you want to cut herbs for use within a day, cut the stems and place them in a small vase or glass of water to keep them fresh.

Prepping herbs for use
After you've clipped stems of edible herbs, rinse the foliage under cold water and pat dry with paper towels. Remove the leaves from tough or woody stems; set aside these stems and don't use them in cooking. Chop the leaves and tender stems with a knife or snip with scissors. Save the woody stems for later use, such as burning in a grill or fireplace to impart an herby aroma.

REAP THE BOUNTY
Summer is prime time to pick, prune, and harvest.

1. DRY Bundle small-leaf long-stem herbs such as sage, tarragon, marjoram, and artemisia, and hang them in a cool, dry, airy place.

2. GRIND AND FREEZE Wash and pat dry large-leaf herbs such as basil and parsley. Combine with oil in a food processor and grind into a paste. Spoon into ice cube trays and freeze to use later in soups, stews, and sauces.

3. ADD THEM TO THE TABLE Create small bundles of fresh herbs, including colorful leaves and flowers, to grace individual place settings.

4. GATHER HERBAL BOUQUETS Place a textural mix of cut herbs in a simple vase as lovely cut-flower arrangement.

5. MAKE INTO WREATHS Wire bundles of herb leaves and flowers to a wreath frame. A fresh herb wreath dries naturally and can be used in recipes all season. It's a flavorful gift from the garden.

Experimenting with flavors
Try fresh and dried herbs in varying proportions in foods to see how you like them best. Use herbs sparingly at first when adding them to recipes. Try them one at a time until you become familiar with the flavors. Mix and match herbs to your taste. Try classic pairings, such as basil and oregano or dill and lemon. Then experiment and create combos of your own.

opposite Gather herbs in the early morning after dew has dried to capture their peak flavor and fragrance.

75

Summer Culinary Herbs

Herbs come into their own during the hot months of summer. Here are some of the season's best.

LEAFY HERBS

Basil
Large-leaf basil varieties produce ample leaves for pastas and pestos. Snip leaves as you need them. For larger quantities, harvest the entire stem.

Thyme
Although savory, thyme is often used in sweets. To coat with sugar, wet leaves lightly with egg white and sprinkle sugar over tops. Let dry two to three hours before using as a garnish.

Mint
Use mint to make simple syrups for summer drinks. Or add leaves directly to iced tea, lemonade, or cocktails. Place leaves in each glass and bruise with a spoon to release their flavor.

Parsley
Cut up flat-leaf parsley to use in salads, soups, and stews. Add parsley to warm foods just before serving so it maintains its flavor and bright green color.

left Rosemary, thyme, lavender—summer produces a bounty of herbal leaves and flowers to use fresh in recipes and bouquets.

FLOWERING HERBS

Hyssop
Use dried or fresh hyssop flowers to add a mintlike flavor to salads, stuffings, or vegetables.

Bee Balm
Pick the frilly flowers of bee balm in full bloom, and break apart for petals to sprinkle into salads and soups.

Lavender
Lavender flowers are used fresh or dried in cooking, as well as in fragrant bath and body-care products.

Clary Sage
The small bracts of clary sage flowers can be used as a skin compress.

SEEDY HERBS

Dill
In late summer yellow dill flowers develop brown seeds. Dill seed is used to flavor pickles and can be added to breads and biscuits.

Coriander
When cilantro plants have bolted, the flowers form seeds in midsummer. When the seeds, coriander, turn dry and brown, they can be used whole or crushed into powder.

Fennel
Infuse a burst of licorice flavor by adding fennel seeds to sweet and savory dishes. To release the flavor, crush seeds in a mortar with a pestle before adding them to recipes.

Caraway
Caraway seeds can be used whole, such as sprinkled on breads and crackers, or ground and used in powder form.

A YEAR OF HERBS

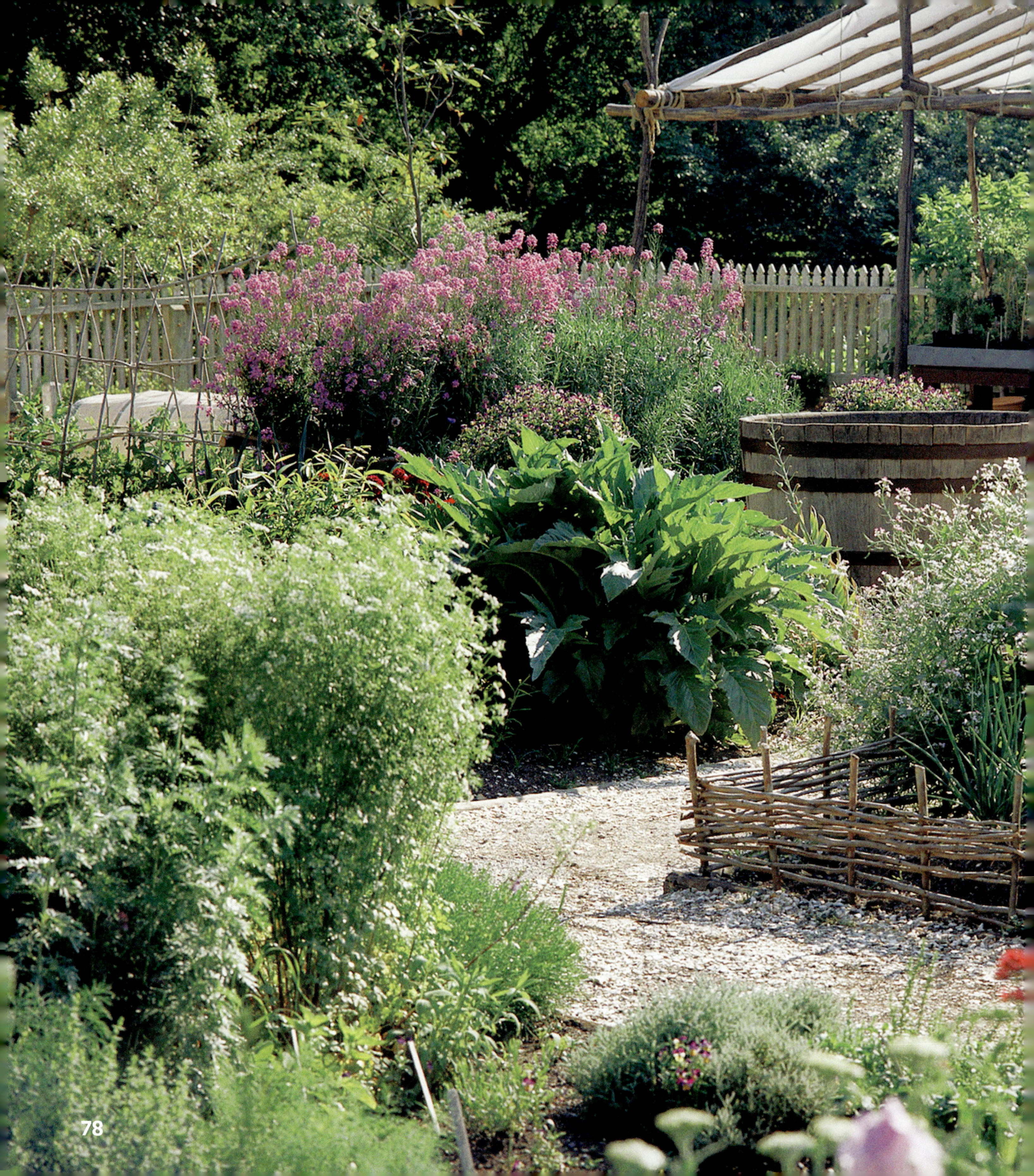

Fall
Propagating Herbs

Take cuttings of your favorite herbs and you'll get a jump start on your next year's herb garden.

Fall is an ideal time to make cuttings from your still-lush, growing herb plants. Cuttings are the most inexpensive way to multiply your plants. Plus, they allow you to overwinter some of your favorite herbs—especially if you don't have room indoors to bring all your tender plants inside.

Start with healthy plants
Choose only the healthiest plants for taking cuttings. Diseased, insect-infested, or stressed plants will not provide good cuttings. Select leafy, nonflowering stems for the best cuttings. Take cuttings in early morning because the plant usually has the most moisture at this time. Clip off stems and keep the cuttings cool and moist until you are ready to root them. Avoid leaving the cuttings in direct sun because they will dry out. You can root cuttings in two ways: in water or in soil.

Root in water
Rooting herbs in water may be the easiest method of propagation; it's a fun project for kids. But water-rooting doesn't work well with all types of herbs. You can generally root soft-stem plants quickly (in less than a couple weeks)—think herbs such as mint, basil, and pineapple sage. Woodier-stem plants, such as lemon verbena and rosemary, will root in water, but they take much longer.

After clipping the stems of the plants you want to start, place the cuttings in a glass of water and set it in indirect sunlight. Change the water every day to keep bacteria from killing the roots. Once the stems have rooted, plant them in a small container in loose potting soil. When they have established a small root ball, plant them in the garden in spring.

opposite The late-summer and early-fall garden is the culmination of the growing season—and it's the perfect time to make cuttings for the next year's garden.

HOW TO MAKE CUTTINGS
Multiply your herbs by taking cuttings to make more plants. Within weeks, you'll have new plants to add to your garden or share with friends and family.

1 CLIP
From summer into fall, cut 3- to 4-inch stems using a sharp pruner, a knife, or shears. Make the cut at an angle just below a node (where a leaf emerges from the stem). Pinch off the bottom leaves and any flowers or buds.

2 DIP
Dip the cut ends of the herb into a rooting hormone powder. This enables the cuttings to root faster. (You can purchase rooting hormone powder at garden centers or online gardening sources.)

3 PLANT
Use a pencil or chopstick to make a planting hole in a container of soilless seed-starting mix (such as peat moss, perlite, and vermiculite). Insert a stem cutting with the rooting hormone powder into the mix. Stand the cuttings 1 inch deep in the cells of seedling flats or in individual pots. The stems should be standing up straight.

4 GROW
Cover the plantings with a sheet of plastic or a dome to help keep the soil moist; prop open the cover to let air circulate. Place the cuttings in bright light but out of direct sunlight. In four to six weeks, transplant into 6-inch pots or the garden as weather allows.

Root in soilless mix
A lot of herbs can be started easily—and inexpensively—from stem cuttings. You can take cuttings throughout summer and into fall from plants grown in the ground or containers. Scented geraniums, oregano, lavender, and rosemary are best propagated through stem cuttings rooted in soilless seed-starting mix. Other herbs, such as tarragon, catmint, feverfew, and hyssop, can be propagated using this method. The stems of woody herbs such as bay laurel should be scraped on all sides before rooting to facilitate growth. Most cuttings root fastest if they're kept in a warm, humid location. Misting the cuttings frequently helps them grow.

Fall
Saving Seeds

Seed saving is one of best ways to save money! Many herb species set a bounty of easy-to-collect seeds in autumn.

As you clean up the garden in fall, gather seeds from your favorite herbs and save them for the next year's garden. Some gardeners get great satisfaction from planting seeds they've collected in their gardens. Some want to propagate a sentimental favorite passed down through generations. Others aim to safeguard seeds' genetic diversity. In fact, seed saving was once the primary way to pass plants down from generation to generation.

Now with so many excellent sources for buying seeds, you may not feel compelled to save them. But if you are looking for a way to cut costs in gardening, this is one of the easiest. Plus, you can share seeds with friends and family.

The best plants for seed saving are old-fashioned varieties and open-pollinated plants. Seeds from these plants will grow into plants that look like their parents. However, seeds harvested from hybrids usually will not grow into plants identical to their parents.

Seeds follow flowers
Most seeds develop after flowers have faded. Herb plants may produce seeds in pods (poppies), seed heads (dill and fennel), or fruits (rose hips). Herb seeds vary in appearance, size, and color.

Collecting seeds
No matter what the seeds look like, their size, or how they're held onto the plant, the key to successfully saving them is to wait until they have matured. You have a small window of opportunity, because you want to harvest seeds before they fall off the plant. The seeds of most flowering herbs can be harvested after they dry on the plant.

Storing seeds
Cool, dry, and dark are the keys to storing seeds. Place thoroughly dried seeds in small paper envelopes. Write the name of the plant, variety, and date stored on each envelope. Plan to use the seeds the next year. Place seed packets in an airtight jar. Store seeds away from light and heat to preserve their viability.

SAVE AND STORE SEEDS
Harvesting herb seeds from your garden is easy—and a great way to jump-start your spring garden.

1 SNIP
Harvest dried seed heads by clipping off the flower head stem at the base. Make sure the seeds are fully formed and starting to dry.

2 HANG
Place the dried seed heads in a paper bag, and tie it shut around the stems. Hang the bag to dry in a warm, dry place. The seeds will drop into the bag as they dry. Allow the seeds to dry for several weeks. Then remove the seeds from the bag.

3 PACKAGE
Place the dried seeds in an envelope, jar, or handmade seed packet. Mark the date and type of seed. Store your dried seeds in a cool, dry place. Many seeds remain viable for several years or more, although it's best to use seeds (whether collected or purchased) within a year of harvest for maximum germination.

opposite Saving seeds from herb plants such as dill (shown), fennel, and caraway allows you to use the seeds in recipes as well as save some for planting the next spring.

81

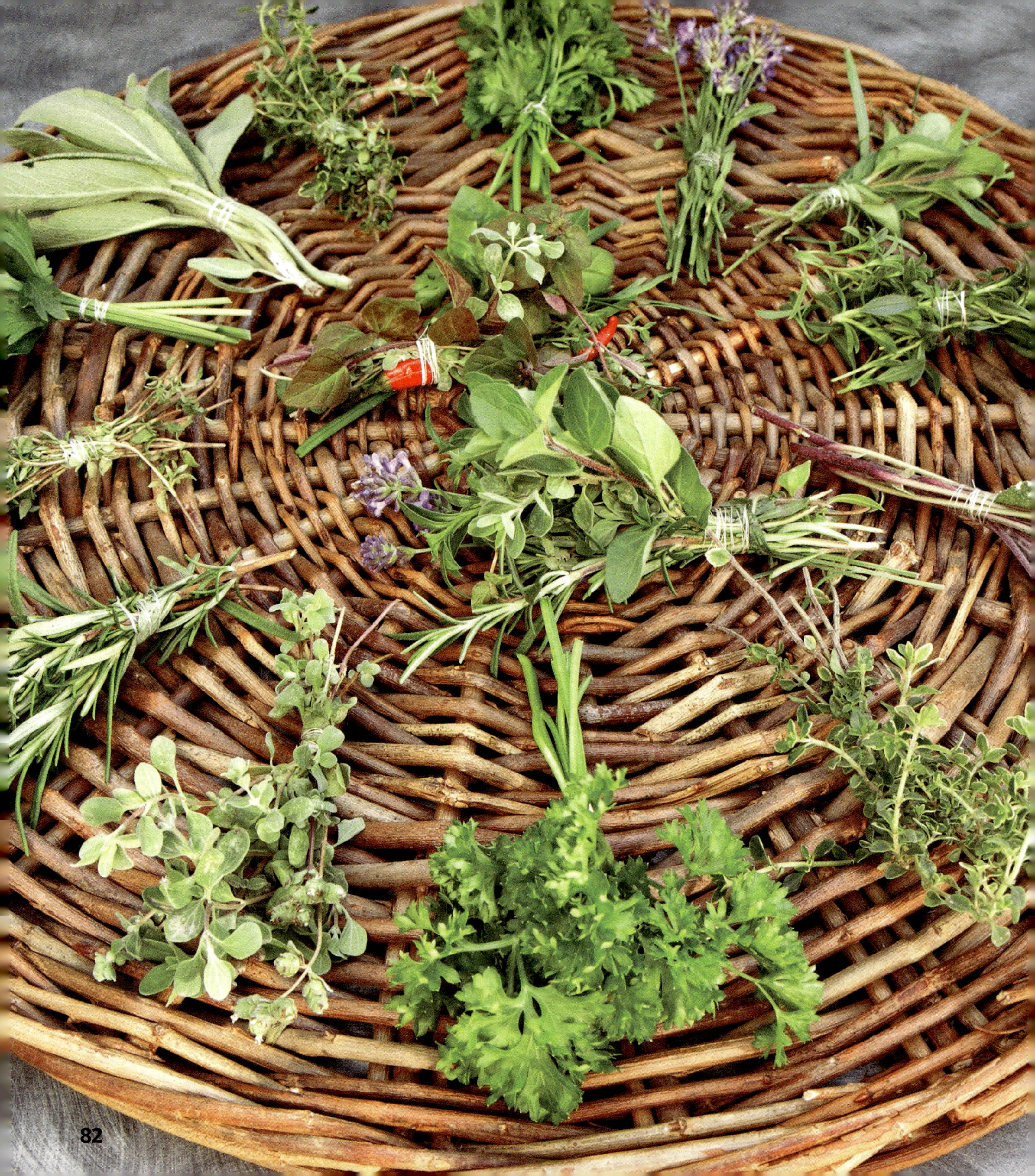

Fall
Drying and Storing

Cut, dry, and store herbs to reconnect with your garden's delicious flavors throughout winter.

For centuries gardeners have dried their herbal bounties, sewing them into sachets and pillows, hanging them on walls, and storing them in jars for fall and winter recipes. You can, too.

Clip at peak
The best time for harvesting herbs is in the morning after dew has evaporated from the leaves but before the afternoon sun and heat sap the plants' color and fragrance. For nonculinary use, select plants in full flower and cut extras to allow for breakage. If you are cutting herbs to use in cooking, do so before they flower. To preserve the health of a perennial, leave a few inches of the stem so it can continue to produce new growth.

Drying herbs
Air-drying. This is the simplest method: You simply cut, bundle, and hang herbs to dry. Gather three to six branches, and secure the stems with a rubber band. The band will hold the stems even as they shrink in drying. Hang the bundles upside down in a dry, dark place where air circulates (sunlight robs color, fragrance, and flavor). A well-ventilated attic or spare room works well. Your herbs will be fully dry and ready for storing within a few weeks.

Using desiccants. Moisture-absorbing substances speed drying as well as preserving the colors and shapes of herb flowers for crafts. Traditional drying agents include sand, borax, and cornmeal. To dry flowers, place them in a container and cover them with clean, dry sand or a mixture of 1 part borax to 3 parts cornmeal. Leave the container open to allow for evaporation. The blooms should be dry in three to five days. Silica gel, available at crafts stores, has lighter granules that are less likely to damage leaves and petals. For most uses, pour about 1 inch of gel into a moisture-tight plastic, metal, or glass container; add your herbs; then cover them

opposite Bundles of clipped herbs can be dried easily—letting you sample the flavors and fragrances of your favorite herbs long past the growing season.

STORE DRIED HERBS
Dried herbs enliven meals throughout winter.

1 GATHER
Assemble your materials: dried herb bundles, a tray to catch them in, and an airtight jar for each herb. Make sure the herbs are dry and brittle. Keep leaves whole. Crumble them only when using.

2 SIFT
Remove the leaves from the stems. Pick out the stems and any other chaff. Place the dried herbs in airtight jars or bags. Mark the herb type, the variety name (if you want to test the flavors of different varieties), and the date.

3 KEEP
Store dried herbs in a cool, dry place (not above a stove) to keep them at their peak of flavor. They will lose much of their flavor after a year—just in time to replenish them with herbs from the next year's garden. Replace your herbs yearly to make sure you are cooking with the best flavors.

4 USE
When cooking, bring out the herbs you will need. Dried herbs are more potent than fresh herbs, so use less of them. If a recipe calls for 1 teaspoon fresh oregano, add ⅓ teaspoon dried oregano (use one-third as much dried herb).

with more gel. Drying time will vary from about two to 10 days. Use a small paintbrush to remove crystals between the petals.

Microwave-oven drying. Wash herbs and pat them dry. Lay them on a paper plate and microwave for intervals of about a minute each; allow standing time between cooking times.

Food-dehydrator drying. Cut, wash, and dry leaves. Place them in a single layer on the tray of a food dehydrator. Dry herbs on the lowest setting possible; if your dehydrator doesn't have setting options, check often to avoid overdrying the herbs.

Fall Prepping Beds

As the temperatures drop, it's time to think about gathering the final bounty and prepping your beds for winter.

In the autumn herb garden, growth slows, seedpods thicken, and the time comes for preparing the garden for the next year and completing the growing season. Here's what needs to be done: Before a hard freeze or frost comes to your area, harvest the stems of the annual or perennial herbs you want to use, freeze, or dry.

Clean up beds
Begin fall cleanup by gathering fallen leaves to add to your compost pile. After the first frost, your annual herbs—such as the lovely, leafy basils—will be reduced to a slimy black mess. Pull out frost-damaged plants, and add them to the compost, too. Avoid composting any leaves that show signs of disease. Empty containers of annual herbs, and compost the soil and foliage.

Compost and cut back
Give perennial herbs an end-of-season nutrition boost by adding a thick layer of compost around the base of the plants. After frost, cut back leafy herbs such as catmint and bee balm. Leave herbs with seed heads intact for winter interest or to feed overwintering birds. For example, poppy, yarrow, and calendula seeds are sold in commercial birdseed mixes, so why not leave them in the garden for a natural snack?

Make design changes on paper
Take notes now about what you want to change in next year's garden. If some plants have become invasive, decide how much you want to cut them back (or whether to remove them). This is also the time to mark perennial herbs to move in spring; they're easier to locate now than when they are just coming up.

MAKE END-OF-SEASON HERB BUNDLES
With cold weather and the holidays in mind, harvest the last of the season's herbs to bundle as gifts.

Fragrant burning bundles Save the dried stems of fragrant herbs, after stripping off the leaves for cooking or crafting. Gather the stems of lavender, mint, rosemary, juniper, and others and use them as kindling in a fireplace. Add a bay leaf to a bundle of twigs; wrap with colorful thread.

Wine bottle bundles Snip stems from your favorite herbs to make tie-on bundles for wine bottles. Forgo gift bags, and make a greener choice by adding these bundles of fresh herbs to dress up gift bottles of wine.

Water perennial herbs
Many perennials expand their root growth during fall's cooler temperatures, so watering throughout autumn is important to your herb plants' health. Strong root systems help protect the plants through winter's freeze-thaw cycles, which can heave weaker perennials from the soil.

Continue planting
End-of-season sales can net some great deals on perennial herbs. And you can still plant these perennials in the warm days of autumn. If you haven't settled on a place for a specific herb, plant it anywhere; you can dig it up and reposition it in spring.

Mulch
After the ground freezes, mulch newly planted perennials, as well as all perennials that are tender in your Zone. Add chopped leaves or straw over the tops of plants. If you live in an area that has severely low temperatures, add up to 6 inches of mulch to your herb beds.

opposite Use season-extending row covers to protect hardy herbs, such as parsley, from frosts. Cover on cold nights and you'll be able to use leafy herbs through fall and into winter.

85

86 GARDENING MADE EASY **HERB GARDENING**

Fall
Bringing Herbs Indoors

Many herbs that excel outdoors can make the transition to houseplants. With a little help, some herbs can grow indoors.

Some herbs will do better than others inside your house. Depending on the amount of space you have—and the amount of south-facing windows—you may need to pick and choose which herbs get the invitation indoors.

Leave annuals outdoors
If you want to bring herbs indoors to use in recipes, it might make better sense to dry or freeze herbs for this purpose. The payoff for raising basil indoors will not be that great; make pesto with what's left of the plant instead. The same goes for other annuals—they've lived for a season and are nearly at the end of their natural life span.

Bring in selected perennials
Tender perennials—especially pricey ones such as topiaries—are definitely worth taking indoors. So are plants you can take cuttings from, such as scented geranium. Perennial herbs that you love to cook with should also make the cut: rosemary, oregano, thyme, and marjoram—you decide.

Check for insects
Before you bring your plant indoors, thoroughly inspect the tops and the undersides of leaves to make sure you aren't bringing along any hitchhiking pests. Insects such as aphids could infect your other indoor plants. Spray all plants with a forceful blast of water to chase away any pests.

Acclimate your herbs
Outdoor plants need to adjust to indoor air and light levels. After you pot the herbs to bring indoors, set them out of direct sunlight outdoors for a few days to help them acclimate to the lower light levels they will experience. Bring them indoors for a few days; then set them back outdoors for a few days. Finally, bring them in to stay.

opposite To enjoy a few herbs indoors over the winter, move plants long before cold weather sets in. A special strap turns the chore of hoisting a heavy container into a quick and easy task for two.

TRANSPLANTING HERBS
Many perennial herbs can transition from outdoors to indoors with the right treatment. Simply dig them up in fall (before frost) and transplant them into a container for indoor use. Clip and enjoy potted herbs all winter.

1 DIG UP
Choose the healthiest herb plants to bring indoors. Herbs that do best being transplanted to an indoor location include chives, garlic chives, lavender, rosemary, thyme, and mint. Dig up herbs before the first frost. Dig up the entire root ball. Divide larger plants (if you prefer), and replant the divisions, keeping one division to take indoors.

2 REPOT
Plant the herb in a container that is slightly larger than the root ball. The container should have a hole in the bottom to facilitate drainage. Fill in spaces with potting soil.

3 WATER WELL
Add extra soil around the root mass, and tamp down soil to eliminate air pockets around the roots. Take your newly potted plant indoors, and set it in a sunny south- or west-facing window.

A YEAR OF HERBS

Winter
The Right Light

Herbs can weather winter indoors if they have enough sunlight. Because these plants are sun lovers, find an indoor spot that will suit their needs.

Whether indoors or out, herbs have a few essential needs: soil, water, nutrients—and sun. When you bring herbs indoors, you need to provide them with enough light to thrive.

Herbs have special needs when growing indoors. And not all herbs can grow indoors (short-lived annuals such as cilantro and dill are poor candidates). Most herbs need at least six hours of sunlight a day, and the short, often-cloudy days of winter make for less-than-ideal growing conditions. But herbs can tough it out indoors with your help. The right light and a few other indoor climate considerations will help them survive.

Winter growth expectations
Unless your indoor location has plenty of light, most indoor herbs will slow or even stop growing during winter. They won't sprout many new leaves or flower as they do outdoors. When their growth slows, you should reduce leaf harvests.

Best natural light
Herbs grow best in south- or west-facing windows where direct light is the strongest. These sun-loving plants can't thrive in north-facing windows or any indoor location that receives less than four hours of direct light a day.

When herbs don't receive enough sunlight, they will grow toward a light source. This is why indoor plants grow elongated stems; they are reaching toward the light and becoming leggy. Plants that don't get adequate light produce thinner, more delicate leaves.

Supplemental lighting
Even if you can grow your herbs in brightly lit south-facing windows, they may still need more light. Weak winter light can be supplemented with grow-lights. Indoor lighting used to grow plants is different from regular lightbulbs.

Grow-lights offer the full-spectrum light plants need to grow. You can purchase stacked, shelflike units with long lights on several levels; these are ideal for starting seeds. Or you can rig your setup using fluorescent shop lights. Use one warm lightbulb and one cool lightbulb to mimic full-spectrum light. Suspend the lights about 4 inches above the plants. Set the fixture to turn on and off with a timer.

Climate control
Most herbs should be kept away from windows and doors where cold drafts and blasts from the outdoors can damage them. Herbs can thrive in consistent indoor temperatures as low as 60–65°F. And, of course, they like it warmer.

Some herbs, such as French tarragon and chives, benefit from a short period of low temperatures; they can be placed in cool locations, such as your garage or basement, as long as the temperatures stay above freezing. These herbs can stay in a cool area for a month or two, then be reintroduced into warmer, brighter locations for the rest of winter. The cool hiatus may stimulate new growth.

Minimizing leaf drop
Plants drop leaves when they are introduced to lower light levels. It's a self-preservation reaction: When plants can't produce enough food because of the lower light levels, they let leaves go. To minimize leaf drop before you bring plants indoors, help them adapt by moving them to a shaded location outdoors first.

> **BHG TEST GARDEN TIP**
> **BRIGHTEN UP**
> Use grow-lights to start seedlings or to grow herbs indoors during winter. You can get kits with fluorescent bulbs or brighter high-intensity lights, also called high-intensity discharge (HID) lights. Check with commercial lighting sources for the best option for your indoor herb-growing situation.

opposite top Potted herbs do best indoors when placed in the bright light of a south- or west-facing window.

GROWING AN HERB GARDEN ON A WINDOWSILL
Create a snippable indoor herb garden in a sunny spot in your home.

1 ASSEMBLE
Bring together all the supplies for your indoor windowsill garden: plants, such as basil, oregano, thyme, and flat-leaf parsley; lightweight potting mix; and terra-cotta pots and saucers.

2 TRANSPLANT
Start with young plants for best results. Give them new homes in terra-cotta pots. If you like, dress up the pots using acrylic paint.

3 WATER
After you transplant each new herb plant, water it well to help it adjust to its new pot.

4 GIVE LIGHT
Place plants in a sunny window; south- or west-facing provides the best and brightest light.

A YEAR OF HERBS

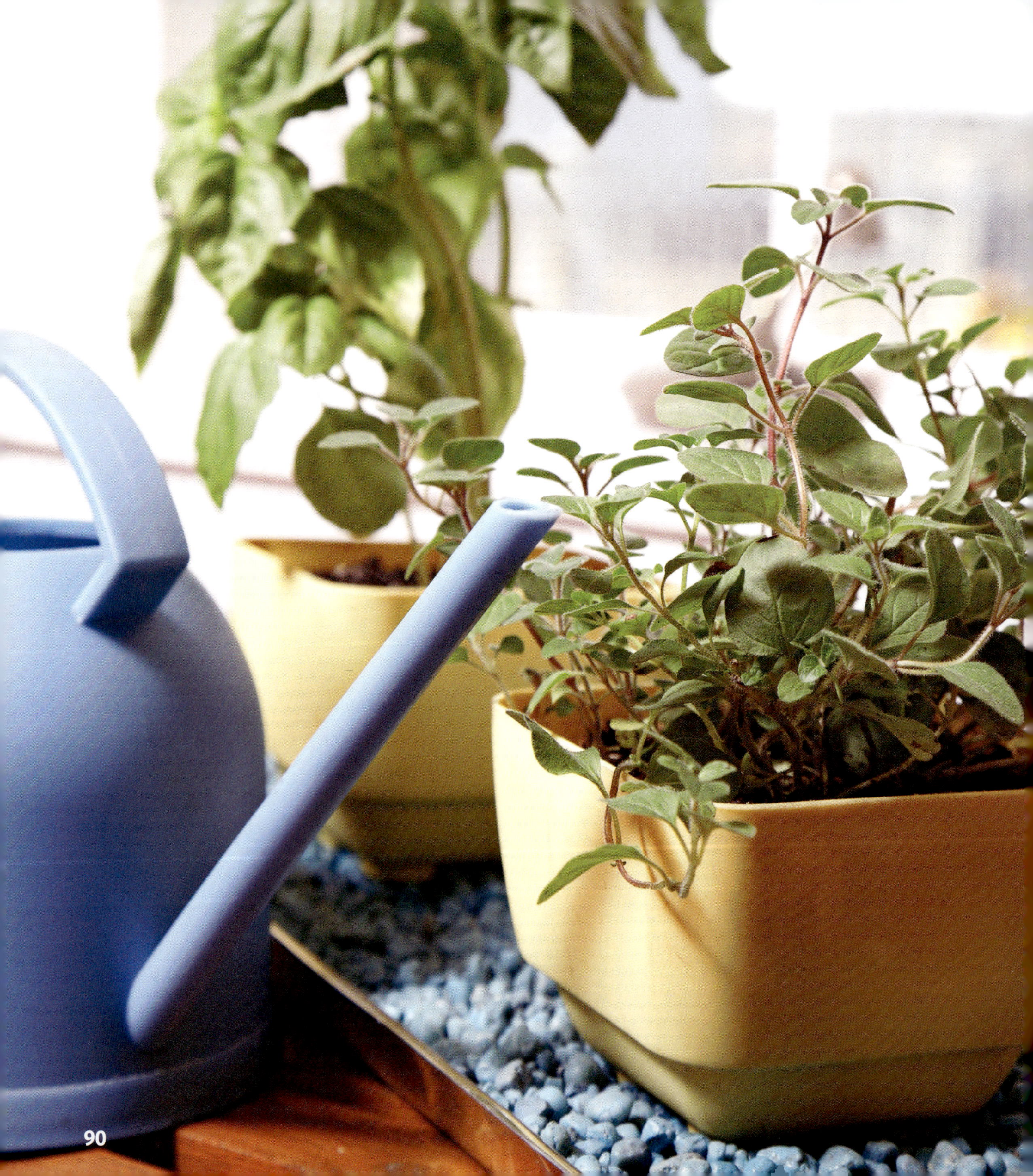

Winter
Watering and Humidifying

Most herbs prefer well-draining soil and hate soggy roots when outdoors—and this doesn't change for indoor plants.

Indoor plants have fewer drying elements to contend with than outdoor plants: There is less sun (and consequently less growth) and less wind. In lieu of that, indoor plants face dry air from forced-air furnaces or fireplaces. Overall, indoor herbs need less water than when they live outdoors.

Water when the soil is dry
To determine when your herbs need water, test the dryness of the soil in the container. If it feels dry to the touch, the plant needs water. The touch test is more accurate than watering on a schedule.

How to water
Use a watering can to water herbs. Direct the flow of water onto the soil; pour the water at the base of the plant rather than wetting the leaves. Keep watering the plant until the water runs out of the bottom of the container. If no water comes out, the pot's drainage hole may be blocked; check and unplug it so the soil can drain properly. You may need to repot the plant.

Misting
To raise the humidity level around your plants in a home with dry forced-air heat, use a mist sprayer. If your herbs develop any fungal diseases, such as powdery mildew, stop misting.

Use mulch in containers
Outdoors, mulch helps keep the soil damp in beds and pots. Indoors, it serves the same purpose. Apply a layer of chopped bark, clean gravel, or other material to cover the surface of the soil in the container. Make the layer 1–2 inches deep. You can use decorative mulch materials to enhance the look of your containers.

opposite Amp up the humidity for your herb plants by setting them on a water-filled tray of stones or gravel. Keep the tray filled with water to the top of the stones. Set herb containers on the stones so plants can benefit from the humidity.

Err on the side of dry
Overwatering your herb plants is the most common way to kill them. Too much water creates soggy soil, which can cause roots to rot. Allow the soil in the container to dry out completely between watering.

PESTS AND DISEASES
Although insect pests and diseases don't bug herbs much outdoors, they can pose a problem indoors.

1. SYMPTOM Holes in leaves
PEST Leaf holes are usually caused by insects, not disease. A number of insects may be the culprit. Check the undersides of leaves for pests. Use a spray of water, soapy water, or insecticidal soap to treat. Start with the least-toxic solution.

2. SYMPTOM Curled leaves; tiny insects
PEST Aphids are small insects that suck the life out of plants along the stems and leaves. Fill a spray bottle with water, add a few drops of liquid soap (not detergent), and spritz the tops and undersides of the leaves. Rinse herb leaves before using.

3. SYMPTOM White powdery foliage
DISEASE Powdery mildew is a fungus that needs humidity and a dry surface to thrive. Good air circulation and growing disease-resistant plant varieties help prevent it.

A YEAR OF HERBS

Winter
Planning Next Year's Garden

Plan your next year's herb garden while the snow flies. Gorgeous summer herb gardens start with herbal dreams during the cold months.

After the first of a new year, seed catalogs begin to arrive in the mailbox. To get a jump on the planting season, order herb seeds in winter. This is especially important if you are planting hard-to-find or rare varieties; seed supplies often sell out fast.

Grow a healthy lifestyle
Rethink your eating habits and incorporate more herbs into your diet. Herbs offer fresh flavors without fat or calories. Plan your next garden to include the herbs you like best as well as some herbs that are especially known for their healthful characteristics, such as chamomile to help you sleep, and oregano and sage, which offer antioxidants.

Plant the way you cook and eat
Before you plan your herb garden for next spring, pull your cookbooks off the shelf and review the herbs you most often use to flavor your favorite recipes. Your standard recipes will taste fresher with herbs you grow yourself (and can harvest anytime you need them). Then pull a world atlas off the shelf and think about which ethnic foods you like best. Create seed lists with herbs that are indigenous to those geographic regions. Do you like Thai food? Add lemongrass and cilantro. Want to try your hand at rolling your own Japanese sushi? Add shiso (perilla) to your list. Herbs add ethnic flavor to recipes—you can taste a place through the use of seasonings.

Plan theme gardens
Let your family's food favorites be your planting guide. If pizza is popular at your home, plant an herb garden with its flavors in mind: savory oregano, leafy basil, spiky rosemary, and pungent garlic. If tacos are a staple, plant a backyard garden with cilantro, peppers, tomatoes, and onions to grow your own salsa.

ENGAGE THE KIDS
Herbs that are tasty and fragrant are the perfect plants for young cooks. Here are some herbs that appeal to the senses:

Taste
Use freshly harvested and rinsed whole basil leaves to top homemade pizzas. A favorite: Margherita pizza with red sauce, leafy basil, and mozzarella cheese.

Planted in pots, mint offers kids delicious leaves for harvest from spring through fall. Make minty simple syrup (with mint leaves, sugar, and water) to drizzle into drinks, over ice cream, or onto a stack of chocolate chip pancakes.

Touch
Rub the leaves of scented geranium varieties to unleash different scents: apples, chocolate, mint, roses, and spices, for example.

Smell
It's amazing how plants can mimic other scents. Plant an all-lemon garden in a bed, container, or window box that includes these citrus poseurs: lemongrass, lemon balm, lemon verbena, and lemon thyme.

Kids with cats can make small aromatic bags of catnip for the family feline. Buy or make small cloth bags, and fill them with dried catnip leaves. Seal a bag tightly before giving it to your pet.

opposite Winter is an ideal time to page through your collection of herb and gardening books for planting inspiration. Your local library will also have a selection of books to help you plan the herb garden of your dreams.

93

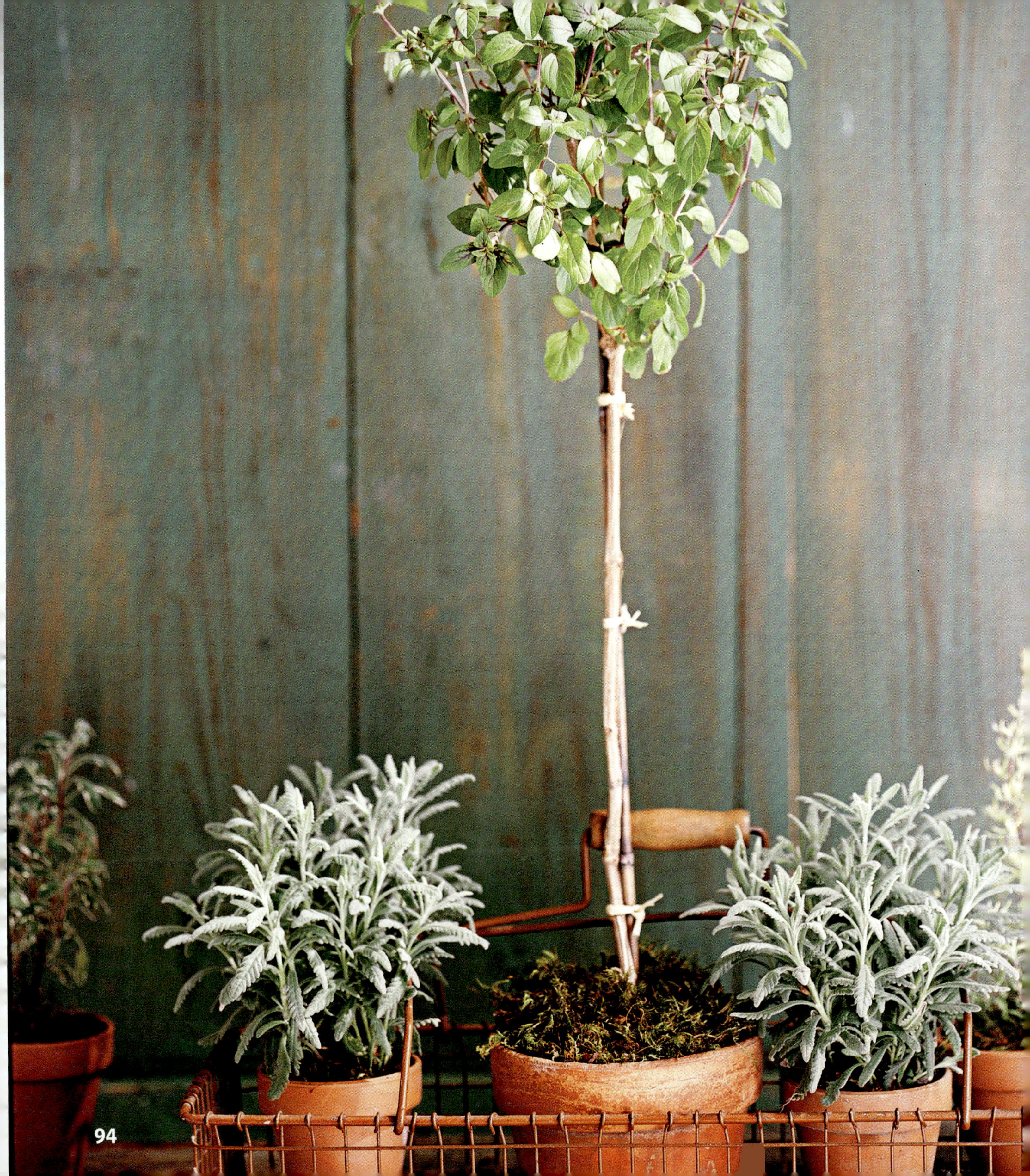

Winter Herbal Decor

Nothing breathes fresh life into indoor spaces like the fragrant presence of herbs.

Decorating with herbs is easy because they have so many pleasing qualities: They are aromatic, colorful, and textural. And best of all, they infuse a bit of the summer garden into your home in the midst of winter.

Herb topiaries

Shapely herb topiaries provide an elegant way to enjoy herbs all winter. The best herbs for topiaries are rosemary, bay laurel, lavender, scented geraniums, and lemon verbena. Topiaries of various sizes and shapes can be grouped for maximum effect. The thought of topiary brings up images of traditional English manor houses or French country estates.

Rosemary centerpieces

Rosemary is a popular choice as a winter gift plant, in part because when the fragrant herb is sheared into a cone shape, it mimics the classic holiday tree in miniature. Set a mini holiday rosemary tree in a colorful container, and it becomes an instant centerpiece with an added value—foliage can be clipped directly at the table and added to soups, salads, and stews.

Indoor kitchen garden

Plants brighten a room and herbs enhance a dish—so indoor herbs in the kitchen pack a double bonus. Place culinary herbs in a bright, south- or west-facing kitchen window. Clip foliage to shape plants. You can harvest leaves and stems for recipes all winter, but don't remove more than one-third of the plant at a time if you want to keep it alive until the next spring. Meting out your herbs to last all winter isn't necessary, because kitchen herbs are now readily available in grocery stores in winter. If you want to make more aggressive harvests (even using the whole plant), feel free; you can replace the plant once you've used up the herbs.

opposite Trimmed herb topiaries add charm to any home. Keep them in a sunny window, and pinch the branch tips often to promote lush growth.

DECK OUT A ROSEMARY PLANT

A cone-shape rosemary becomes a fragrant holiday centerpiece when dressed up with flowering lavender sprigs and twinkle lights.

1 BUY A PLANT
Start with a large, unadorned cone-shape rosemary plant from a grocery store or nursery. Rosemary plants are often available around the holidays as gift plants. Look for a healthy plant; avoid plants with dried leaves or dead spots.

2 ADD FLOWERS
Select long-stem dried or fresh flowers, including fragrant sprigs of lavender. Choose flowers to match the color theme of your holiday table. Simply insert the flower stems into the dense foliage of the rosemary plant; the foliage will hold the stems in place.

3 LIGHT UP
Twine a strand of twinkle lights around the rosemary tree. Start at the top of the plant and encircle the rosemary with the light strand. Use a battery-operated light string when displaying the tree as a centerpiece to avoid contending with a cord. If you like, add a small garland or other holiday decor.

4 ENJOY
A lavender-studded, twinkle-lit rosemary topiary makes a festive decoration that lasts beyond the holidays. The warmth of the twinkle lights subtly releases the rosemary and lavender fragrances.

Herb garlands

For holiday celebrations and special winter dinners, cut fragrant sprigs of rosemary, lavender, thyme, and sage, and bind them into bundles with green florist's wire. String the bundles to make an herb garland to drape along a stair railing or fireplace mantel.

A YEAR OF HERBS **95**

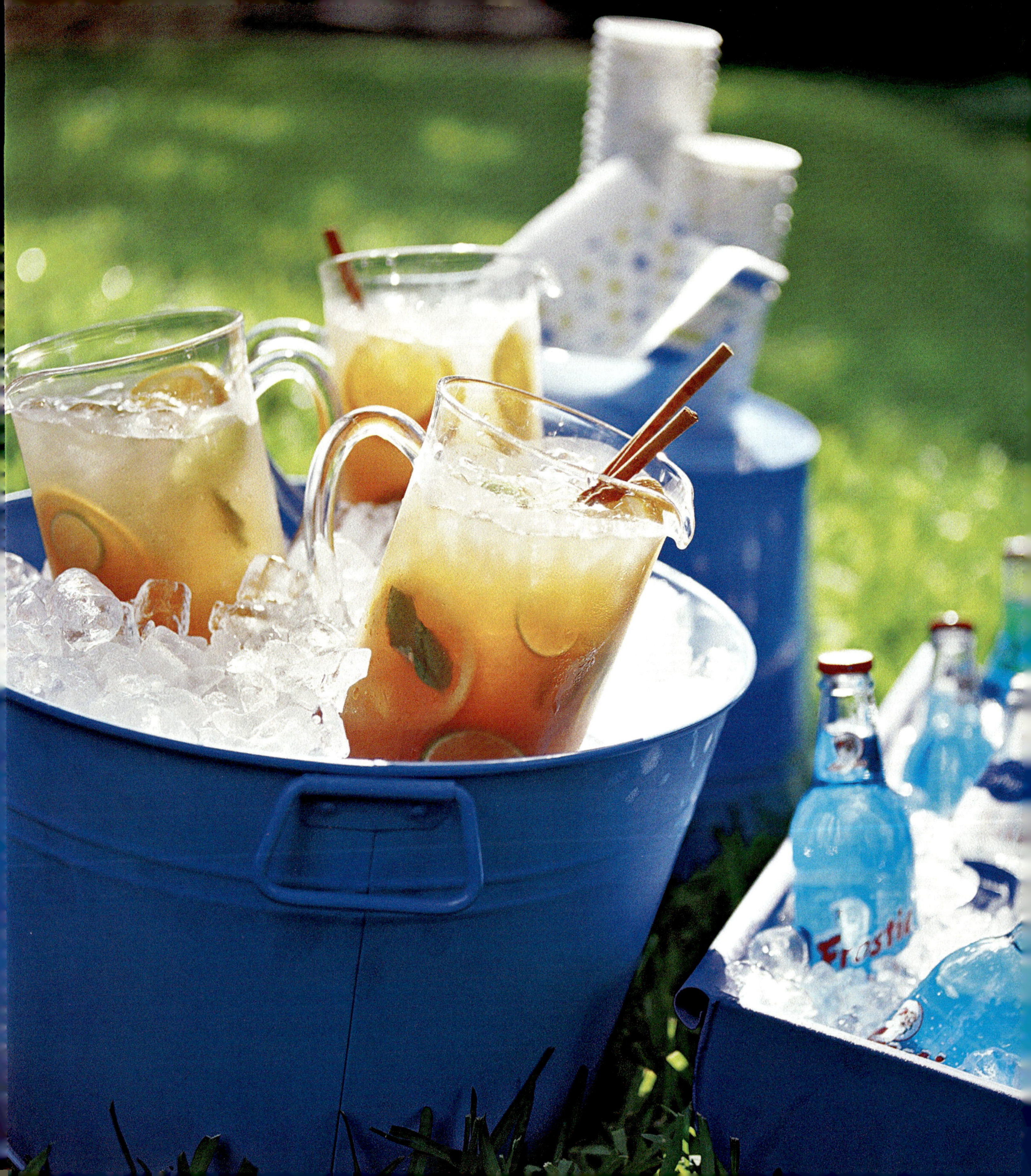

CHAPTER FOUR

Using Herbs

Versatile herbs can be used fresh and dried in recipes, as well as to imbue lovely fragrance in crafts projects. Use herbs in every season.

May Basket

Herb Butter

Mint Julep

Herb Bouquet

Spring Herbal Entertaining

Spring brings a flush of fresh herbs ready for picking. Add them to soups, spreads, drinks, and bouquets.

Get out your clippers. Snip perennial chives for soups and salads, as well as sorrel for tarts and soups. Mint and parsley leaves can be clipped as garnishes for sweet and savory dishes. Cilantro, self-seeded from the previous year's crop, can be picked just inches tall and tossed into salsa. Dill, with its ferny fronds, can be harvested as it develops—the newest leaves have a mild flavor. Plus, spring herbs offer materials for crafting, decor, and gift possibilities.

May basket
Celebrate the first day of May with an herbal May Day basket made with herb plants for the garden. Include fragrant herbs, such as lavender and thyme, and flowery violas, too. Tradition would have you offer this gift anonymously, but you can add a card to make sure your recipient knows who was so thoughtful.

Herb butter or cheese
Almost any culinary herb makes a delicious herb butter. Some of the best options include herbs you can harvest in spring: parsley, chives, dill, garlic chives, tarragon, and chervil. Mix ¼ cup butter with 2 teaspoons chopped fresh herbs. Let stand at room temperature for 30 minutes. Spread the butter on crackers or bread, corn on the cob, grilled or cooked vegetables, or pasta. You can also add herbs to soft cheeses, such as ricotta, cream cheese, or chèvre. Allow the cheese to soften by bringing it to room temperature. Add minced herbs and shredded hard cheese (such as cheddar or Asiago), and shape the cheese into a ball, log, or rectangle. Chill before serving.

Mint juleps
Just in time for a Kentucky Derby party, harvest fresh mint leaves and serve mint juleps. Ingredients include crushed ice, 1 tablespoon mint simple syrup, 2 to 4 large sprigs of fresh mint, and 3 to 4 tablespoons bourbon. To make one serving, fill a tall glass with crushed ice. Pour the mint simple syrup into a glass. (For a sweeter cocktail, add more syrup.) Slightly crush mint sprigs and add to the glass. Pour bourbon into the glass. Stir. Garnish with a mint sprig, if desired. To make mint simple syrup: Pour ½ cup boiling water over ½ cup sugar in a small bowl; stir until the sugar dissolves. Stir in ¼ cup lightly packed fresh mint leaves. Cover and chill for at least 4 hours. Strain the mixture through a sieve. Discard the mint leaves. Store the syrup, covered, in the refrigerator for up to 2 weeks. Makes about ¾ cup.

Herb bouquet
Flowering herbs, such as chamomile and lavender, make a fragrant floral centerpiece for a spring party. Choose aromatic and textured foliage from other herbs, such as artemisia, anise hyssop, and lemon balm.

EDIBLE FLOWERS
Clip, snip, and enjoy edible flowers from spring-blooming herbs. Always rinse herbs before serving.

1. CHIVES Crumble these peppery-tasting flowers into salads and soups. The purple blossoms of chives retain their color when dried.

2. GARLIC Garlic flower stalks are called garlic scapes. They offer a delicious oniony flavor.

3. ROSES The petals of late-spring-blooming roses can be shredded into salads to add color and flavor.

4. CALENDULA Sprinkle these orange and yellow petals directly into salads.

USING HERBS 99

Spring Herb Recipes

Snip early-sprouting perennial and annual herbs to add zip to recipes.

Thyme-Garlic Chicken Breasts
Flavorful thyme pairs well with chicken.

PREP 10 minutes COOK 6 to 7 hours (low) or 3 to 3½ hours (high)

- 3 to 4 pounds bone-in chicken breast halves
- 6 cloves garlic, minced
- 1½ teaspoons dried thyme, crushed
- ½ teaspoon salt
- ¼ cup orange juice
- 1 tablespoon balsamic vinegar
- 1 8- to 10-ounce package mixed greens
- ½ cup cherry tomatoes, halved or quartered
- ¼ cup pitted Kalamata olives, halved
- ¼ cup crumbled feta cheese (1 ounce)
- ½ cup bottled vinaigrette dressing

1. Remove and discard skin from chicken. Sprinkle chicken with garlic, thyme, and salt. Place chicken in a 3½- or 4-quart slow cooker. Pour orange juice and vinegar over chicken.
2. Cover and cook on low-heat setting for 6 to 7 hours or on high-heat setting for 3 to 3½ hours. Remove chicken from slow cooker; cover and keep warm. Discard cooking juices.
3. In a large bowl toss together greens, tomatoes, olives, and feta; divide among serving plates. Slice chicken from the bones, discarding bones. Top each salad with some of the chicken. Drizzle dressing over salads. Makes 6 to 8 servings.

Fresh Tarragon Yogurt Cheese
A tart cheese flavored with fresh tarragon makes a refreshing spread.

PREP 15 minutes CHILL 24 hours

- ½ of a 32-ounce carton plain yogurt or plain goat's milk yogurt*
- 1 tablespoon finely snipped fresh tarragon
- ⅛ teaspoon salt

1. Line a strainer or sieve with cheesecloth. Place over a bowl. Spoon yogurt into lined strainer. Cover with plastic wrap. Refrigerate for 24 hours. Remove from refrigerator; discard drained liquid.
2. Transfer yogurt cheese to a bowl. Stir in tarragon and salt. Store covered in refrigerator for up to 1 week. Makes 16 to 20 (1-tablespoon) servings.
***Tip:** Use yogurt that contains no gums, gelatin, or fillers, which may prevent the whey from separating from the curd.

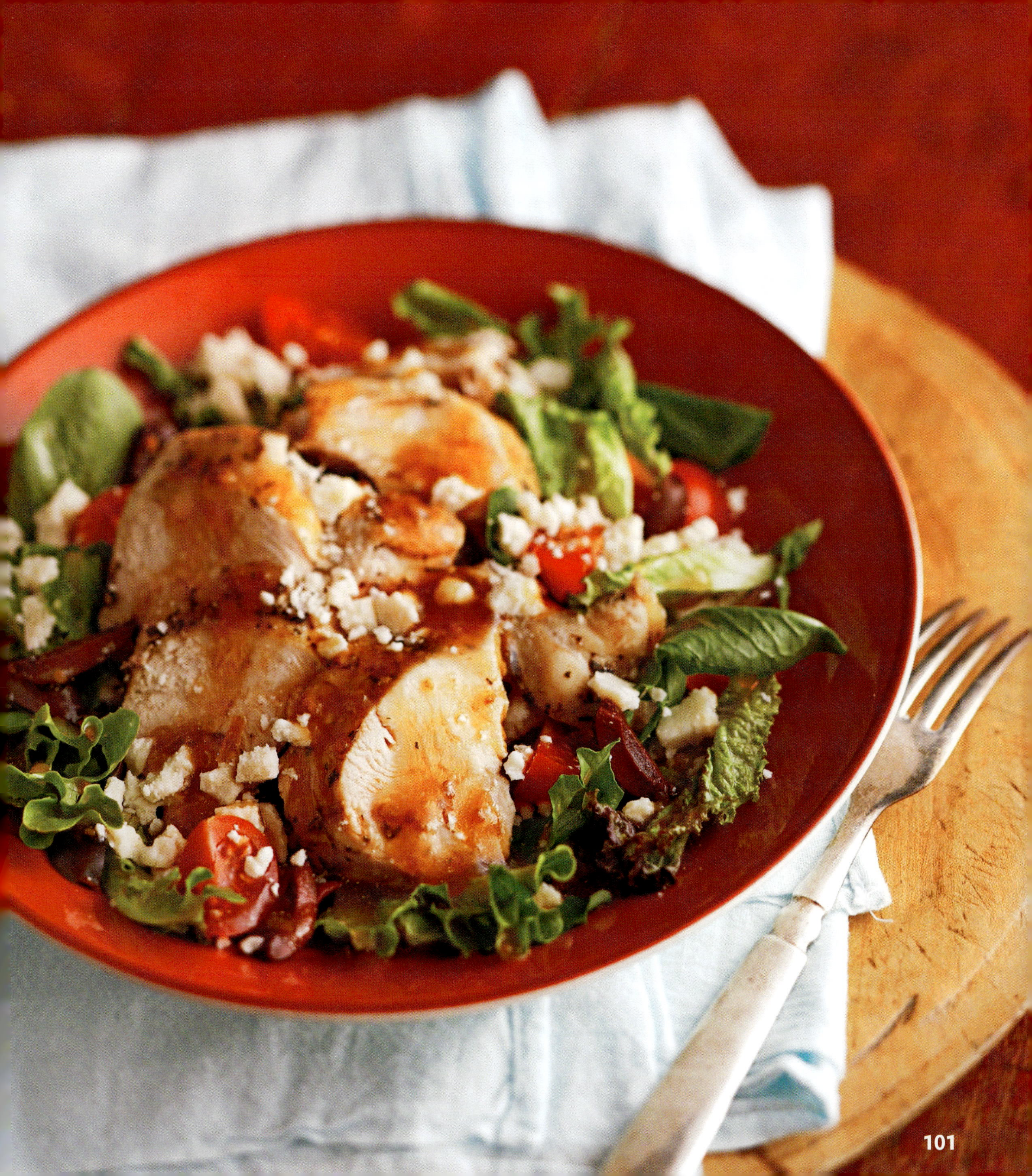

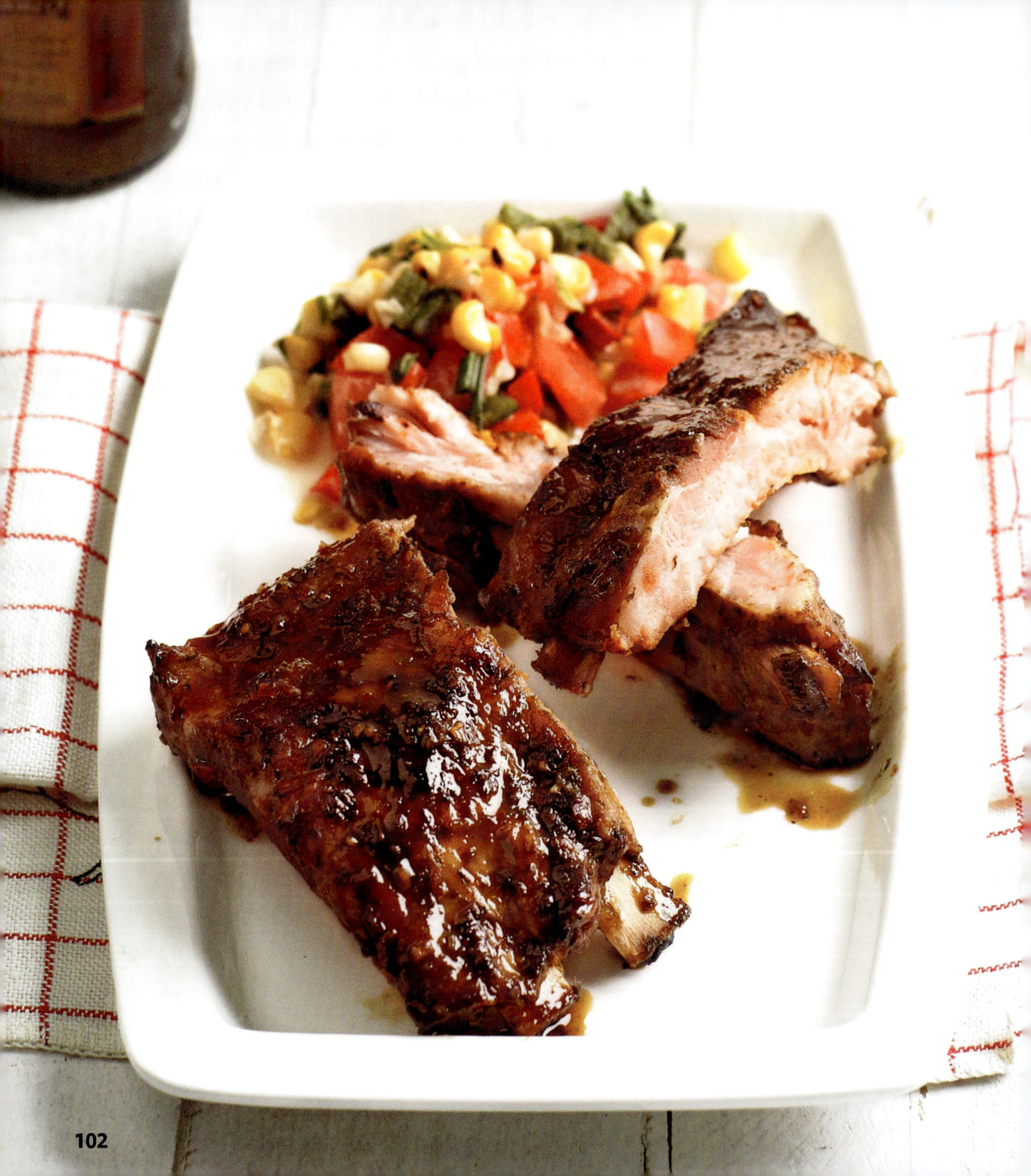

Spring

Hearty Boys Cilantro-Garlic Ribs
Pungent cilantro leaves add distinctive flavor to ribs.

PREP 20 minutes MARINATE overnight GRILL 12 minutes
BAKE 3 hours at 250°F

- 2 tablespoons minced garlic
- 1 large bunch cilantro, washed, and leaves coarsely chopped (1 cup)
- 1 tablespoon sugar
- 1 cup reduced-sodium soy sauce
- ½ cup Asian sweet chili sauce (from Asian aisle of supermarkets or Asian specialty markets)
- ¼ cup vegetable oil
- 3 pounds pork back ribs, cut into 2 racks
- Vegetable oil

1. In a blender or food processor combine garlic, cilantro, and sugar; blend or process until ingredients form a paste. Add soy sauce, sweet chili sauce, and vegetable oil. Pulse until well combined. Place ribs in a large glass, plastic, or stainless-steel container. Pour sauce over ribs, turning ribs to coat well. Cover and refrigerate overnight.
2. Preheat oven to 250°F. Preheat grill. Remove ribs from the sauce, shaking off any excess. Reserve remaining sauce. Place the ribs on the grill rack meaty side down. Grill for 8 minutes. Flip and grill for 4 minutes more. Transfer ribs to a 13×9×2-inch baking dish; pour reserved sauce over ribs. Cover with foil and bake for 3 hours. Remove and serve immediately.
Makes 2 to 4 servings.

Spinach, Sorrel, and Orange Pesto
A fresh take on pesto, this tangy paste is excellent on bread or pasta.

START TO FINISH 15 minutes

- ¼ cup slivered almonds, toasted
- 1½ cups loosely packed fresh spinach leaves
- 1½ cups loosely packed fresh sorrel, arugula, or watercress leaves
- ⅓ cup olive oil
- ⅓ cup grated Parmesan or Romano cheese
- ½ teaspoon finely shredded orange peel
- 3 tablespoons orange juice
- ¼ teaspoon ground red pepper
- ⅛ teaspoon salt

1. Place almonds in a food processor or blender. Cover and process or blend the almonds until finely chopped. Add spinach and sorrel; cover. With the machine running, gradually add the oil in a thin, steady stream, processing until the mixture is combined and slightly chunky. Add Parmesan cheese, orange peel, orange juice, ground red pepper, and salt. Cover and process or blend just until combined.
2. To store, divide pesto into ¼-cup portions and place in airtight containers. Store in the refrigerator for up to 1 week. To serve, bring pesto to room temperature. Makes ¾ cup (twelve 1-tablespoon servings).
Note: Instead of storing in the refrigerator, divide into freezer containers and freeze up to 1 month. To serve, thaw pesto in the refrigerator, then bring to room temperature. Toss with cooked pasta, spread on pizza crust, or use as a burger topper.

Summer Herb Blends

Savor the summer herb garden with blends and recipes that combine fresh flavors in classic ways.

Making blends of herbs you grow yourself allows you to create customized flavors for your food. Several classic herb blends—including herbes de Provence and bouquet garni—are used in a variety of recipes. Here's how to make them:

Herbes de Provence
Herbes de Provence is a blend of herbs commonly used in the South of France—in Provence—as well as throughout the Mediterranean. The plants used offer strong flavors and resinous leaves, and can be added to foods that cook a long time. Typical herbes de Provence mixes include thyme, marjoram, savory, fennel, and basil. Both the leaves and flowers can be used. Dried lavender leaves and flowers are often added, giving the blend a flowery taste. Herbes de Provence is used to flavor grilled fish, meat, and poultry, as well as stews. This dried herb blend can also be added to oils and used as a marinade or added to food during cooking. Here's how to make a classic recipe: In a small airtight storage container combine 1 tablespoon each of dried marjoram, dried thyme, and dried savory. Add 1 teaspoon each of dried basil and dried rosemary. Then add ½ teaspoon each of dried sage and fennel seeds. Cover and store for up to one month. Crush before using. Makes ¼ cup (twelve 1-teaspoon servings).

Bouquet garni
This classic French herb bundle is bound with string or added to a small sachet made with cheesecloth. It typically includes parsley, thyme, and bay leaf. It's tossed into soups, stocks, and stews to add rich and aromatic herbal flavors. The bundle is boiled with the other recipe ingredients and removed before serving. Bouquets garnis can include a variety of herbs, depending on the recipe. You can create bundles of basil, salad burnet, chervil, rosemary, savory, and tarragon. Vegetables can also be bundled with the herbs.

VARIATIONS ON A THEME: BOUQUET GARNI
Make several versions of this French classic using herbs and vegetables that suit your recipe.

1. ITALIAN Some Italian cooks tie their flavorings between two snug-fitting pieces of celery, making removal from a hot dish simple and quick.
2. FRENCH TWIST A traditional French bouquet garni includes thyme, parsley, and bay leaf, but you can create a twist on the original by substituting other French herbs, such as rosemary, tarragon, and lavender.
3. AMERICAN Casual American cooks often toss flavorings right into the pot, sticking cloves into an onion and poking a toothpick through garlic, helping diners avoid unwelcome bites of seasoning.

Fines herbes
An herb blend that also hails from the Mediterranean region, fines herbes is less pungent than bouquet garni. This mix is traditionally a combination of chopped parsley, tarragon, chives, and chervil. Marjoram and savory can also be added. Start with the same amounts of all herbs (for example, 1 tablespoon). Then experiment with the ratios to find the taste you like best. Use fines herbes fresh, or make a mix of dried herbs.

Italian seasoning
Create a mix of fresh or dried herbs to season your favorite Italian foods. Chop equal amounts of basil, oregano, and thyme; then add 1 bay leaf. This blend can be used to flavor red pasta sauces, or toss it with olive oil and fresh garlic and serve over pasta for a fast and flavorful summer meal.

opposite Customize your own herb blends—using the herb combinations you like best—to dry or use fresh in soups, stocks, and stews.

105

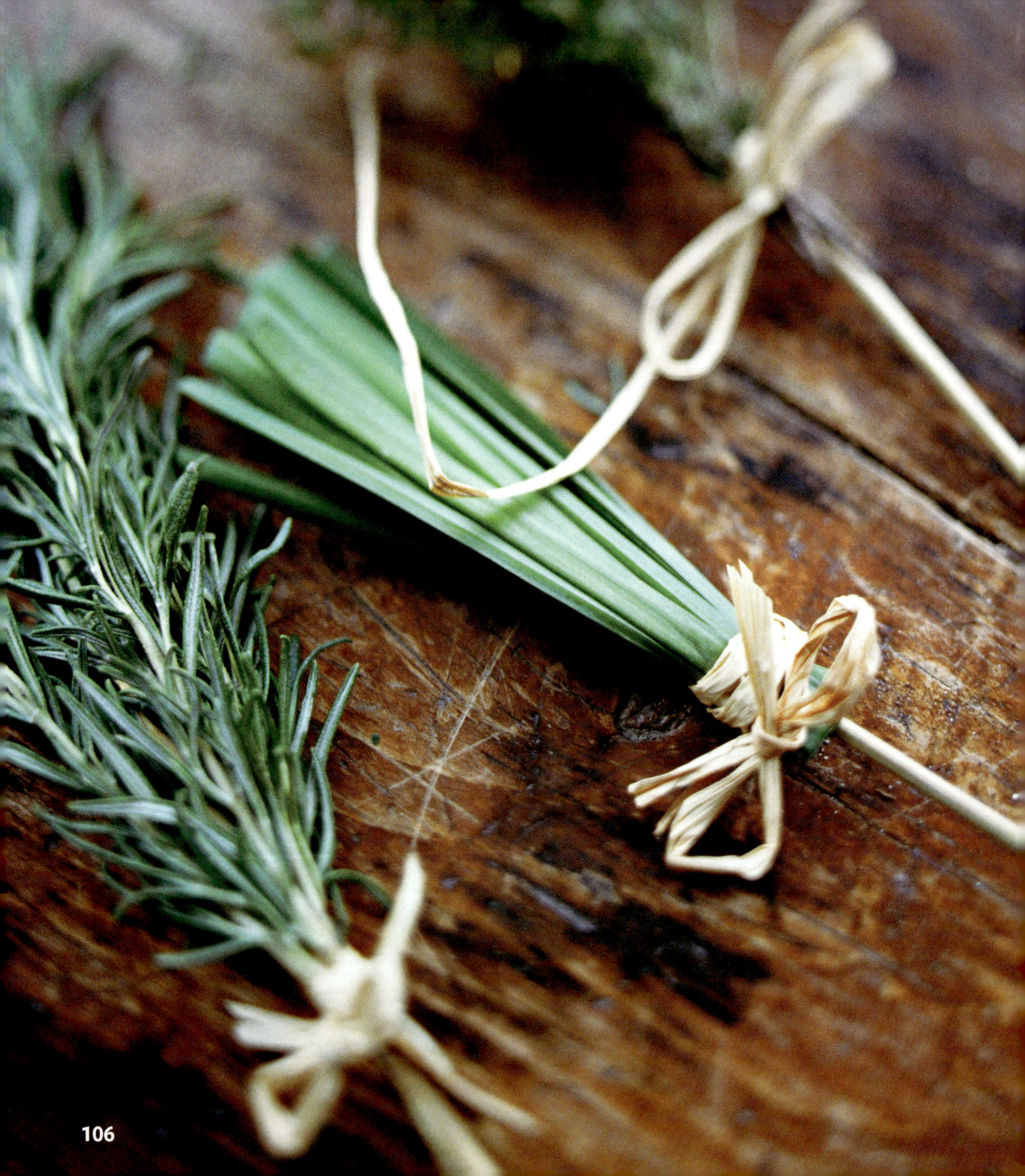

Summer
Savory Selections

Summer herbs come into their own and offer flavor at its peak. Use them in every course.

Summer brings lots of outdoor entertaining possibilities: grilling parties in the backyard, afternoon drinks on the patio, appetizers in the garden. Herbs lend fresh taste and leafy beauty to a variety of dishes—from drinks to appetizers to main meals. Here is an assortment of savory options.

Herbal meat brushes
Marinate meats with brushes made from herbs. Some favorite culinary herbs, such as rosemary and thyme, can be used to make flavorful brushes for dabbing marinade or sauce onto food as it cooks on the grill.

Grilled apricot appetizers
Grill lavender-infused apricots on lavender-stem skewers for a surprising (and easy!) appetizer. Remove and reserve half of the buds from the lower portion of 6-inch woody lavender stems. Thread halved, pitted apricots onto the stems. In a saucepan combine ½ cup honey, ¼ cup butter, and ½ teaspoon of the lavender buds. Cook over medium-high heat until boiling. Reduce heat; cook, uncovered, for 10 minutes. Pour mixture through a sieve to remove lavender buds. Brush strained mixture onto apricots. Grill on a greased grill rack directly over medium-hot coals for 1 minute on each side.

Cilantro pesto
Enjoy this bright green and flavorful pesto as an accompaniment with Thai or Mexican food. In a food processor place 1 jalapeño pepper halved and seeded; 2 cups cilantro leaves, stems removed; ½ cup loosely packed basil; ¼ cup loosely packed fresh mint leaves; and 2 large cloves garlic. Cover and process with several

opposite Rosemary, garlic chives, thyme, and other herbs with stiff or woody stems make handy basting brushes for marinades. They also add flavor of their own.

DRESSINGS, SAUCES, AND MARINADES
Use these herb-inspired recipes to enhance a variety of meals.

1. TARRAGON DRESSING In a blender combine ¼ cup mayonnaise, ¼ cup buttermilk or yogurt, 2 green onions, 2 tablespoons parsley, 1 teaspoon fresh tarragon, and 1 clove garlic. Cover and blend until smooth. Makes about ½ cup dressing.

2. LEMON-DILL SAUCE In a small saucepan melt ¼ cup butter over medium heat. Combine 1½ teaspoons cornstarch and ½ cup chicken broth; stir into butter in saucepan. Cook and stir until thickened and bubbly; cook and stir for 2 minutes more. Stir in ½ teaspoon lemon zest, 2 tablespoons lemon juice, and 2 to 3 tablespoons snipped dill. Makes about ¾ cup sauce.

3. ROSEMARY MARINADE Stir together 1 teaspoon finely shredded lemon peel, ⅓ cup lemon juice, ¼ cup olive oil, ¼ cup Worcestershire sauce, 1 tablespoon sugar, 1 tablespoon snipped fresh rosemary, ¼ teaspoon salt, and ⅛ teaspoon ground black pepper in a small bowl. Pour over fish, chicken, or pork in a resealable plastic bag set in a bowl or shallow dish; seal bag and turn to coat. Refrigerate 1 to 2 hours, turning bag occasionally. Makes 1 cup (enough for 2 pounds of fish or meat).

on-off turns until finely chopped. With processor running, gradually add ½ cup olive oil and ¼ cup water. Stir in 1 to 2 tablespoons lime juice and ½ teaspoon sea salt. Makes 1 cup.

Lemongrass kabobs
Thread firm-flesh fish cubes onto flavorful skewers to make a gorgeous, fast main dish. Strip the tough outer layers of 6 lemongrass stalks until they're pencil-thin. In a bowl combine ½ cup coconut milk, 1 to 2 teaspoons green curry paste, and 1 tablespoon chopped lemongrass. Add 1 pound fish cut into 1½-inch cubes. Marinate for 30 minutes. Use a sharp knife to cut a point at one end of each lemongrass stalk. Skewer the fish cubes onto stalks. Grill over medium heat for 2 to 3 minutes on each side or until fish flakes easily when tested with a fork.

USING HERBS **107**

Summer
Sweet Delights

Sweeten summer days with fresh herbs from the garden. Herbs add refreshing flavors to cool drinks and desserts.

Although most herbs don't offer a sweet taste (with the exception of stevia), they have their sweet sides.

Sugared herb flowers and leaves
Sprinkle sugar onto herb flowers and leaves to add to cupcakes, cakes, cookies, and other sweets. Rinse flowers or leaves gently. Let them air dry. Place an egg white in a cup. Using a food-safe brush, dab small amounts of egg white onto both sides of the petals and leaves. Sprinkle superfine sugar over both sides. Shake off excess sugar. Let dry for 1 hour before placing on sweets.

Verbena vanilla sugar
Infuse sugar granules with the citrusy flavor of lemon verbena and the mellow tones of vanilla. Use the sugar in teas, in baking, or sprinkled on your morning bowl of cereal. Harvest 1 branch (about 12 inches) of lemon verbena with leaves. Use a heavy-duty knife or sharp kitchen shears to cut the verbena stem in pieces about 3 inches long. Layer the verbena in the bottom of a glass container large enough to hold 4 cups sugar. Pour 2 cups sugar into the container. Stick 3 vanilla beans (split in half lengthwise) into the sugar at even intervals. Add another 2 cups sugar. Seal the jar tightly and store for at least one week before using. Once sugar is aromatic, remove verbena and vanilla. If sugar becomes hard or clumped, break pieces with a wooden spoon and sift before using. Makes 4 cups sugar.

left Sugared herb flowers and leaves—such as viola, rose, borage, lavender, and mint—can be used fresh or dried and stored for up to two weeks in an airtight container.

Lavender whipped cream

Add a generous dollop of this herb-inspired whipped cream to a fruit crisp or pie. Or serve lavender whipped cream with scones for a summer afternoon tea party. In a small saucepan combine 1 cup whipping cream and 1 tablespoon crushed dried lavender. Bring just to simmering. Remove from heat. Strain mixture and discard lavender. Cover and chill cream mixture at least 2 hours or until completely chilled. In a chilled metal mixing bowl beat whipping cream and 2 tablespoons superfine sugar with an electric mixer on medium speed, beating just until soft peaks form (tips curl). Use at once or cover and chill up to 2 hours. Makes 16 (2-tablespoon) servings.

Stevia extract

This leafy plant offers a natural alternative to sugar. Use this sweetened extract in teas, coffees, and other recipes. Add 1 cup hot water to a heat-resistant jar. Drop in 1 cup freshly picked and lightly bruised stevia leaves. Cover tightly. Let the mixture steep for a day at room temperature, then strain out the solids; discard solids. Store, covered, in the refrigerator up to 2 weeks. Makes 1 cup syrup.

Stevia-sweetened mint syrup

Minty simple syrup is great to have on hand when you're whipping up summer drinks, such as mint juleps or mojitos. This recipe uses the sweetening charms of stevia instead of sugar. Add 1 cup hot water to a heat-resistant jar. Add ½ cup freshly picked mint leaves and ½ cup freshly picked stevia leaves. If desired, to thicken the syrup, add ¼ teaspoon unflavored gelatin to the hot liquid. Cover tightly. Let the mixture steep for a day at room temperature, then strain out the solids; discard solids. Store, covered, in the refrigerator up to 2 weeks. Makes 1 cup syrup.

BHG TEST GARDEN TIP: FRESH/DRY HERB RATIOS

When you substitute fresh herbs for dried, the general rule is to use three times as much. For example, 1 teaspoon dried tarragon equals 1 tablespoon (or 3 teaspoons) fresh tarragon.

HERB SUBSTITUTIONS

Although each herb has its own distinct flavor, you can replace herbs in recipes with others that have comparable flavors. Whether you're making an emergency substitution or experimenting with a new flavor, follow these suggestions for herb alternatives.

MINT = BASIL

TARRAGON = CHERVIL

CILANTRO = PARSLEY

SAGE = SAVORY

OREGANO = THYME

USING HERBS **109**

Hair Rinse

Herbal Spritz

Foot Soak

Liniment

Summer
Herbal Cooldowns

Enjoy the spa-like options of garden herbs. Make your own rinses, sprays, and soaks to beat summer's heat.

Cool down summer's heat with herbal concoctions—there are so many scented ways to refresh and revive. Make these custom spa treatments at home, and treat yourself to the charms of herbs for your skin, hair, and feet.

Herbal hair rinse

Rosemary brings out the natural highlights in hair and is also great for the scalp; it helps reduce dandruff. Place 1 large handful of fresh rosemary, sage, and/or chamomile in a 1-quart jar and pour 2 cups boiling water over the herbs. Cover loosely with a lid or saucer, and steep for 10 to 15 minutes. Allow the infusion to cool. Strain and discard herbs. To use, shampoo your hair, then pour the cooled infusion over rinsed hair. Do not rinse out.

Herbal spritz

Herbal refreshment is just a spray away when you make your own herb-infused cooling mist. Fill a quart jar with your favorite herbs, such as mint, lavender, rosemary, lemon balm, and rose petals. Cover with apple cider vinegar. Let steep for several days; strain out the solids, and pour the herb-infused vinegar into an atomizer or spray bottle. Keep the spritz in the refrigerator for an extra-cooling effect. Spray on your arms, legs, and face to enjoy a quick herbal refresher.

Peppermint foot soak

Enjoy a foot soak every week of summer, thanks to the ease of this recipe and mint's assertive growth. Bring 8 cups (½ gallon) water to boiling in a large pot; remove from heat. Add 4 cups loosely packed fresh peppermint; cover with lid and steep for 15 minutes. Transfer the infusion to a basin. Add enough warm or cool water to make a comfortable footbath. Sit in a shady area of your garden, soak your feet in the footbath for at least 10 minutes, and relax.

HERBAL LIBATIONS

Herbs offer delicious possibilities for refreshing summer sips.

1. LEMON VERBENA TISANE Place 12 sprigs fresh lemon verbena and 4 sprigs fresh mint in a warm teapot. Add 4 cups boiling water. Steep for 3 minutes; serve warm. To serve chilled, remove herbs and mint sprigs with a slotted spoon; refrigerate.

2. BASIL/CHAI PUNCH Pour a 32-ounce container of chai tea concentrate (black tea) into a large pitcher. Stir in ½ cup sugar. Add 8-inch stick cinnamon, ¼ cup torn fresh basil leaves, 1 medium sliced lime, and 1 medium sliced orange. Cover and chill for 4 hours. Strain mixture, discarding solids. Before serving, add 32 ounces of club soda to chai mixture. Serve over ice. Garnish with whole basil leaves.
Makes 10 (6-ounce) servings.

Soothing liniment

Create a calendula-infused oil for dry skin or massage. In an 8-ounce glass jar combine 1 cup fresh calendula petals and 1 cup olive or almond oil. Allow the petals to steep in the oil for 1 week. Strain the oil, pressing the petals with the back of a spoon to extract as much of the oil as possible. Pour the oil back into the jar and discard the petals. Refrigerate the infused oil for up to 1 month.

Summer Herb Recipes

Harvest and use summer herbs when they are at their peak flavor.

Chicken Breasts with Herbs

Spice up chicken with a lemony herbal mix.

PREP 15 minutes COOK 14 minutes

- ⅓ cup chopped Italian (flat-leaf) parsley
- 1 tablespoon chopped fresh oregano
- 1 tablespoon finely shredded lemon peel
- 1 tablespoon finely chopped garlic (about 3 cloves)
- 3 tablespoons butter
- 4 skinless, boneless chicken breast halves
- ¼ cup chicken broth

1. In small bowl stir together parsley, oregano, lemon peel, and garlic. Set aside. Season chicken with *salt* and *black pepper*.
2. In a 10-inch skillet heat butter over medium-high heat. Cook chicken in hot butter for 6 minutes or until browned, turning once. Transfer chicken to platter. Remove skillet from heat; stir in half of herb mixture. Return to heat. Add broth; bring to boiling, stirring to scrape up browned bits from the bottom of the skillet. Return chicken to skillet; reduce heat. Simmer, covered, for 8 minutes or until chicken is no longer pink.
3. Serve chicken with pan sauce; sprinkle with remaining herb mixture. Makes 4 servings.

Lemon-Basil Pasta

Basil leaves and lemon make a refreshing pasta dish.

START TO FINISH 25 minutes

- 10 ounces dried linguine or desired pasta
- 1 19-ounce can white kidney (cannellini) beans, rinsed and drained
- ½ of a lemon
- 3 tablespoons olive oil
- 1 cup packed fresh basil leaves

1. Cook pasta according to package directions, adding beans for the last 2 minutes of cooking time. Remove ½ cup of the pasta cooking liquid; set aside. Drain pasta and beans; cover to keep warm.
2. Meanwhile, finely shred peel from the lemon half (about 2 teaspoons). In a small skillet heat 1 tablespoon of the oil over medium heat. Add lemon peel; cook and stir for 1 minute or until lightly golden.
3. In a food processor combine cooked lemon peel, the basil, the remaining 2 tablespoons oil, the juice from the lemon half, ½ teaspoon *salt*, and ¼ teaspoon *black pepper*. Cover and process until smooth. Add the reserved pasta cooking liquid, 1 tablespoon at a time, until desired consistency, processing mixture after each addition.
4. To serve, toss hot cooked pasta mixture with lemon-basil mixture. Makes 4 servings.

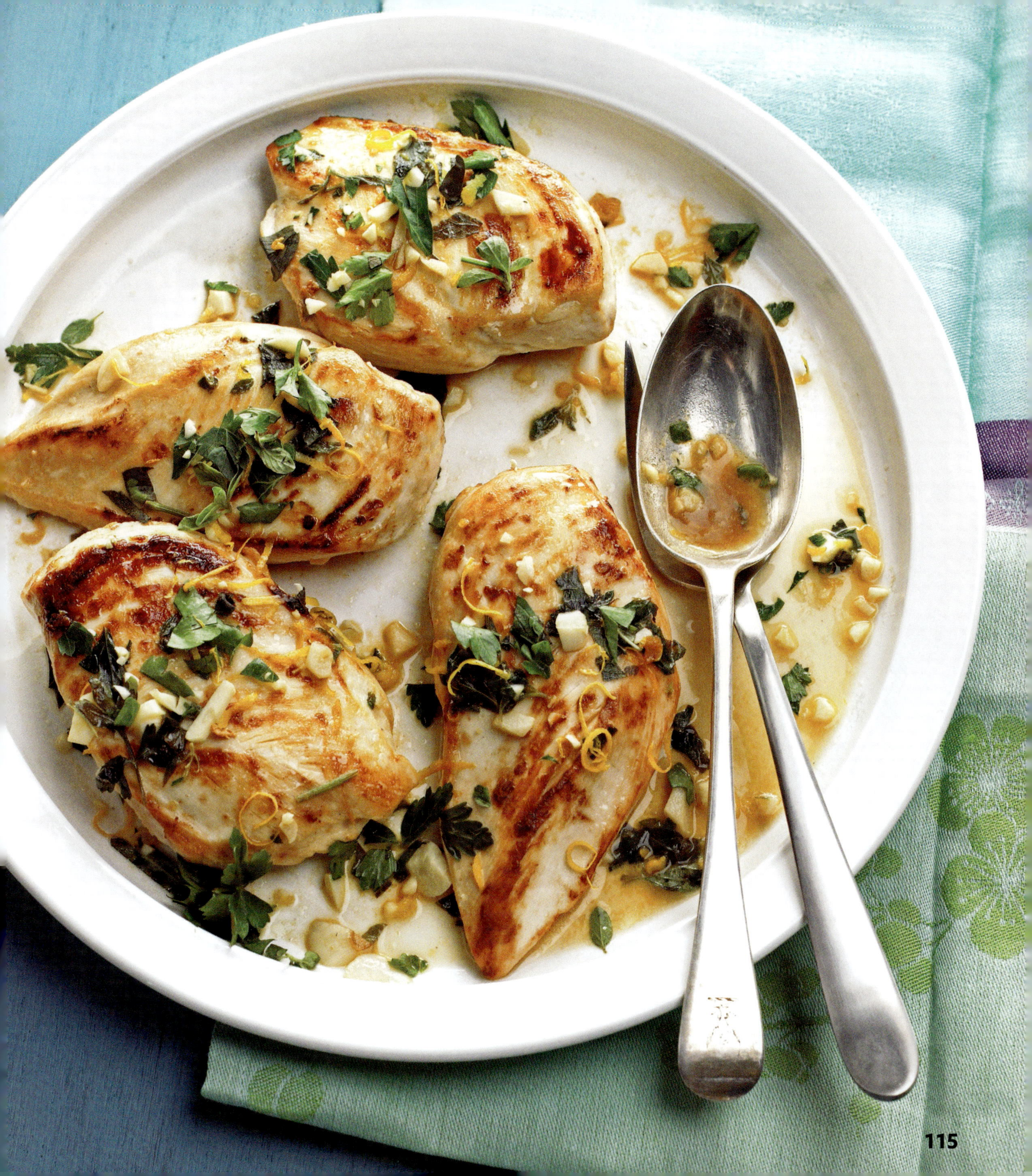

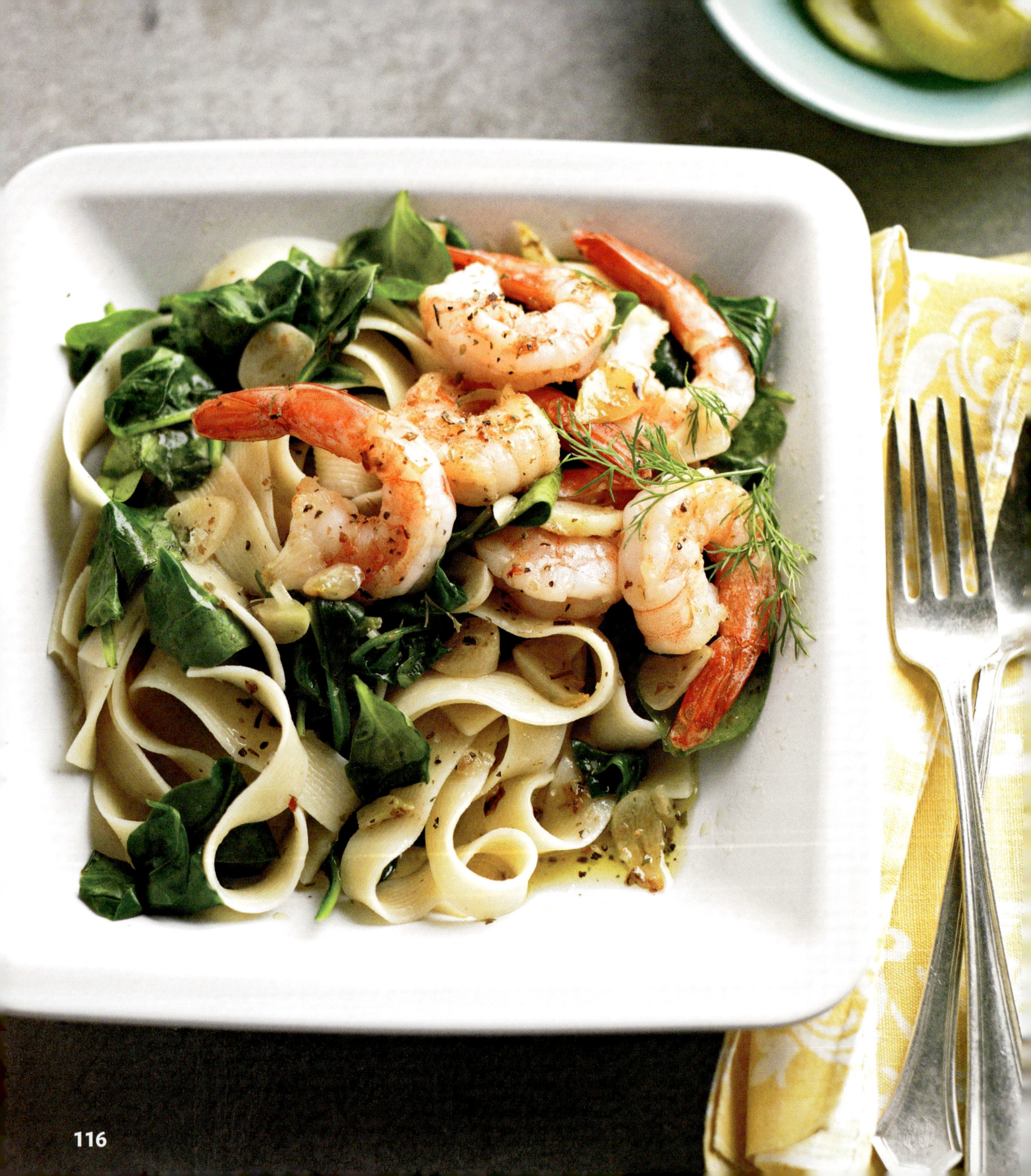

Summer

Lemon-Dill Shrimp and Pasta

This one-dish meal gets fresh flavor from spinach and dill.

START TO FINISH **25 minutes**

12	ounces frozen peeled and deveined medium shrimp, thawed
1	lemon
8	ounces dried fettuccine
2	tablespoons olive oil
3	to 4 cloves garlic, thinly sliced
6	cups baby spinach
½	teaspoon Italian seasoning, crushed
	Salt and ground black pepper
	Fresh dill (optional)

1. Rinse shrimp; pat dry with paper towels. Finely shred 1 teaspoon peel from the lemon; set aside peel. Juice the lemon over a bowl; set aside juice. Cook pasta according to package directions.
2. Meanwhile, in a 12-inch skillet heat olive oil over medium heat. Cook garlic in hot oil for 1 minute. Add shrimp; cook for 3 to 4 minutes, turning frequently, until shrimp are opaque. Add spinach and drained pasta; toss just until spinach begins to wilt. Stir in Italian seasoning, lemon peel, and 2 tablespoons of the lemon juice. Season to taste with salt and pepper. If desired, top with fresh dill. Serve immediately. Makes 4 servings.
Variation: Substitute bite-size pieces of deli-roasted chicken for the shrimp. For a peppery bite, replace half the spinach with arugula.

Sparkling Basil Lemonade

Make a refreshing twist on a summertime classic.

PREP **15 minutes** COOK **20 minutes** CHILL **2 hours**

4	cups water
3	cups sugar
2	cups fresh basil leaves (about 1½ ounces)
2	1-liter bottles club soda, chilled
2	cups lemon juice
	Ice cubes
1	fresh jalapeño chile pepper, sliced*
	Fresh basil leaves

1. For basil syrup, in a large saucepan combine the water, sugar, and the 2 cups basil. Bring to boiling over medium-high heat. Reduce heat; simmer, uncovered, for 20 minutes. Strain syrup and discard leaves. Cover and chill syrup for 2 to 24 hours.
2. For lemonade, in a very large punch bowl combine chilled syrup, club soda, and lemon juice. Serve over ice, and garnish with jalapeño slices and fresh basil leaves. Makes 16 (8-ounce) servings.
***Tip:** Because chile peppers contain volatile oils that can burn skin and eyes, avoid direct contact with them as much as possible. When working with chile peppers, wear plastic or rubber gloves. If bare hands touch the peppers, wash hands and nails well with soap and warm water.

Fall Herb Recipes

Gather the last of the season's bounty in fragrant armloads of foliage and flowers.

Autumn herb harvests offer tasteful possibilities. Use fall leaves and flowers in recipes and crafts. Here are some ideas:

Herb-baked olives
Preheat oven to 375°F. In a 15×10×1-inch baking pan combine 1½ cups mixed imported Greek and/or Italian olives, ½ cup dry white wine, 1 tablespoon olive oil, and two 4-inch sprigs fresh rosemary. Bake for 45 to 60 minutes or until most of the liquid is absorbed, stirring occasionally. Meanwhile, for dressing, in a small bowl combine 3 tablespoons olive oil, 1 tablespoon finely shredded orange zest, 2 tablespoons orange juice, 1 tablespoon snipped fresh rosemary, 1 tablespoon snipped fresh parsley, 3 cloves garlic, minced, and ⅛ teaspoon ground black pepper. Pour dressing over olive mixture; toss gently to coat. Transfer to a serving bowl. Cover and chill for at least 2 hours. Makes 6 servings.

Thyme wreath
Harvest thyme by cutting at the base of plants so the branches are as long as possible and about the same length. Use a wire wreath form and attach bunches of fresh thyme to it with fine-gauge wire. Wrap the wire tightly around the cut ends of a bunch, securing it to the base. Keep adding bundles until you have completed the wreath. The wreath can be hung fresh and allowed to dry. Use the leaves in cooking, if you like.

Herb bowl centerpiece
Plant small herb plants in a decorative bowl and present with dinners as the freshest way to add seasonings—just clip fresh herbs directly into food. You can also make a cut-herb bowl by harvesting small bundles of fresh herbs and standing them in water. Use a flower-arranging frog to hold them in a bowl.

BREW HERBAL TEA
Infuse herbs in steaming-hot water to make tea—it's healthful, soothing, and satisfying. Use mint, chamomile, rose hips, licorice root, or ginger.

1 PLACE TEA IN A POT
Use 2 teaspoons of dried herb leaves for each cup of water. Popular herbs for tea-making include mint, chamomile, rose hips, licorice root, and ginger. Sprinkle herbs directly into the base of a teapot, or make your own tea bags.

2 BOIL WATER
Bring water to boiling, then allow it to cool for a few minutes. Pour the water directly over the dried herbs. Cover the cup (or place the lid on the teapot), and allow the herbs to steep for 5 minutes. If you like stronger tea, let the herbs steep for a bit longer.

3 SERVE TEA
Pour the prepared tea into a cup. Remove any floating herb leaves from the tea using a strainer.

4 SIP AND ENJOY
Allow your tea to cool. If you like, add honey or agave syrup to sweeten. Then sip, relax, and savor the flavor of your own homegrown herbal tea.

Sage stuffing
Preheat oven to 325°F. In a large skillet cook 1½ cups chopped celery and 1 cup chopped onion in ½ cup hot butter over medium heat until tender but not brown. Remove from heat. Stir in 1 tablespoon snipped fresh sage and ¼ teaspoon ground black pepper. Place 12 cups bread cubes in a large bowl; add onion mixture. Drizzle with enough chicken broth to moisten (1 to 1¼ cups); toss lightly to combine. Place stuffing in a 2-quart casserole. Bake, covered, for 30 to 45 minutes or until heated through. Top with fresh sage. Makes 12 to 14 servings.

Herbed Olives

Thyme Wreath

Herb Centerpiece

Sage Stuffing

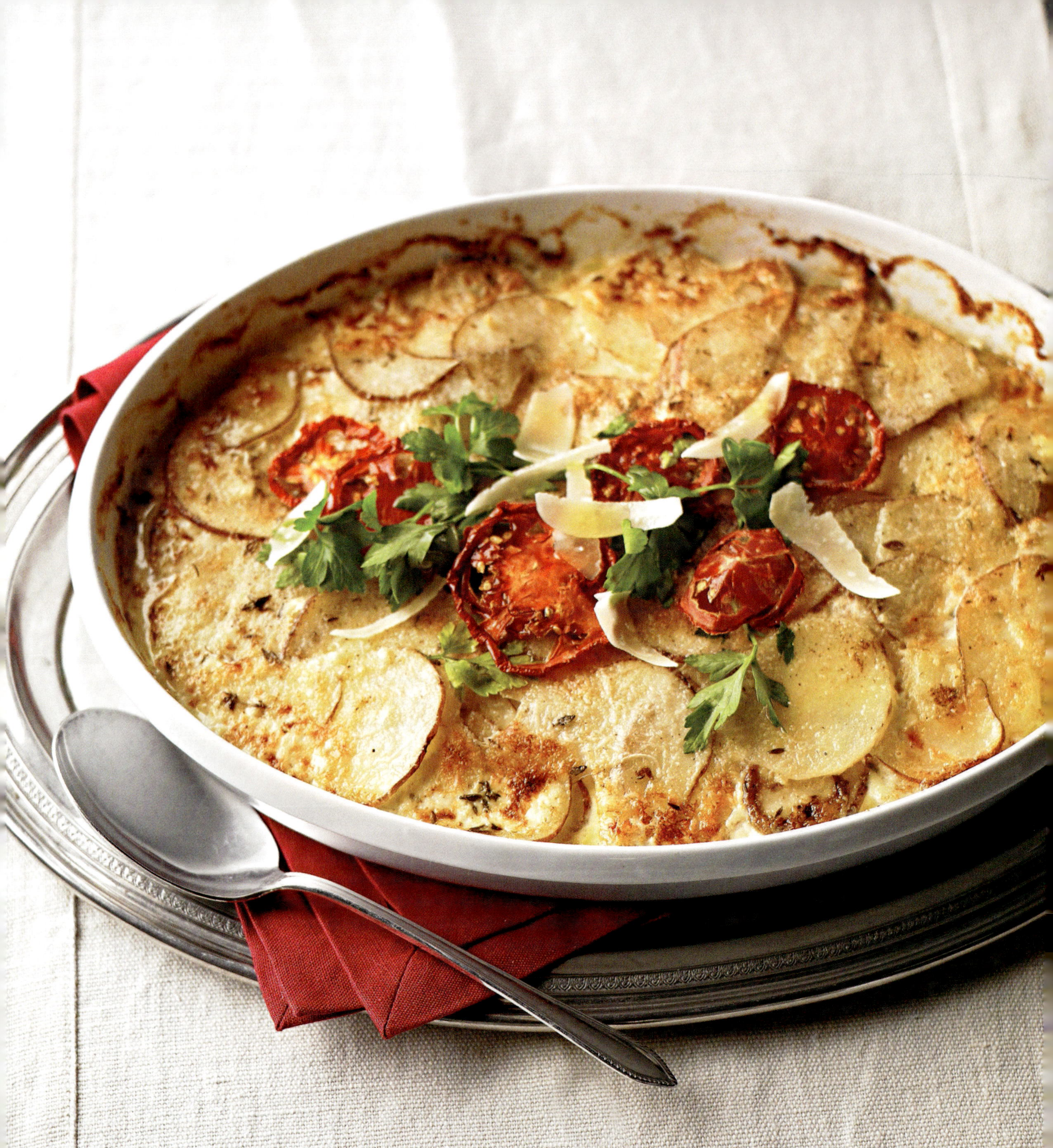

Fall

Thyme Potatoes au Gratin
Autumn potatoes and fresh thyme are excellent partners.

PREP 40 minutes **BAKE** 1 hour 35 minutes at 350°F
STAND 10 minutes

- 3 cups whipping cream
- 1 large clove garlic, minced
- 2 tablespoons butter, softened
- 4 pounds red potatoes, peeled and thinly sliced
- 4 ounces Parmesan cheese, grated
- 2 tablespoons snipped fresh thyme
- ¼ teaspoon freshly grated nutmeg
- ¼ teaspoon freshly ground black pepper
  Shaved Parmesan cheese, Italian (flat-leaf) parsley, and dried tomato slices (optional)

1. Preheat oven to 350°F. In a medium saucepan combine cream and garlic; bring to simmering over medium heat. Simmer, uncovered, for 5 minutes; do not boil. Remove from heat.
2. Use the butter to generously grease a 3- to 3½-quart baking dish. Arrange one-third of the potato slices in a layer. In a small bowl combine grated cheese, thyme, 1 teaspoon *salt*, nutmeg, and pepper. Sprinkle one-third cheese mixture over the potatoes; pour on one-third of the hot cream. Repeat layers twice. Cover with foil.
3. Bake for 1¼ to 1½ hours or until potatoes are almost tender and liquid is mostly absorbed. Uncover; bake for 20 to 30 minutes, until liquid is absorbed and potatoes are browned and moist. If dish is broiler-safe, broil 3 to 4 inches from the heat for 2 to 3 minutes, or until top is crisp and brown. Let stand for 10 minutes. Makes 8 servings.
Make-Ahead Tip: Prepare as directed through Step 2. Chill for up to 2 days before baking. Remove dish from refrigerator and let stand 20 minutes at room temperature. Preheat oven to 350°F. Bake as directed in Step 3. (You may notice some darkening on the edges of the potatoes when you remove the dish from the refrigerator. This is to be expected as the raw potatoes are exposed to the air. This is not harmful and does not affect the taste of the potatoes.)

Cranberry-Sage Rolls
Pungent sage and tart cranberries make a sweet pairing.

PREP 30 minutes **RISE** 30 minutes **BAKE** 20 minutes at 350°F

- 1 16-ounce loaf frozen white bread dough
- 2 tablespoons butter, melted
- ½ cup finely chopped dried cranberries
- 2 tablespoons chopped crystallized ginger
- 2 tablespoons snipped fresh sage
- 1 egg
- 1 tablespoon water
- 12 small fresh sage leaves (optional)

1. Thaw dough according to package directions. Grease a large baking sheet; set aside. On a lightly floured surface, roll dough into a 12×10-inch rectangle. Brush with melted butter; sprinkle with cranberries, crystallized ginger, and snipped sage. Starting from a long side, tightly roll up rectangle into a spiral. Cut into twelve 1-inch slices. Place rolls on prepared baking sheet, standing rolls upright with seam sides down. Cover and let rise in a warm place until double in size (about 30 minutes).
2. Preheat oven to 350°F. In a small bowl whisk together egg and the water. Brush rolls with egg mixture. If desired, gently press a small sage leaf into the top of each roll; brush leaves with remaining egg mixture. Bake about 20 minutes or until golden brown. Makes 12 rolls.
Make-Ahead Tip: Prepare as directed in Step 1, except after shaping dough and covering loosely, chill in the refrigerator for up to 24 hours. Let stand at room temperature for 30 minutes before baking. Bake as directed in Step 2.

USING HERBS **121**

Fall

Pumpkin, Barley, and Sage Soup

Sage adds subtle flavor to this hearty soup.

START TO FINISH 30 minutes

8	ounces cooked andouille or smoked sausage links, chopped
1	small onion, chopped
1	tablespoon snipped fresh sage
1	tablespoon vegetable oil
1	cup quick-cooking barley
4	cups water
1	teaspoon instant chicken bouillon granules
1	15-ounce can pumpkin
2	tablespoons maple syrup
1	tablespoon cider vinegar
	Salt and ground black pepper

1. In 4-quart pot or Dutch oven cook sausage, onion, and sage in hot oil over medium heat for 3 minutes, stirring often. Add barley, the water, and bouillon granules. Bring to boiling. Reduce heat; simmer, covered, for 12 minutes, stirring occasionally.
2. Stir in pumpkin, maple syrup, and vinegar; heat through. Season to taste with salt and pepper. Makes 4 servings.

Rosemary-Potato Frittata

Fresh or dried rosemary brightens this creamy potato dish.

START TO FINISH 20 minutes

4	ounces tiny new potatoes, cut into ¼-inch slices (1 cup)
¼	cup chopped red onion or onion
¼	cup chopped red, green, or yellow sweet pepper
	Nonstick cooking spray
1	cup refrigerated or frozen egg product, thawed, or 4 eggs, beaten
½	teaspoon snipped fresh rosemary or ¼ teaspoon dried rosemary, crushed
⅛	teaspoon salt
¼	cup shredded Swiss cheese (1 ounce)
	Cracked black pepper

1. In a covered medium nonstick skillet cook potatoes and onion in a small amount of boiling water for 7 minutes. Add sweet pepper. Cook, covered, for 3 to 5 minutes more or until vegetables are tender. Drain vegetables in a colander. Cool and dry the skillet. Lightly coat the skillet with cooking spray. Return vegetables to the skillet.
2. In a small bowl combine egg, rosemary, and salt. Pour over vegetables in the skillet; do not stir. Cook over medium heat. As mixture sets, run a spatula around the edge of the skillet, lifting egg mixture so uncooked portion flows underneath. Continue cooking and lifting egg mixture until it is nearly set (top will be moist).
3. Remove skillet from heat. Sprinkle with cheese. Let stand, covered, for 3 to 4 minutes or until top is set and cheese is melted. Sprinkle with cracked black pepper to serve. Makes 2 servings.

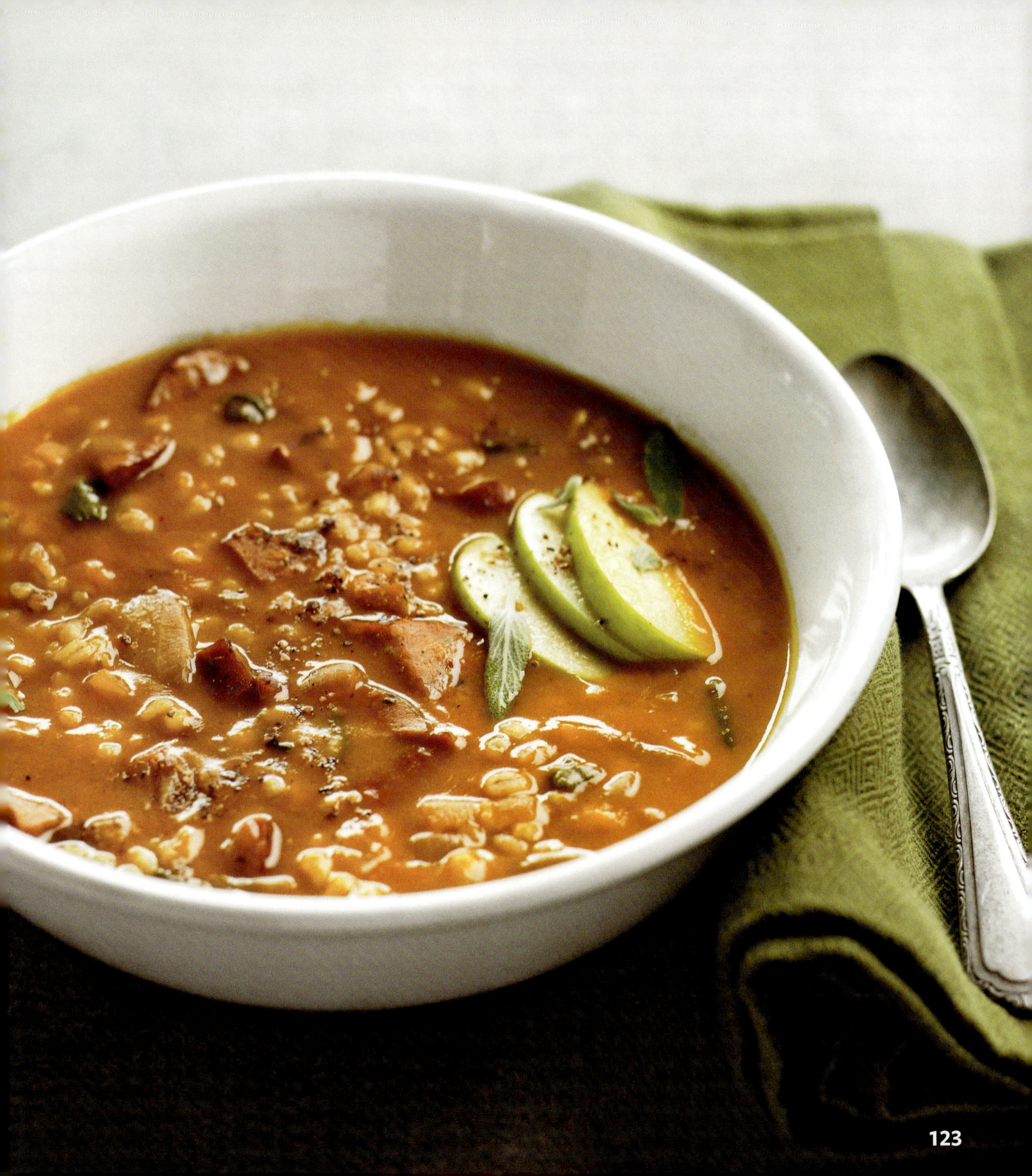

Winter
Herb Recipes

Brighten winter meals with the pungent tastes of the garden.

Recall the glories of the summer garden with the herbal flavors you've harvested. Here are some ideas:

Orange-fennel marinade
In a small bowl stir together ⅔ cup orange juice, ⅔ cup water, 2 tablespoons thinly sliced green onion, 1 tablespoon snipped fresh sage (or ½ teaspoon ground sage), 1 tablespoon Dijon-style mustard, and 1 teaspoon fennel seeds, crushed. Pour over meat or fish and turn to coat. Marinate in the refrigerator at least 30 minutes or up to 4 hours. Drain the meat or fish, discarding the marinade. Grill. Makes enough for ¾ pound meat.

Lemon-mint water
Place the slices of 4 lemons in a large pitcher. Gently squeeze 1½ cups mint leaves to slightly bruise them. Add the mint to the pitcher with lemon slices. Pour in water. Cover and chill for 1 to 8 hours. Strain the lemon-water mixture; discard herbs and lemons. Divide additional lemon slices and fresh mint (or basil sprigs) equally among 6 to 8 tall glasses or pint canning jars. For each serving, add 1 cup of ice cubes; fill with the lemon-mint water. Makes 6 to 8 servings.

Five-spice powder
Combinations vary, but this fragrant blend usually includes cinnamon, anise seeds or star anise, fennel seeds, black or Szechwan pepper, and cloves. In a blender combine 3 tablespoons ground cinnamon, 6 star anise or 2 teaspoons anise seeds, 1½ teaspoons fennel seeds, 1½ teaspoons whole Szechwan peppers or whole black peppercorns, and ¾ teaspoon ground cloves. Cover and blend until powdery. Store in a covered container. Makes about ⅓ cup.

left Bring potted rosemary plants indoors in late summer, and they'll prosper throughout winter when placed in a cool room and watered often enough to keep the soil damp. Tuck baubles at the base of the plants for a festive touch.

Jamaican jerk seasoning

In a bowl, combine ¼ cup sugar, 2 tablespoons dried thyme, 2 tablespoons ground allspice, 1 tablespoon ground black pepper, 1½ teaspoons salt, 1½ teaspoons cayenne pepper, 1½ teaspoons ground nutmeg, and ¾ teaspoon ground cloves. Rub seasoning into meat before grilling. Makes about ⅔ cup, or enough for 3 pounds poultry, pork, seafood, or vegetables.

BHG TEST GARDEN TIP

FREEZE A BOUQUET

You can prepare and freeze ready-to-use herb blends such as bouquet garni. Prepare sprigs of parsley, thyme, and a bay leaf. Wrap in cheesecloth and tie with kitchen twine. Place the bouquets in a freezer bag, and use each as needed in sauces and soups.

HERBAL FLAVOR RANGES

Herbs are generally categorized as strong or mild. Most foodies agree that using just one strong-flavor herb per dish keeps herbs from overpowering a recipe. Mild-flavor herbs can be combined freely.

Strong Herbs

These herbs are more resinous than mild herbs, and their flavors tend to dominate a dish. Generally, use just one of these herbs per dish.

1. WINTER SAVORY
2. ROSEMARY
3. SAGE

Mild Herbs

These herbs add subtle undertones of flavor to a dish. Use them fresh or dried, and add to a dish just before serving. You can use multiple mild herbs in the same preparation.

4. PARSLEY
5. DILL
6. CHERVIL

USING HERBS

Winter Garden Gifts

Share nature's scents and flavors with herb-inspired gifts you can grow and make.

Fresh and dried herbs make excellent gifts for the holidays. Here are some ideas:

Good-taste basket
Give each pot a colorful paper wrapper, then insert four different herbs into a compartmentalized basket. Go with a culinary theme: French herbs, Italian herbs, tea herbs, or sweet herbs. For the gift marker, insert a fork (handle first) into the soil of one of the pots. Thread a gift tag hand-printed on a slip of paper between the tines. If you like, include an envelope with a few of your favorite herbal recipes written onto recipe cards.

Exfoliating scrub
To make a soothing exfoliating scrub, use coarse kosher salt or sea salt. Combine with a natural oil, such as jojoba, grapeseed, olive, or sweet almond. Drop in the oil from a couple of punctured vitamin E capsules. Add a handful of dried powdered rosemary and lavender. Add 10 drops of your favorite essential oil (rose, lavender, lemon verbena) and mix well. The salt scrub will have a grainy consistency. Spoon it into decorative jars or tins. Tie on a sprig of rosemary and a label with a length of cotton twine.

Mini greenhouse
Fill cups with potting soil and sow three to five basil seeds in each. Cover lightly with soil and add water. Set under grow lights or in a south-facing window. After the seedlings sprout, pinch them back to make bushier plants. Wrap the base of the cup with yarn, twine, or ribbon. Add a matching gift tag, and top the cup with its greenhouse dome.

Herb-infused bath oils
First sterilize and let dry any small, pretty bottles you have on hand. Drop into each bottle a few fresh or dried stems of lavender or rosemary. In a measuring cup with a spout mix together the oils. For a soothing bath oil, mix 16 ounces almond oil with 24 drops lavender essential oil and 8 drops rose essential oil. For a stimulating bath oil, blend 16 ounces soy or olive oil with 24 drops rosemary essential oil and 8 drops juniper essential oil. For each mixture, break open 8 capsules of vitamin E and stir the contents into the oil mixture. Using a funnel, pour the oil mixture into each bottle and cork it. Seal the cork with paraffin. Tie dried flowers to the neck of each bottle with raffia or ribbon.

MAKE LAVENDER SACHETS
With cut and dried lavender bundles, you can make your own lavender sachets that will scent your clothing and keep away insect pests.

1 REMOVE FLOWERS
Remove the dried lavender flowers from the stems by holding a flower bundle between your hands and rubbing the stems together. The flowers will drop off the stems. Keep rubbing until all the flowers have fallen from the stems.

2 SIFT FOR STEMS
Place the lavender blossoms in a large bowl. Sift through the flowers and pick out any small stems or chaff.

3 FILL THE SACHETS
Using a small scoop, place lavender buds into a small cloth bag with a pull string. You can also use fine mesh bags, which allow you to see the lavender flowers.

4 WRAP AND GIVE
Box up several of your sachet creations and give them all as a gift. Or use individual bags as fragrant stocking stuffers. The fragrance from lavender sachets will last for months. To refresh sachets with a lavender scent, spray with linen water or dab with lavender essential oil.

Good-Taste Basket

Exfoliating Scrub

Mini Greenhouse

basil

Bath Oil

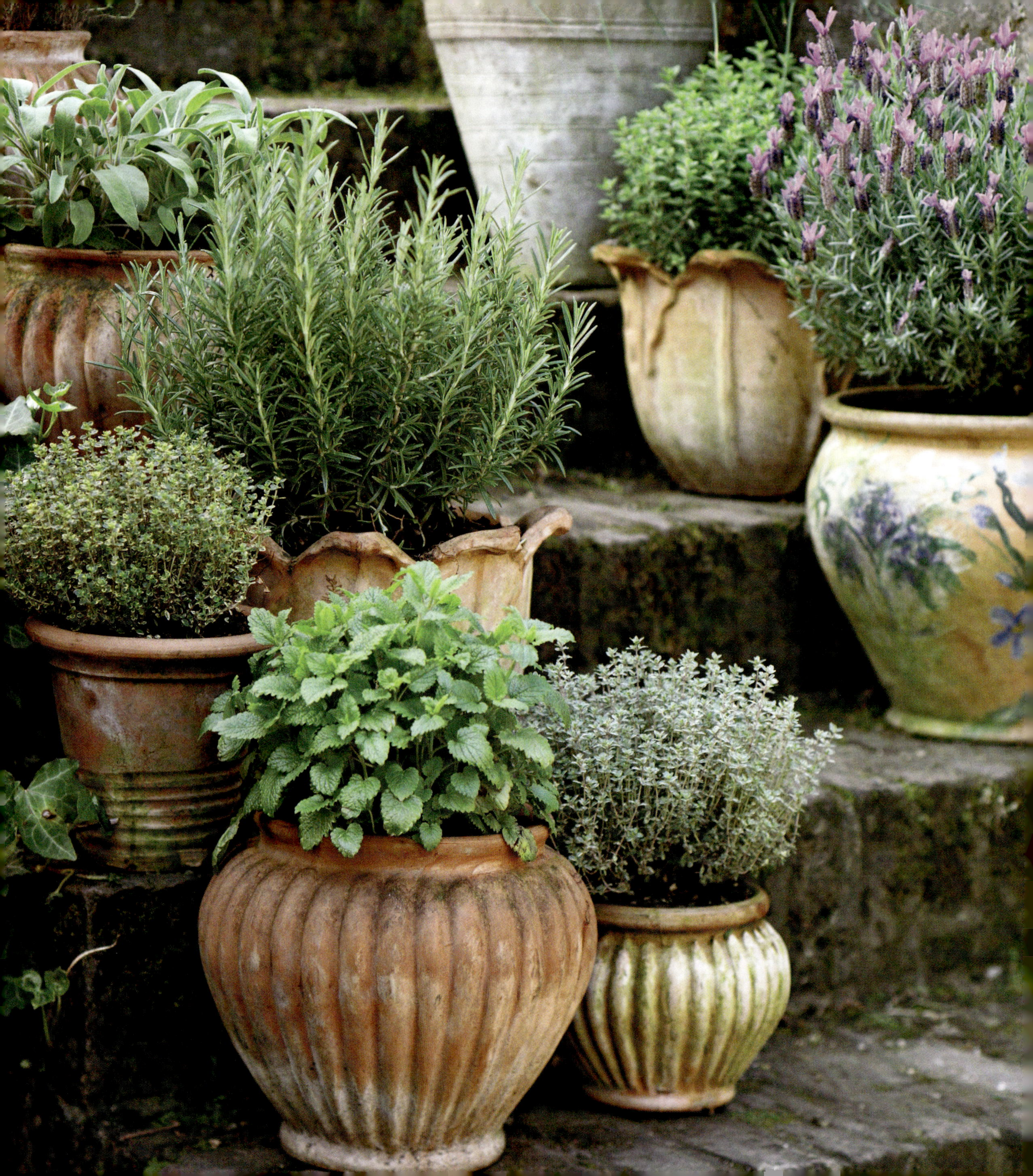

CHAPTER FIVE

Herb Encyclopedia

Discover the charms of herbs. Learn how to grow and harvest them, and how to use them in your garden, kitchen, and bath.

> **YOU SHOULD KNOW**
> Aloe vera is a versatile plant that grows just as well in a container indoors on a sunny windowsill as it does outdoors.

Aloe Vera
Aloe vera

Talk about easy care. Aloe vera has simple needs: Sunshine and a little water make it very happy. In return, the plant provides you with handsome, spiky foliage that contains a gellike sap used to soothe burns and moisturize skin.

Aloe vera is a perennial tropical plant native to hot, dry regions of Africa. It has been used in traditional medicine around the world and can be traced to early Egypt (nearly 6,000 years ago), where an image that resembles an aloe vera plant is depicted in stone carvings. Carl Linnaeus identified and named aloe vera in 1753 as *Aloe perfoliata* var. *vera*. It is referred to as the plant of immortality and the first-aid plant because of its healing properties.

Best site
Full sun is ideal. This plant does best in arid climates. Throughout much of the country, aloe vera is grown in containers that can be moved indoors when frost threatens. In frost-free regions, it can be grown outdoors.

Planting
Aloe vera can be grown from seed, but it's faster and easier to buy young plants at your local garden center or greenhouse. Pot them in a soil mix designed for succulents. As plants mature, they develop offsets that can be divided and potted individually.

Growing
Set aloe vera in a location that receives at least six hours of sun a day. Because this is a succulent plant, the leaves have a high water content, so it's important not to expose it to freezing temperatures. Water when the soil feels dry to the touch. Indoors during winter, keep plants in bright light; water less often. In spring, give your plants a diluted solution of liquid houseplant fertilizer. Zones 9–11.

Harvest
Leaves can be broken off and used at any time.

Uses
Try aloe vera in these ways:
Healing touch Aloe vera gel can be applied as a soothing balm for cuts or second-degree burns and is thought to have antioxidant and anti-inflammatory properties. It is found in many skin products, including lotions, sunblocks, and salves. Aloe vera gel is not to be confused with aloe juice and should not be taken internally.
Landscape design Aloe vera makes a dramatic edging plant for garden beds.
Succulent bowl Combined with other succulents, such as jade plant, panda plant, and echeveria, aloe vera is an excellent addition to succulent containers.

Angelica
Angelica archangelica

Angelica is a tall, hardy biennial. It has dramatic stalks that can be candied and used on cakes and cookies. It also is used to flavor liqueurs such as Chartreuse. It bears ball-shape pale green to cream flowers with a pleasant fragrance.

In ancient times angelica was an herb of protection from witchcraft and illness, including the plague. Angelica is associated with protector angels—specifically Michael the Archangel—from which the herb gets the species name *archangelica*.

Best site
Plant angelica in full sun in a location where it has plenty of room. It can take dappled shade. This easy-care herb grows 4–6 feet tall. Place it at the back of a border.

Planting
Angelica can be grown from seeds, root divisions, or transplants purchased at your local garden center or nursery. The first year, the plants produce lots of beautiful frilly green foliage. The second year, angelica shoots up flower stalks and then produces seeds.

Growing
This herb does best in a rich, organic soil that remains slightly moist. In poor soil, add rotted manure or compost to the bed at planting time. Angelica is somewhat drought-tolerant. Plants may self-sow, but as a precaution, plant new angelica each year. Mulch the soil around the plants to prevent weed competition and to maintain consistent soil moisture. Zones 5–9.

Harvest
Use all parts of the plants: seeds, stems, and roots. Pick leaves and stems in the plant's second year—early in the season, when they are tender. Gather seeds in autumn, then dig the roots.

Uses
Try angelica in these ways:
In garden beds This big, bold bloomer offers flowers and foliage as a tall, back-of-the-border accent in perennial gardens.
Tea Angelica root can be dried and used for tea.
Candied treats The celery-flavor stems can be candied. The stems can be eaten raw.

YOU SHOULD KNOW
Bees love angelica, so if you want to increase the pollinators in your garden, include this plant.

VARIETIES
1. PURPLE ANGELICA (*Angelica gigas*) has pretty reddish-purple stems and flowers.

HERB ENCYCLOPEDIA

Anise Hyssop
Agastache foeniculum

This 2- to 5-foot-tall plant produces upright columns of fuzzy purplish-blue blooms in late summer. The scent of anise hyssop is a marriage of licorice (anise and licorice are synonymous) and mint (because this plant is also a member of the mint family).

Anise hyssop was used extensively by Native Americans, who called on it to relieve depression. It was also used in medicine bundles.

Best site
Plant in full sun in moist to well-draining soil. Anise hyssop can also grow in light shade. To improve the fertility of the planting area, add 2 inches of compost to the soil.

Planting
Plants spread 1–3 feet wide, so space them accordingly. Plant transplants or seedlings (if you have a friend who has this plant, self-sown seedlings should be readily available).

Growing
Start anise hyssop from seeds about eight weeks before your last frost date. You can also sow seeds directly in the garden. If buying seedlings, wait until the threat of frost has passed before planting. For established plants, divide large clumps in spring. Zones 4–10.

Harvest
Gather leaves from established plants any time of the season. Start from the base of the plant, and harvest leaves in the morning. To dry leaves to use as seasoning later or for tea, cut whole stems, make into bundles, and hang upside down to dry. Remove dried leaves and store. Cut fresh flowers when they are about three-fourths open. Use the flowers in bouquets.

Uses
Try anise hyssop in these ways:
Deer-resistant gardens These plants don't taste good to deer, so they are ideal for gardens in deer-heavy areas.
Pollinator attractant Loved by hummingbirds, butterflies, and bees, anise hyssop is a must-have plant for wildlife.

YOU SHOULD KNOW
Anise hyssop self-seeds with abandon. If you don't want this lovely herb to spread, deadhead the flowers as soon as they fade.

VARIETIES
1. **'BLUE FORTUNE'** (*Agastache foeniculum*) grows 3 feet tall and blooms July through September. Zones 4–9.

2. **'GOLDEN JUBILEE'** (*A. foeniculum*) produces chartreuse foliage and lavender-purple flower spikes. It grows 2–3 feet tall in Zones 4–10.

Artemisia
Artemisia

Artemisias are prized for their beautiful silvery foliage that complements other perennials and herbs in a border. The different members of the family go by various common names, such as wormwood, prairie sage, and sagebrush.

Artemisia was used as a folk remedy to treat digestive-system disturbances. Chinese herbalists used artemisia to treat fevers in ancient times.

Best site
Plant in full sun and well-draining soil. Artemisia thrives in hot, dry conditions. All species can grow quite large and make poor candidates for containers.

Planting
Start artemisia from nursery-grown plants, spacing them at least 2–3 feet apart. Many species will self-sow, providing you with artemisia seedlings for friends and family. Taller species can topple in high winds and may require staking.

Growing
Artemisias are drought-tolerant. They thrive in sandy soil with only an occasional watering to keep them looking good. Hold off on fertilizer; these plants prefer soil low in nutrients.

Harvest
Artemisia foliage can be clipped at any time. You may also cut the plants back severely if they start to flop over their neighbors in a border.

Uses
Try artemisia in these ways:

Insect repellent This pungent herb can be used to deter insects in closets or dresser drawers.

Nature gardens Artemisia is the host plant for several species of butterfly larvae. Plants are so vigorous that caterpillar leaf damage is typically not noticeable.

Everlastings The frosty-gray foliage dries well and provides an ideal addition to wreaths, swags, and other decorative arrangements. Cut 4-inch stems, gather them into bundles, and attach the sprays to a base for an elegant wreath.

YOU SHOULD KNOW
Trim the new growth of artemisias by a few inches to shape them and prevent them from flopping over later in summer. Cut plants to 6 inches in fall.

VARIETIES

1. WHITE SAGE (*Artemisia ludoviciana*), the variety used to make Owyhee oil, is a fruity-smelling artemisia with a hint of peach. Zones 4–9.

2. 'POWIS CASTLE' grows 3 feet tall with feathery, finely serrated silver leaves. Zones 4–9.

3. 'SILVER KING' (*A. ludoviciana*) grows 4 feet tall, creating a tower of silver foliage for back-of-the-border locations. It spreads easily. Zones 4–9.

HERB ENCYCLOPEDIA

> **YOU SHOULD KNOW**
> A few full-size basil plants provide plenty of leaves to make several batches of pesto, a paste made of basil, garlic, nuts, and oil. 'Genovese' makes excellent pesto.

Basil
Ocimum

If summer had a flavor, it would taste like basil. An ideal companion to tomatoes, basil offers spicy flavors when used fresh or cooked in sauces. This popular annual herb is easy to grow and comes in many varieties: sweet big-leaf selections, lemon-flavor, purple-hue, and compact dwarf types. The flavors range from citrus to spicy, with a touch of anise.

Basil has a rich history. It is a sacred herb in India and Thailand; in Italy it is a traditional symbol of love and romance. As a medicinal, it has been used to relieve sore throats, headaches, and nausea. There are more than 150 varieties of basil.

Best site
Plant basil in full sun. Although it grows best in moist soil, it will tolerate drought conditions for short periods as long as it has an established root system, which develops about six weeks after planting. Basil grows well in garden beds, whether in a traditional kitchen garden or mixed with perennials and annuals in a flower garden. It also grows well in containers. Use a well-drained potting mix, and plant in a container that holds at least 5 gallons of soil.

Planting
Start from seeds or transplants. Basil is a tender herb; plant only after the threat of frost has passed. It grows slowly in cool weather, but once the weather warms, basil flourishes. Sow seeds indoors in early spring, and transplant into the garden after the danger of frost is over. Thin seedlings to 1–3 feet apart. Seedlings provide a great way to grow different basil varieties.

Growing
Cover plants with cloches, cold frames, or protective cloth in cool regions or anytime frost is predicted. To encourage bushy growth, cut or pinch off flowers as they form. Basil does not need extra fertilizer; in fact, excessive nutrients result in poor flavor. Average garden soil provides all the necessary nutrients. Keep the soil around

VARIETIES

1. 'GENOVESE' grows 2–3 feet tall and 2 feet wide. The large, fragrant leaves can be harvested all summer.

2. 'PESTO PERPETUO' has variegated foliage (cream-edge pale green leaves) and forms a columnar plant that reaches 3 feet tall. Use it in pots or the landscape.

3. 'MRS. BURNS' LEMON' is a tall and narrow basil that's a green-leaf version of 'Pesto Perpetuo'. It grows 18 inches tall. It has a delightful lemony fragrance and flavor.

134 GARDENING MADE EASY **HERB GARDENING**

plants consistently moist and free of weeds. To help satisfy moisture needs and stifle weeds, spread a 2-inch-thick layer of mulch around plants when they are about 6 inches tall.

Harvest

Begin harvesting basil as soon as the plant has at least four sets of leaves. For the most intense flavor, harvest leaves just as the flower buds begin to form. Pinch out the topmost set of leaves and any flowers as needed for use in the kitchen. After harvesting, store unwashed basil in plastic bags in the refrigerator for a day or two. Basil cuttings won't last long; the foliage begins to turn black after a few days. You can also stand cut stems in a glass of water and keep them handy on your countertop. Preserve fresh leaves by pulverizing them in a food processor with olive oil, then placing the paste in an airtight bag or other container and storing it in the freezer for up to a year. Basil can be dried, but dried basil is neither as flavorful nor as colorful as basil preserved with oil.

Uses

Try basil in these ways:

Tea Steep 2 teaspoons dried or fresh leaves in 1 cup boiling water. Strain out the leaves and sweeten the tea with honey or sugar.

Chiffonade Large-leaf basils are ideal for cutting into thin strips and sprinkling on dishes. This preparation technique is called chiffonade: Stack large basil leaves, roll them tightly, then cut across the roll using a sharp knife. Use the ribbons of flavorful basil to top soups, sauces, and salads.

Edible flowers The spicy sprays of basil flowers can be used to spark salads and soups.

Breath freshener Chew a basil plant stem to freshen your breath.

VARIETIES

4. 'RED RUBIN' looks as gorgeous in flower borders as it does in bouquets. This purple-leaf beauty grows 2 feet tall and 14 inches wide.

5. 'CINNAMON' has tasty cinnamon-flavor leaves. Plants grow 18 inches tall.

6. 'SWEET THAI' has a pronounced spicy anise flavor and pretty reddish-purple stems on 12- to 18-inch-tall plants.

7. 'SPICY GLOBE' is one of the best basil varieties for use in small spaces, reaching only 6–10 inches tall. It has a spicy flavor, tiny leaves, and a compact form.

HERB ENCYCLOPEDIA

> **YOU SHOULD KNOW**
> Bay is a slow-growing plant, so buy the largest plant you can find. The bigger the plant, the more leaves you can harvest.

Bay Laurel
Laurus nobilis

A mainstay in every chef's inventory, bay is a warm-climate tree that's easily grown in containers in Northern gardens. Where it is hardy outdoors, bay can grow to 30 feet tall, but in a container it typically tops out at 3–5 feet.

The leaves of bay laurel have a heralded and symbolic past. In ancient Greece laurel wreaths indicated high status, and in Rome laurel was a symbol of victory and accomplishment.

Best site
Bay needs a sunny spot that receives at least six hours of direct sunlight a day. Start with a young plant from a local nursery or greenhouse, or start cuttings taken from branch tips.

Planting
Plant bay in a good-quality potting soil that drains well. Water whenever the soil's surface feels dry to the touch; bay prefers to be on the dry side and will suffer in wet soil.

Growing
Bay is a slow-growing plant that benefits from a dose of liquid houseplant fertilizer in spring. In late spring or early summer, move the plant outdoors to spend the season in a sunny spot. New leaf growth can be targeted by aphids. If you notice the tiny green insects on the plant, blast them off with a jet of water from the garden hose. Bay cannot tolerate temperatures below 25°F and must be moved indoors to protect it from cold weather. Once indoors, keep the plant in bright light and away from cold drafts. Indoors, if a bay tree becomes infested with scale, spray the plant with insecticidal soap. Zones 9–11.

Harvest
Leaves can be harvested at any time, but you can snip off extra leaves in late spring as the plant puts out new growth. Bay leaves can be dried and used for up to three months after harvest. Their flavor dissipates quickly.

Uses
Try bay laurel in these ways:

Soup and stew seasoning Use fresh or dried bay leaves to season food. Bay is an ideal seasoning for poultry and fish dishes. Add the whole leaves to soups and stews, and remove them before serving to eliminate a choking hazard.

Topiary Bay can be clipped into shapes, most commonly the classic ball topping a bare trunk.

Wreaths Bay's stiff almond-shape leaves make it ideal for making wreaths.

Bayberry
Myrica pensylvanica

A North American native, bayberry forms a beautiful semievergreen shrub that can grow up to 8 feet tall. An adaptable coastal shrub, bayberry is most prized for its grayish-white berries, which have a waxy covering.

The Choctaw tribe used the bark of bayberry for a variety of medicinal uses, including fever reduction. In the Colonial era, bayberry was favored for its waxy berries, which were used for candle making. Bayberry candles are fragrant when burned and offer a bright light. Bayberry is also called candleberry and tallowbush.

Best site
Bayberry will grow in full sun or partial shade. It prefers coastal areas, where it thrives in poor, sandy soils. The roots of bayberry have nitrogen-fixing bacteria on their surface that allows the shrub to grow in extremely poor soil. Bayberry tolerates salt spray, making it a good choice for landscapes along the East Coast.

Planting
Buy bayberry plants at your local nursery or garden center. Because these plants can grow 8 feet tall and wide, be sure to give each plant enough space to stretch out. Plants are either male or female; to ensure berry production, always plant at least two or three shrubs in the same landscape.

Growing
Once planted, bayberry requires little care. The plants bloom in early spring, developing small white or green flowers that eventually form prized grayish-white, waxy berries. The berries are about $\frac{1}{8}$ inch in diameter and are popular with a wide range of songbirds. Pruning is rarely necessary, but the plants can be shaped at any time. Zones 3–6.

Harvest
The berries appear on the plants in late fall and, if left alone, they will remain throughout the winter. To harvest the berries, simply pluck them from the branches.

Uses
Try bayberry in these ways:
Essential oils Bayberry leaves can be used to produce a delightfully fragrant essential oil.
Candle-making Harvest the berries, cover them with water, and boil. The waxy coating from the berries will harden on the surface of the water as it cools. Skim the wax and use it to make candles. Four pounds of berries yield a pound of wax.

YOU SHOULD KNOW
If you live in an Eastern coastal area, bayberry makes an excellent landscape plant. You need to plant several shrubs to ensure the best berry production.

Bee Balm
Monarda didyma

Bee balm, also known as bergamot, attracts pollinators such as butterflies, hummingbirds, and bees in droves. For that reason alone, it's good to have this plant in your garden. Herb fans enjoy this plant for its flowers because they are edible. The aromatic citrusy-minty leaves are a plus.

Also called Oswego tea, the leaves of bee balm were used by the Oswego tribe of New York. Native Americans discovered medicinal uses of bee balm and shared them with the settlers in America. They used the plant for poultices to cure skin infections and tea that promoted dental health. It's no surprise that bee balm has been found to contain antiseptic qualities.

Best site
Although bee balm prefers full sun, it tolerates some shade. Plants grown in partial shade, however, produce fewer flowers. Bee balm can grow in a wide variety of soil conditions, although it does best in moist, well-draining soil. In dry soils plants do not grow as vigorously. This plant does not do well in climates where winters are warm and humid.

Planting
Bee balm is slow to start from seed, so buy established plants. Transplants will generally bloom the first year. Plants vary in size by variety but are generally 3 feet tall and wide. Allow room between plants to avoid fungal diseases.

Growing
This perennial is loved by flower gardeners because it blooms all summer, producing shaggy flowers in lavender, pink, white, red, or magenta. Plant bee balm in perennial borders where it can spread out. Prune plants almost to the ground in fall. Powdery mildew and rust can affect plants, but most bee balms are resistant to most wilts and viruses. Slugs can be a pest early in the season. Zones 3–10.

Harvest
Both the leaves and flowers are edible. To dry leaves and flowers, cut stems, bundle them in small groups, and hang upside down in a cool, dry location. Or dry stems, leaves, and flowers on a screen.

Uses
Try bee balm in these ways:
Sage substitute Use dried bee balm leaves as a citrusy substitute for sage in seasonings for poultry and pork. It makes a tasty dry rub.
Potpourri Because of its minty and citrusy scents, bee balm leaves and flowers are ideal for sachets and potpourris.
Edible flowers Remove the flower petals from the fringy bee balm heads and scatter them into salads or use to garnish dips.
Pollinator attractant Bees love bee balm—hence the name.

YOU SHOULD KNOW
Bee balm, or bergamot, is not the source for the essential oil known as bergamot. That citrusy essence is derived from a fruit (*Citrus bergamia*) that provides the distinctive flavor in Earl Grey tea.

VARIETIES
1. **'CAMBRIDGE SCARLET'** has leafy clumps of 3-foot-tall stems clothed with aromatic oval leaves. The terminal whorls of bright red two-lipped flowers are surrounded by brownish-red bracts. Zones 3–9.
2. **MONARDA DIDYMA** has a citrusy aroma. Plants grow 2–3 feet tall in Zones 3–9.

Betony
Stachys officinalis

Commonly called wood betony or Bishop's wort, betony is a close relative of the common perennial lamb's-ears. This sturdy herb has nectar-rich flowers that attract bees and butterflies to the garden in late summer.

For centuries betony was credited as a cure-all for many ailments and was used as a talisman against evil spirits. In Europe it was frequently planted in physic gardens and churchyards. Ancient healers prescribed betony for nearly everything from curing coughs to deworming. Today it is grown mostly to draw pollinators to the garden.

Best site
Betony prefers a sunny spot, but it will grow in partial shade. The drought-tolerant plant prefers soil enriched with organic material such as compost. Although drought-tolerant, it does best when watered regularly.

Planting
Start betony from seeds, cuttings, or divisions. Because it's not a particularly common plant, you may have some difficulty finding seeds locally, but seed sources are available online. Once started, betony requires little care. Sow seeds ½ inch deep.

Growing
As plants sprout, cultivate frequently to eliminate weed competition. Betony thrives in moist conditions. Mulch between young plants to help conserve soil moisture. It takes two years for betony to mature and flower. The plant's attractive flowers are a deep reddish purple and they lure bees and other pollinators. Mature plants grow to about 2 feet tall. Zones 4–8.

Harvest
Cut stems just as the flowers are beginning to open. Pluck the leaves and dry them on a rack or screen in a well-ventilated, dark location. Store the dried leaves in an airtight container.

Uses
Try betony in these ways:
Tea Use the whole dried leaves to make tea. Use 2 teaspoons of leaves for every cup of boiling water. Allow the tea to steep, covered, then remove the leaves. Betony tea is reputed to cure headaches, sore throats, and nervousness.
Cut flowers Harvest flowers as they are just opening to use in herbal bouquets.
Pollinator attractant The sweet nectar of betony flowers attracts bees and butterflies.
Perennial garden The purple blooms of this plant make stunning additions to perennial gardens alongside yellow flowers such as yarrow and daylily.

YOU SHOULD KNOW
Early herbalists claimed betony could cure a variety of ailments and often called this versatile plant self-heal or heal-all.

VARIETIES

1. 'ROSEA' (*Stachys officinalis*) provides a summerlong display of spires of small pink flowers above compact, healthy clumped foliage. Zones 5–8.

2. 'SUPERBA' (*S. macrantha*), also called big betony, grows 24 inches tall and is topped with lovely pink flowers. Zones 4–8.

YOU SHOULD KNOW
Borage has a reputation as a self-seeding plant. To prevent the herb from becoming too gregarious, weed out early-spring seedlings.

Borage
Borago officinalis

Borage has an outstanding presence in a garden, growing 1–3 feet tall and 2 feet wide. The plant appears as natural in an herb garden as it does mingling with perennials. The plant has notably fuzzy stems and leaves. Gardeners especially appreciate this herb for its edible periwinkle blue blooms—and so do bees!

Borage was thought to instill courage in ancient times. A native of the Mediterranean region, this distinctive herb was used as a remedy for sore throats and skin disorders. You can buy borage seed oil pills, which have shown anti-inflammatory effects. Borage is also called starflower for its bright blue blooms, and its leaves and flowers are edible.

Best site
Plant borage in a sunny spot in well-draining soil. Borage will, however, do well in poorer soils if fertilized with compost.

Planting
Start seeds indoors a month or so before the last frost in cold climates. Transplant seedlings or purchased plants into the garden once the threat of frost has passed and the soil is warm.

Growing
Although borage is classified as an herb, flower gardeners use it in mixed perennial borders. It is also a popular addition to vegetable gardens because of its ability to attract pollinating insects. Borage is considered a good companion plant for tomatoes, strawberries, and squash. Allow enough space for this rangy plant to spread out to 2 feet. Borage continues to bloom throughout summer. This herb is an annual but it readily self-sows to come back each year.

Harvest
Harvest borage flowers when they are fully open. Harvest new leaf growth; the leaves are fuzzy, but blanching them makes them more palatable.

Uses
Try borage in these ways:

Edible flowers Harvest the bright blue (and sometimes pink or white) flowers to dress up salads, summer drinks, and desserts. Pluck flowers moments before serving time, remove the prickly back, and rinse flowers. Sprinkle these bright edibles into fresh greens. Because vinegar discolors flowers, add borage flowers to salads just before serving. If not using the blooms right away, store them in a glass or plastic container in the refrigerator.
Dessert garnishes Borage flowers can be candied in sugar and used to decorate cakes or cupcakes.
Ice cube adornments Freeze borage flowers with water in ice cube trays to add to summer drinks.
Leaves Borage leaves can be used in recipes such as rustic ravioli, soups, and fritters.
Salads Harvest young leaves of borage plants for salads. The flowers and the leaves have a cucumber flavor.
Herbal bouquets Borage leaves and flowers make beautiful additions to herbal bouquets to give as gifts or use as centerpieces.

Calamint
Calamintha nepeta

Calamint looks as much at home in the perennial border as it does in the herb garden. This compact plant develops small leaves that have a refreshing minty fragrance. Calamint is dotted with masses of tiny white flowers that attract butterflies.

Calamint, because of its minty aroma, was historically often used in the kitchen and as an herbal remedy for stomach problems. It's also called lesser calamint.

Best site
Calamint grows well in any sunny location with well-draining soil. It tolerates heat and drought, and because it only grows 18 inches tall, it makes an excellent edging plant along walkways and paths. In the extreme southern part of its range, plant calamint where it's protected from the hot afternoon sun.

Planting
This herb can be grown from seeds that germinate easily. Start four to six weeks before the last frost date in spring. For faster results, buy transplants at your local garden center or from a mail-order garden catalog. Space plants about 15 inches apart.

Growing
Once established, calamint requires almost no maintenance. It develops pretty, light green leaves that resemble oregano. In late summer the plant produces waves of tiny white or lavender flowers until frost. Although calamint is resistant to dry spells, mulch between plants to maintain soil moisture. This healthy plant has few problems with pests or disease. Typically, calamint is a short-lived perennial and may not return after four or five years. Otherwise, the plant may self-sow and reappear in your garden. Zones 4–9.

Harvest
Use leaves as needed from spring to fall to make teas or to flavor soups and stews. Harvest whole stems. Leaves can be used fresh or dried.

Uses
Try calamint in these ways:
Deer garden As a member of the mint family, this herb is uninteresting to deer.
Pollinator attractant The tiny flowers attract butterflies and bees.
Oregano substitute This herb is sometimes used in Italian cuisine as an oregano substitute. In Tuscany, it is used to flavor mushroom and meat dishes.

YOU SHOULD KNOW
You can't beat calamint for its minty foliage and beautiful late-summer flowers. It's also a snap to grow in any sunny spot.

YOU SHOULD KNOW
Calendula is versatile. It looks great in herb gardens, in mixed flowerbeds, and even in containers planted with salad crops, such as Swiss chard or lettuce.

VARIETIES
1. **'CANDYMAN ORANGE'** develops showy orange double flowers on compact 1-foot-tall plants.
2. **'DAISY MIX'** has single flowers in a variety of colors that include yellow, apricot, and orange on 1-foot-tall plants.

Calendula
Calendula officinalis

Beautiful and edible, calendula flowers will brighten your spring garden. The cool-season annual is easy to grow. You can harvest the bright petals and use them to add color and zip to soups and salads. These bright beauties also make long-lasting cut flowers.

A native of southern Europe, calendula was named by the ancient Romans for its nonstop blooming habit. It was used by ancient Egyptians as an herb of rejuvenation. In Europe, calendula flowers were used to color cheese.

Best site
Calendula requires a sunny spot in the garden that receives at least six to eight hours of direct sunshine a day. The plants prefer well-draining soil enriched with organic material.

Planting
Calendula grows easily from seed, whether started indoors or planted directly in the garden. Or start with transplants from a local nursery or garden center. Space plants 6–8 inches apart. They will grow up to 3 feet, depending on variety. Calendula also grows beautifully in containers. It goes by the common name pot marigold.

Growing
The key to success with calendula is to remember it prefers cool weather, so plant early in spring or fall. Heat is calendula's biggest enemy. When the temperature soars, calendula will die back. In the southernmost parts of the United States, you can grow calendula for winter color. To keep plants blooming, remove flowers as they fade. However, at the end of the season, let a few flowers mature and form seeds. Your calendula may sow itself for the next season's display.

Harvest
The petals of calendula can be harvested at any time, but it's best to pick them as soon as the flowers open. The petals of young blooms will be more tender than those of older flowers. Dry the petals on screens for use later.

Uses
Try calendula in these ways:
Saffron substitute For rice dishes such as paella, use calendula flowers to take the place of the more-expensive saffron.
Skin oils Infuse flowers in olive or jojoba oil to make skin treatments for bee stings, bug bites, and rashes.
Edible flowers The cream, orange, apricot, or yellow flower petals of calendula add vibrant color to salads.

Caraway
Carum carvi

Caraway has been cultivated for centuries. This versatile plant—a member of the carrot family—produces tasty edible seeds. The leaves and parsniplike roots are also edible. As a biennial, the plant blooms in its second year.

In ancient times caraway was favored as a remedy for digestive-tract disturbances. The seeds were used in various other medicines. It is still known for its antiflatulence qualities. Today, caraway seeds bring their distinctive flavor to rye and other breads. All parts of the plant are edible.

Best site
Caraway prefers a sunny location and rich, well-draining soil. Because the plant develops a large taproot, loose soil is best. Although the plant tolerates drought, the soil should not be allowed to dry out completely.

Planting
Grow caraway from seeds sown directly in a garden bed. Sow seeds about ½ inch deep. The seeds may be slow to germinate. When seedlings have developed several sets of leaves, thin them to about 8 inches apart. Gently pull out or snip off the extra plants.

Growing
Cultivate around caraway plants every few weeks to eliminate weeds. Once the plants are several inches tall, spread mulch between them to help keep weeds at bay. Weed prevention is essential while the plants are young. Water the plants thoroughly during dry spells. Caraway has few insect pests, but some foliage diseases may affect your crop. To avoid this, keep the foliage as dry as possible by hand-watering with a hose early in the day or using drip irrigation. Zones 5–8.

Harvest
Gather seeds before they fall. Cut the stalks as soon as the seeds begin to ripen and turn brown. Then bundle the stems and hang them upside down in a dry, airy place over a large tray until the seeds are completely dry. Hold the dried seed heads inside a large paper bag, and shake them to release the seeds. Store the seeds in an airtight container, and use them within one year.

Uses
Try caraway in these ways:
Salads Harvest the young leaves for use in salads and as a seasoning for soups and stews.
Root dishes The roots can be boiled in the same manner as parsnips and carrots.
Seasoning for baking The seeds are a flavorful ingredient in breads, cakes, cookies, soups, sauces, and vegetable dishes.

YOU SHOULD KNOW
Caraway is a biennial, meaning you'll have to wait until its second year in the garden for the plant to produce flowers and seeds.

HERB ENCYCLOPEDIA

YOU SHOULD KNOW

Catmint is easy to divide. After the flowers fade in late summer, dig up large plants, separate them into smaller plants, and replant them with room to grow.

Catmint
Nepeta × faassenii

Catmint is a tough perennial herb that excels in hot, dry weather. Plants feature mounding sprays of silvery-green foliage with a flush of blue flowers. Although the name suggests cats are attracted by this herb, they aren't as tantalized by it as they are by catnip.

Catmint was used historically for brewing tea enjoyed as a relaxing hot beverage as well as a medicinal drink to relieve fever. In ancient times it was thought that catmint gave strength to timid people.

Best site
For best results, choose a sunny location with average, well-draining soil. Catmint is drought-tolerant and can grow in partially shaded locations, although it will not bloom as well.

Planting
Sow catmint seeds indoors or directly in the ground. Mature plants self-seed. Transplant these seedlings elsewhere in your garden. Space plants according to the variety's mature size. Most varieties range from 6 to 36 inches tall and from 2 to 4 feet wide.

Growing
Catmint is easy to grow. The tall types may need gentle staking, but otherwise it is an easy-care plant. Deadhead or cut back hard after the first flush of bloom to encourage more flowers. Zones 5–9.

Harvest
To dry leaves, cut the stems and bundle them; hang the bunch to dry in a cool, airy location. After the stems are crisp-dry, strip off the whole leaves and store them in an airtight container.

Uses
Try catmint in these ways:
Tea Catmint makes an interesting tea with a mild minty-spicy flavor.
Rock gardens Catmint is a long-blooming option for rock gardens.
Lavender substitute In cold climates, include the blue-purple bloomer in the perennial garden as an alternative to tender lavender.
Garden edger Catmint is a pretty edging plant. It spills over pathways and blooms nearly all summer long.

VARIETIES

1. 'SIX HILLS GIANT' is one of the tallest catmints, growing up to 3 feet tall. Zones 5–9.

2. JAPANESE CATMINT (*Nepeta subsessilis*) reaches 30 inches tall and develops bluish flowers. Zones 5–9.

Catnip
Nepeta cataria

A member of the mint family, catnip is the recreational drug of choice for cats. The fragrance of fresh or dried leaves attracts some cats. You may find your cat rolling around near your plant in ecstasy. The leaves are used as filler for cat toys. Catnip is also a proven mosquito repellent.

Best site
Give catnip a sunny location and evenly moist, well-draining soil.

Planting
Start from seed about eight weeks before the last frost in your area. Or plant transplants directly into the garden after frost.

Growing
Plant this aromatic perennial in flowerbeds or near vegetables to deter flea beetles and aphids. Zones 3–9.

Harvest
Snip fresh leaves all summer. To dry, cut stems in early morning and hang bundles upside down in a dry, airy, shaded place. Strip the dried leaves from the stems and store in a glass jar.

YOU SHOULD KNOW
Used as a mosquito repellent, catnip has been found to be 10 times more effective than DEET, the chemical found in many commercial insect repellents.

Celery
Apium graveolens dulce

Growing celery in your garden allows you to try smaller, more tender, and milder-flavor celery than you get at the grocery. This crunchy, low-calorie vegetable offers its fresh flavor for soups, stuffings, and stews. Celery seeds are used widely in French and Indian cuisine.

Best site
Plant celery in full sun or partial shade. Mulch the soil to help keep it evenly moist.

Planting
Celery takes 80–120 days to mature. Start seeds indoors 10–12 weeks before your usual spring planting time. Transplant seedlings when the soil has warmed.

Growing
Space plants at least 6–8 inches apart. If you plant in rows, leave 2–3 feet between the rows.

Harvest
When the stalks reach about 10 inches tall, cut them at the base of the plant using a sharp knife. Allow the plant to flower and set seeds, then harvest them before they dry and scatter.

YOU SHOULD KNOW
Blanching gives celery stalks a milder flavor. To blanch stalks, place a light-blocking structure, such as a terra-cotta drainage tile or a PVC pipe, over most of a plant.

VARIETIES
1. CUTTING CELERY (*Apium graveolens*) grows well in containers. It produces flavorful leaves for vegetable salads. The greens also add flavor to homemade tomato juice.

> **YOU SHOULD KNOW**
> Roman chamomile offers a fast-spreading, aromatic groundcover for moist climates. It can be mowed and smells delicious when cut or walked upon.

Chamomile
Chamaemelum nobile, Matricaria recutita

Two plants called chamomile are easily confused. Both have an applelike scent and similar white-and-yellow daisylike flowers that bloom from late spring into summer. Yet the plants have subtle but notable differences.

Chamomile was considered one of the nine sacred herbs by the Anglo-Saxons. It was strewn on floors to improve the ambience (and odor) during gatherings. Chamomile comes from the Greek *chamaimelon*, meaning ground apple—a reference to the plant's fragrance.

Best site
Plant chamomile in full sun or partial shade and well-draining soil.

Planting
Sow seeds indoors four to six weeks before the last frost date. You can also sow seeds directly in the ground. If you garden in a warm climate, you can sow seeds in fall. Plant chamomile seedlings 12 inches apart. If you use chamomile as a groundcover, set the plants 6 inches apart.

Growing
In spring, sow seeds directly in the garden where they will germinate readily. Set out transplants, if you prefer. For best results, keep the soil evenly moist. Cold climates are hard on Roman chamomile. Cover plants with 4–6 inches of mulch after the ground freezes to protect them from the damage of freeze-thaw cycles. German chamomile may reseed itself and come back year after year.

Harvest
In spring and summer, gather flowers and leaves to use fresh or dried. To dry the harvest, gather stems into a bunch, secure with a rubber band, and hang upside down in a dry, airy place. Or spread the plant material on a rack or screen. Store dried flowers and foliage in an airtight jar.

Uses
Try chamomile in these ways:
Groundcover The foliage of Roman chamomile is deep green, finely cut, and matlike, making it an ideal groundcover.
Tea Brew a relaxing tea using 2 teaspoons of chamomile flowers and 1 cup of freshly boiled water; cover and steep for 5 minutes. Women who are pregnant or lactating shouldn't use chamomile. People allergic to ragweed may react to chamomile. Handle it carefully and use sparingly.

VARIETIES

1. ROMAN CHAMOMILE (*Chamaemelum nobile*) is a perennial herb that grows 6–12 inches tall. Some gardeners use it as a lawn alternative. It has a stronger flavor than German chamomile. Zones 4–8.

2. GERMAN CHAMOMILE (*Matricaria recutita*) is a more common plant, an annual that reaches 2 feet tall. The flowers are apple-scented, but the foliage has no fragrance.

Chervil
Anthriscus cerefolium

This cool-season annual has fine-texture, fernlike leaves and grows 12–18 inches tall. Chervil has a mild flavor and appearance similar to parsley. Used to flavor eggs, soups, sauces, vinegars, and butters, this herb is essential in French cooking.

This native of Eastern Europe has long been associated with new life, which is why chervil soup may be served as part of a traditional Easter feast. It is also reputed to cure hiccups.

Best site
Grow chervil in a partially sunny location. Plants prefer well-draining but moist soil and shaded roots.

Planting
This annual grows easily from seed. Scatter seeds in beds or containers several times throughout the growing season for an ongoing harvest. Sow seeds where you want them to grow because the plants do not transplant well. The seeds need light to germinate. Leave them uncovered after sowing, and keep the soil well watered until the seeds germinate.

Growing
In the garden, let a few flower stalks set seeds and self-sow for a continuing crop of chervil. If aphids become a problem, remedy it with a strong spray of water from the garden hose.

Harvest
Snip tender young chervil leaves often to enjoy the plant's best flavor. Pick leaves from the outside of the plant. To prolong the leaf harvest, pinch off flower stalks as soon as they begin to form. Use chervil fresh; dried leaves have little flavor. Chervil retains its freshness up to a week when stored in a plastic bag in the refrigerator. Preserve chervil's flavor in white wine vinegar.

Uses
Try chervil in these ways:

Fines herbes Chervil is a key ingredient in the traditional French herb mix fines herbes. Use the blend in preparing omelets and salad dressings.

Chervil pesto Freeze chervil for later use in soups and sauces by making a flavorful paste. Blend $\frac{1}{3}$ cup olive oil with 2 cups of chervil leaves in a food processor until smooth. Press the pesto into ice cube tray compartments. When frozen, drop the pesto cubes into a freezer bag, label with the contents and date, seal well, and keep in the freezer for up to one year.

Parsley substitute Use chervil instead of parsley in spring salads, soups, and sauces. Chervil has a more complex flavor, with a hint of anise. Chervil is also rich in vitamin C, beta-carotene, iron, and magnesium.

YOU SHOULD KNOW
Chervil is an annual herb, but it self-sows easily. Allow the flowers to form seed heads and you'll have lots of new plants.

> **YOU SHOULD KNOW**
> This plant is not to be confused with Belgian or French endive, which is also called chicory in Germany and the United Kingdom. Endive is a closely related species, *Cichorium endivia*.

Chicory
Cichorium intybus

Bearing pretty blue flowers, chicory is a common roadside flower. It has tough, twiglike stems and is known by other common names including blue sailors, succory, wild chicory, and coffeeweed. This European native has naturalized throughout the United States.

Chicory has been cultivated for at least 5,000 years. It was used by the Egyptians and included in the gardens of Charlemagne and Thomas Jefferson. Chicory is valued as a dye plant and grown for animal fodder.

Best site
Plant chicory in full sun and well-draining soil. It will grow in poor soils and is not demanding—this is why you see chicory growing along roadsides and in ditches.

Planting
Sow seeds indoors in spring about six weeks before the last frost date. Or plant seeds directly in the garden once the soil has warmed. Chicory is not usually sold in plant form because it is commonly found in the wild.

Growing
Chicory is a biennial and blooms its second year in the garden. The plant has a long taproot that helps make it drought-tolerant.

Harvest
Pick chicory leaves when they are young. Harvest the roots once the plant has matured—from midsummer into fall.

Uses
Try chicory in these ways:

Salad greens Pick young tender chicory leaves to use fresh in salads as you would dandelion foliage. Blanching makes young chicory leaves less bitter.

Coffee enhancer or substitute Chicory earned the name coffeeweed because the long white taproots can be harvested, dried, and used as an additive to substitute for coffee. This practice is common in Europe as well as New Orleans.

Chives
Allium schoenoprasum

This easy-to-grow perennial herb thrives in beds or pots. The grassy, hollow leaves can be harvested from early spring through autumn. This clump-forming member of the onion family also boasts edible, fragrant pink-purple flowers that appear in spring.

Chives are native to Europe and Asia, where this herb grows wild. Medieval gardeners planted chives around the borders of gardens because of their decorative value and the belief that the herb deterred insects. It was also thought that chives warded off evil.

Best site
Plant chives in full sun and in average, well-draining soil. Although chives tolerate light shade—especially in regions with hot, dry summers—they grow best in an area that receives six to eight hours of sun a day. Improve soil drainage by working in loads of organic matter such as chopped leaves before planting. Chives also grow well in containers; plant in a well-draining potting mix.

Planting
Plant divided chunks of chives or new plants anytime during the growing season. Divisions and transplants usually produce flowers the first year (the foliage can be clipped for use anytime). Chives can also be planted successfully from seed; sow in early spring or, in mild-winter areas, in fall. Seed-grown plants may require a full year of growth before you harvest leaves and flowers.

Growing
Perennial chives grow for years, blooming in early spring. They are generally drought-tolerant and do not require fertilizer. Deadhead faded flowers to prevent self-seeding and spreading throughout the garden. In warm climates, chives stay green all season; in cooler zones, plants die back to the ground over winter. Zones 3–10.

Harvest
When grown from seed, chives are ready to harvest in 75–85 days. Harvest the leaves as needed by cutting them just above soil level using scissors or a sharp knife. Chives can be dried but retain their color and flavor better when frozen.

Uses
Try chives in these ways:
Edible flowers Snip chive flowers and break them up into soups and salads.
Vegetable ties Use the long, strong leaves as simple-yet-decorative ties around wraps or bundles of vegetables.
Onion substitute Just before serving, sprinkle potato and egg dishes with freshly chopped chives for a subtle zip of onion flavor.

YOU SHOULD KNOW
As chive plants mature, the clumps become overcrowded. Dig and divide them every couple of years. Replant divisions in new locations or share them with friends.

VARIETIES
1. GARLIC CHIVES (*Allium tuberosum*) grow taller than common chives, producing flat leaves and white flowers. They can be invasive; remove the flowers before they develop seeds. As the common name suggests, the leaves have a mild garlic flavor. Zones 4–10.

HERB ENCYCLOPEDIA

YOU SHOULD KNOW
Newer varieties of cilantro are slower to bolt (when plants mature and set seeds). They provide a longer harvest of leaves than earlier cilantro varieties.

Cilantro, Coriander
Coriandrum sativum

Cilantro is a two-for-one annual. The leafy part of the plant, called cilantro, is a favorite seasoning in Mexican and Asian foods. The seeds of a mature plant are called coriander and have a spicy, citrusy flavor.

Cilantro and coriander have been cultivated since 5000 BC and used commonly throughout the Middle East and Asia. The herb was introduced to Latin America, where it also became a staple ingredient in food preparation.

Best site
Plant cilantro in full sun to part shade and well-draining soil. Cilantro grows easily in containers, too. Sow seeds in a pot, and grow plants outside your door for quick and easy harvests.

Planting
Start from seeds or transplants. Sow seeds in early spring after the last frost. In regions with mild winters, sow seeds in fall for winter harvests. Elsewhere, if you prefer, purchase and plant seedlings in spring after the threat of frost has passed.

Growing
Water plants consistently during hot, dry weather to prevent them from bolting. To extend your cilantro crop, sow successive plantings two to four weeks apart. In colder climates, grow cilantro in a cold frame in early spring or fall for an extended growing season. Plants self-sow readily, so remove seed heads to keep cilantro from sprouting everywhere. If you like, keep a potted plant indoors over winter on a sunny windowsill.

Harvest
Harvest leaves from the lower part of the plant once several stems have developed. The lower or outermost leaves have a more spicy flavor than the upper foliage. The white or lavender flowers are also edible. But once the flowers appear, the flavor of the leaves becomes less palatable. To harvest the seeds, cut the stalks when the seedpods turn brown. Hang the dry stalks upside down in paper bags to catch the seeds.

Uses
Try cilantro/coriander in these ways:
Cilantro leaves Add cilantro leaves to cooked food just before serving; heat dissipates the flavor. Cilantro is best used fresh. It can be dried, but the flavor is milder.
Coriander seeds Grind coriander seeds with a mortar and pestle to release their bright flavor just before adding to a dish.
Dukka Coriander seeds play a big part in the North African nut, herb, and spice mix called dukka. The traditional way to eat dukka is to dip a piece of flatbread into olive oil, then dip into a bowl of powdery dukka. You get a burst of coriander flavor in every bite.

VARIETIES
1. **'DELFINO'** is an All-American Selections winner with ferny foliage. It tolerates warm weather well and is slow to bolt.
2. **VIETNAMESE CORIANDER** (*Persicaria odorata*) is used in Southeast Asian cuisine. Hardy to Zone 10, it is grown elsewhere as an annual.

Citrus
Citrus

Citrus—including lemons, oranges, and limes—produces juicy, sweet, or tart fruit. Planted in the landscape (in warm climates) or in containers (best for cold climates), these small trees add structure to a yard or patio and are true components of an edible landscape. Enjoy their flowers, fruits, and leaves.

Citrus fruit can be traced to Southeast Asia as far back as 4000 BC. It traveled the world with early explorers, who introduced these sweet and tart fruits to the Americas in the 16th century.

Best site
Plant citrus in full sun. Plants grow best in well-draining soil. In hot, dry climates, place citrus where it will receive light shade at the hottest time of day. In cool climates, plant in the warmest spot in the yard against a south-facing wall.

Planting
Where winters are mild and summers are hot, plant citrus in fall. Elsewhere, plant in early spring after frost. Dig a hole as deep as the nursery pot and slightly wider. For best results, plant with the graft (bulging area at the trunk's base) at least 2 inches above soil level.

Growing
Water regularly during dry periods. Trees need about 1 inch of water per week. Fertilize two or three times from February through September, and avoid overfertilizing. Protect the young frost-sensitive trees by wrapping them with an insulating material. In cold climates, grow citrus trees in pots and keep them indoors over winter. Zones 9–11.

Harvest
Citrus fruits mature at various times of year. To determine orange maturity, taste the fruit. Color doesn't indicate ripeness. Lemons, limes, and other acidic citrus fruits can be picked whenever they reach acceptable size and juice content.

Uses
Try citrus in these ways:
Patio planters Dwarf varieties of lemon, lime, and orange do well in roomy containers.
Asian bouquet garni Combine Kaffir lime leaves with lemongrass and ginger.
Citrus zest To zest citrus fruits, use a vegetable peeler, paring knife, or zesting tool (available at kitchen shops) to remove the outermost colored peel in long strips. Avoid the fruit's white membrane, or pith, which has a bitter flavor.

YOU SHOULD KNOW
Keep citrus trees in good health and well irrigated to minimize fruit drop.

VARIETIES

1. KAFFIR LIME (*Citrus hystrix, C. papedia*) is native to Indonesia. The peel, zest, and whole leaves are used in soups and curries, or cut into thin strips and added to salads and meat dishes.

2. 'IMPROVED MEYER LEMON' (*Citrus liman*) is a favorite hybrid because of its excellent flowery flavor. The fruit is orange-yellow when mature and holds well on the tree. The small to medium tree is nearly thornless and well-suited to growing in a container.

HERB ENCYCLOPEDIA

YOU SHOULD KNOW
Stake clary sage in early spring to prevent it from flopping over in the garden. It grows about 2 feet tall.

Clary Sage
Salvia sclarea

Clary sage has been cultivated for centuries for use as a medicinal plant. In modern times the herb is prized for its showy pink, white, and lilac flowers. It's a short-lived perennial or biennial. The plant self-sows easily, so once you plant clary sage, you may not have to replant.

Clary sage is native to southern Europe. Historically it was used to flavor wine and as a substitute for hops in beer brewing.

Best site
Like many herbs, clary sage prefers a sunny site and well-draining, nutrient-rich soil.

Planting
Clary sage is easily grown from seeds sown directly in the garden. Sow the seeds about ½ inch deep in a well-prepared seedbed. Once the seeds have sprouted, thin them to stand a foot apart.

Growing
Once established, clary sage requires very little care. Keep weeds at bay with seasonal cultivation and a 2-inch layer of mulch. Clary sage eventually grows about 2 feet tall and usually needs staking unless it is planted between stouter plants that will support it. At the end of the season, let some flower heads mature to produce seeds for following years. Zones 4–9.

Harvest
The leaves and seeds can be harvested and used either fresh or dried. Harvest young leaves for use in fragrant blends of dried herbs and flowers, such as sachets, potpourris, and bath herbs (tub teas). Cut the flowers and add their fragrant beauty to bouquets.

Uses
Try clary sage in these ways:
Aromatherapy Clary sage has a spicy haylike scent. The plant's essential oil (distilled essence) is a favored ingredient in massage oils and bath salts with its refreshing effect. It is also used to balance other scents when blending potpourris and sachets.
Flower gardens The colorful spires of clary sage stand out in a perennial garden. Catmint and fennel make handsome companion plants.

Comfrey
Symphytum officinale

Comfrey leaves are full of nutrients that make a natural fertilizer or addition to compost. This vigorous perennial sends down deep roots that pull nutrients into the plants' large, hairy leaves.

A native of Europe, comfrey was once used medicinally to help heal bone fractures (and had the common name knitbone). Now it is not recommended for internal use; this herb can cause liver damage in humans if consumed.

Best site
Comfrey is a heavy feeder requiring a rich, organic soil with a high moisture content. In its native Europe, this plant is often found growing wild along streams and waterways. Plant in full sun or partial shade.

Planting
Plant comfrey in spring. Start with seedlings from a garden center or mail-order nursery, or root divisions from a fellow gardener. When dividing a plant, dig deeply to get as many of the roots as possible. Replant a division and water it every four or five days until it resumes growing.

Growing
Comfrey can grow up to 4 feet tall. To keep it looking good, shear it back once or twice a season to a few inches tall; it grows back quickly. Zones 4–9.

Harvest
Gather leaves anytime during the growing season. Wear gloves when harvesting and handling comfrey because the prickly leaves and stems can irritate skin.

Uses
Try comfrey in these ways:
Comfrey salve Make a soothing salve to help reduce swelling. Chop comfrey leaves, place in a jar, cover with warm olive oil, and allow to stand for 24 hours. Strain out the leaves and add melted beeswax to the oil to thicken.
Fertilizer Soak the leaves for a week or so in a bucket of water to make a nutrient-rich comfrey tea that you can use as a liquid fertilizer for plants.

YOU SHOULD KNOW
Plant comfrey where you can control it. The plant spreads by its rootlike rhizomes and can become invasive.

VARIETIES
1. **'VARIEGATA'** is a variegated form of common comfrey with white-edge leaves.

HERB ENCYCLOPEDIA

YOU SHOULD KNOW

This easy-to-grow annual herb self-seeds with gusto. To keep it from growing all over the garden the next year, snip off seed heads before they mature in late summer and early fall.

Dill
Anethum graveolens

This tall annual herb reaches 2–4 feet tall and adds frilly foliage and flowers to the garden. It attracts butterflies and bees. The distinctive tangy leaves of dill add flavor to fish dishes and potato salads. The leaves and seeds provide the headline ingredient in dill pickles.

Dill, native to the eastern Mediterranean and western Asia, is mentioned in Egyptian medical books dating to 3000 BC. It's a common herb in Scandinavian, Russian, and Greek cuisines.

Best site
Plant dill in full sun and moist, well-draining soil. Because dill grows tall, select a growing site that is protected from high winds—a back-of-the-border location is good. Dill thrives in rich soil; dig in a 2-inch-thick layer of compost before planting.

Planting
Start dill from seeds or transplants. Plant seeds indoors a month before the usual spring planting time or directly in the garden in spring. Sow seeds in fall in warm-climate areas. Plant seeds ¼ inch deep, and cover them with a fine layer of soilless seed-starting mix. Water gently. For a continuous supply of new plants, sow seeds once a month throughout summer.

Growing
If planted from seed, dill plants should be thinned when they are 6–8 inches tall. Use the thinned seedlings in cooking. Once established, dill tolerates short periods of drought. To help maintain consistent soil moisture, spread a 2-inch layer of mulch between plants. As flowers develop, snip them off to encourage foliage growth and prevent plants from self-sowing. Dill withstands cool weather, making it one of the year's first herbs to sprout in the spring garden and one of the last herbs standing in fall.

Harvest
Fresh dill leaf has better flavor than dried. Harvest the foliage 30–55 days after seeding. Snip leaves for use in cooking or as garnishes. Air-dry leaves or freeze for long-term storage. Dill sets seed in 75–100 days, and seeds turn brown when they are ready for harvest. To collect seeds, cut stems 6 inches below the mature seed heads. Hang the seed heads upside down inside a paper bag to catch the seeds as they dry and fall.

Uses
Try dill in these ways:
Tzatziki sauce Dill is a predominant flavor in Greek tzatziki sauce, which is made with yogurt, garlic, and cucumber.
Flower arrangements The plants are topped with umbels of yellow flowers in summer. Cut these blooms for lasting additions to bouquets.
Swallowtail host plant The striped (yellow, black, white, and green) caterpillar or larval form of the swallowtail butterfly feeds on dill.

VARIETIES
1. 'FERNLEAF' is a dwarf blue-green variety with high leaf yield that makes a superior addition to kitchen gardens and containers.

Egyptian Onion
Allium × proliferum

Called walking onions, these unusual members of the *Allium* genus have 2-foot-long stems with curly topknots of little onion bulblets. The weight of the bulbs causes the stems to fold over, allowing the onions to root in the ground and become ambulatory, hence the name.

Best site
Egyptian onion plants require a full-sun location and well-draining soil.

Planting
Plant the small bulbs in fall in loose soil amended with loads of compost and rotted leaves. Or you can allow the bulblets to plant themselves and spread.

Growing
These hardy onions do well in cold climates. Zones 3–9.

Harvest
In early spring, dig the onions to use the green stems while they are tender—before the bulbs form; use as you would green onions. After the bulblets form on the top of the plant, pick them off to use fresh.

YOU SHOULD KNOW
The little bulblets that top Egyptian onions are extremely spicy—like garlic. They are excellent chopped and used fresh in dishes that benefit from onion flavor.

Elderberry
Sambucus

A vigorous shrub that grows to 12 feet tall, elderberry or elder is prized for its pretty white flowers as well as its round, shiny blue-black fruit. In the wild, elderberry is often found along streambeds and at the edge of woodlands, where it thrives in sunny and moist conditions.

Best site
Elderberry thrives in a sunny or partially sunny location with rich, moist soil.

Planting
Start elderberry from seed or young plants found near mature specimens. Purchase native species as well as newer cultivars from local garden centers or mail-order sources.

Growing
Mulch the plant to maintain soil moisture, and give it extra irrigation during periods of drought. Zones 3–9.

Harvest
Cut the flower clusters as soon as they open. When the large heads of fruit ripen, clip off the entire cluster, shake the berries into a bucket, and use them to make delectable syrup or jelly.

YOU SHOULD KNOW
Sambucus nigra 'Black Lace' is an easy-care ornamental shrub with dark, almost black foliage and edible berries. It makes a showy accent in contemporary gardens.

Epazote
Dysphania ambrosioides

Also called Mexican tea, epazote is a pungent tender perennial most commonly used in Mexican cooking. It has a strong scent some people compare to that of gasoline or kerosene. Use the leaves fresh or dried in bean dishes and soups. Epazote blends well with oregano, cumin, and chiles.

Best site
Epazote isn't fussy about growing conditions but prefers a sunny site and dry soil. This herb is highly invasive. Grow it in a container or in a place where you can easily control its spread.

Planting
Epazote grows readily from seed. You can also purchase seedlings. Space plants about 10 inches apart.

Growing
Mature plants reach 2–3 feet tall. By midsummer epazote develops pale greenish-yellow flowers. Zones 8–11.

Harvest
Epazote leaves can be harvested at any time.

YOU SHOULD KNOW
Often the biggest challenge with epazote is how to stop it from spreading throughout your garden. To prevent this, remove flower stalks before the seeds mature.

Eucalyptus
Eucalyptus

The silvery leaves of eucalyptus trees are as beautiful as they are aromatic. Eucalyptus oil is a staple in spa treatments because of its sinus-clearing fragrance. The plants, native to Australia, are ideal for warm climates. In colder climates, grow eucalyptus in a patio container, then move it indoors for winter.

Best site
Eucalyptus requires a sunny location and thrives in consistently moist, well-draining soil.

Planting
Varieties of the tree take years to grow from seed. Start with nursery-grown plants, and transplant hardy young trees.

Growing
Grow aromatic eucalyptus in a sunny location, near a patio or a front entryway where you can enjoy the leaves' fragrance as it is released by the warmth of sunlight. Zones 8–10.

Harvest
The leaves and bark have a camphorous scent, comparable to a blend of menthol and sage. Cut stems and leaves for use in potpourris, sachets, long-lasting fragrant bouquets, and wreaths.

YOU SHOULD KNOW
Eucalyptus oil is flammable as well as poisonous. Take care when working with essential oils, and avoid ingesting this herb.

Fennel
Foeniculum vulgare

If you appreciate the flavor of anise or licorice, you may already be a fan of fennel. The perennial green herb differs from the annual vegetable or Florence fennel (*Foeniculum vulgare azoricum*), which has a white, edible base. 'Purpureum', a cultivar of the herb, has bronze foliage and grows 4 feet tall.

Best site
Plant fennel in a sunny spot with well-draining soil. Plants can take some light shade.

Planting
Sow seeds in early spring directly into the ground. Established plants transplant poorly.

Growing
Keep plants well watered. Avoid deadheading flowers because they attract beneficial and beautiful bugs including butterflies, ladybird beetles, and bees. Zones 5–9.

Harvest
Collect leaves all season. When seeds turn brown, clip flower heads and suspend them upside down inside paper sacks, so dried seeds fall into the bags. To release their strong flavor, crush seeds in a mortar prior to using.

YOU SHOULD KNOW
Graceful, ferny fennel adds structure, texture, and airy beauty to any herb garden. The 2- to 4-foot-tall plants are also pretty enough to tuck into a perennial border.

Feverfew
Tanacetum parthenium

The daisylike flowers of feverfew were once believed to be a fever reducer, but today this little perennial is enjoyed more for its ornamental and crafting value. Feverfew grows about 2 feet tall. The edges of the foliage are finely serrated, and the leaves release a strong odor when cut or brushed.

Best site
Feverfew needs at least six to eight hours of sun a day. It will not thrive in partial shade. The plant is not picky about soil types.

Planting
Start feverfew from seed, nursery-grown transplants, or divisions in spring.

Growing
The plants are a bit weedy in character and look more at home in an informal or wild garden. The blooms begin to appear in midsummer and continue until fall. Deadhead flowers as they fade to promote additional blooms. Zones 4–9.

Harvest
Clip the flowers when they are fully open. Hang stems to dry upside down in a dark, airy place. Store the dried flowers in an airtight container.

YOU SHOULD KNOW
Although feverfew is thought to help reduce fever, headache, and arthritis, self-diagnosis and treatment are not recommended. Consult a physician instead.

YOU SHOULD KNOW
Three types of garlic are widely grown. Softnecks have strong garlic flavor. Hardnecks have a mild flavor. Elephant garlic is a leek, similar to garlic in flavor but less pungent.

Garlic
Allium sativum

Sautéed, baked, or used fresh, this perennial bulb adds its unmistakable pungent flavor to stir-fries and sauces. Easy to grow, garlic is a big producer: One pound of cloves can yield 7–10 pounds of garlic the following year. Garlic is often listed among the top good-for-you foods.

Garlic is native to Central Asia, and is a staple seasoning in the Mediterranean region, Asia, and Africa. Its use is traced back 6,000 years, when it was worshipped, used as currency, and thought to repel evil (including vampires).

Best site
Plant garlic in full sun and well-draining soil. Garlic thrives in slightly dry sites. Add a 2-inch-thick layer of compost to the soil.

Planting
Plant garlic around the first frost date in fall. In mild-winter areas, you can plant until January. Plants form deep roots and then mature the following summer. You can also plant garlic in early spring, but plants will yield smaller bulbs. Garlic grows best during cool weather and stops growing at temperatures above 90°F. Plant individual cloves (not the whole bulb) pointy side up 2–3 inches deep. Space cloves 6 inches apart in rows 1–2 feet apart. Plant elephant garlic 6 inches deep and 8 inches apart.

Growing
Water garlic well after planting in fall to promote good root growth. In cold-winter areas, mulch after a few hard freezes with a 4- to 6-inch-thick layer of straw to prevent the bulbs from heaving out of the ground. In spring, weed around plants; weeds compete with bulb production. To boost your garlic harvest, add a high-nitrogen fertilizer in spring. Begin fertilizing once three leaves have formed, and continue monthly until bulbs begin to develop. Rotate crops and keep beds weed-free to reduce troublesome insect populations. You can also grow garlic in containers. Zones 3–9.

Harvest
In summer, when about half of the garlic leaves begin to yellow and wilt, stop watering and knock over the tops. Allow the garlic to cure for one week in the garden, then harvest the bulbs. Remove excess soil, and hang the garlic to dry in a cool, shady location with good air circulation. When the tops are dry, trim to ½ inch above the bulb and trim the roots at the base of the bulb. Store the garlic in mesh bags in a cool room.

Uses
Try garlic in these ways:
Bread spread Bake whole garlic bulbs with olive oil and salt, and squeeze the warm soft cloves over crusty bread.
Garlic scapes Cut immature flower stalks, called green garlic or scapes, to prompt bulb growth. Use them in stir-fries and pasta dishes.

VARIETIES
1. 'RUSSIAN RED' is a hardneck garlic with purple stripes. Bulbs produce six to nine large cloves. This variety has good winter hardiness.

2. 'SPANISH ROJA' is a hardneck type with medium-hot flavor. The brown-skin cloves are excellent for roasting.

3. 'NEW YORK WHITE' is also called 'Polish White'. This hardy, disease-resistant softneck variety is well-suited to gardens in cold-climate areas.

Germander
Teucrium chamaedrys

Easily sheared to form a low hedge, germander is an ideal choice for shapely knot or parterre gardens. The herb's shiny green leaves and mauve flowers make it a great garden plant. Because germander only grows 12–18 inches tall, it makes a wonderful edging plant along pathways.

Best site
Germander requires a sunny location with well-draining soil.

Planting
Germander grows slowly from seed. Start with transplants instead. Space plants 6 inches apart for a knot garden; otherwise, space plants about 1 foot apart.

Growing
Trim plants in early spring to encourage new growth. The plants develop pretty mauve flowers in midsummer. Zones 5–9.

Harvest
Cut stems and use them fresh in crafts projects.

Uses
Try germander in these ways:
Container plants Germander grows well in pots, planters, and window boxes.
Crafts projects Fresh branches and leaves can be used as greenery in wreaths and floral crafts.
Bonsai Prune upright germander plants into bonsai forms.

YOU SHOULD KNOW
Germander is a widely grown but little-recognized herb. You'll find this shrubby perennial in patterned knot or parterre gardens around the world.

Ginger
Zingiber officinale

This spicy herb is as healthful as it is flavorful. Ginger is a tropical plant that grows outdoors in frost-free regions or in containers in cold climates. Buy gingerroots (the same ones you cook with) from the grocery store and plant pieces of the tubers. Culinary ginger does not produce showy flowers.

Best site
Ginger requires a sheltered location out of direct sunlight. It needs warm, humid conditions. Plants must be overwintered indoors in cold climates.

Planting
Choose firm, fresh rhizomes. Soak the thick tubers overnight, and break them into pieces, making sure each piece has at least two eyes or growing points. Plant pieces about 8 inches apart; cover with about 1 inch of potting soil.

Growing
Amend soil with compost or well-rotted manure. Keep the soil damp but not wet. Humidity is crucial for the plants, so mist them daily using a garden hose. In the garden, mulch ginger to maintain consistent soil moisture.

Harvest
In late summer, ginger foliage begins to die back. Dig up tubers. It takes about 10 months for ginger to reach harvestable size. In tropical regions, dig the tubers as you need them.

YOU SHOULD KNOW
Culinary ginger is not as showy as its ornamental cousins, but you can reap a small harvest even from a container-grown plant.

HERB ENCYCLOPEDIA

YOU SHOULD KNOW

When growing hops for their conelike flowers, start with female rootlike rhizomes. The plant can become invasive. Pull out excess plants, including the rhizomes.

Hops
Humulus lupulus

Widely grown as a key ingredient in beer making, hops are the flowers and seed heads of a perennial vine. This hardy vine is also beautiful, so it's an excellent option for use in the landscape—even for gardeners who don't drink beer. Hops require 120 frost-free days to produce usable flowers.

Cultivated since the eighth century, hops were used medicinally to treat nearly everything from fevers to fits to worms. In the 11th century, the herb became associated with beer production in Germany. Today, Germany is the largest producer of hops.

Best site
Hops requires a sunny location and well-draining soil. Because hops are rampant vines that can quickly grow up to 30 feet in length, you must be sure to plant them next to a sturdy trellis or arbor. Avoid planting near power poles.

Planting
You will need a female plant to produce flowers and a male plant to pollinate it. Start with rhizomes or container-grown vines from a local garden center or mail-order supplier. Keep the plants watered until they become established, and mulch them to keep weeds at bay.

Growing
There's no secret to planting hops. Just put them in the ground and stand back. By the second year the female plant will develop yellowish conelike flowers. Prune the vines back to ground level every spring. Hops generally do not produce flowers their first year in the ground. Hops can be attacked by the hop aphid, which sucks the juices of young stems. To control these pests, spray with an insecticidal soap. Hops vines can also become infected with downy mildew. Prevent mildew by keeping the plants' foliage dry. Use drip irrigation or hand-water to avoid wetting foliage. Remove the vine's lower leaves to ensure better air circulation. Zones 4–9.

Harvest
It is estimated that each hops vine can produce 1–2 pounds of dried flowers. Harvest hops when they feel dry and light to the touch. Spread them on a window screen to dry in an airy, shady place. Stir the hops every day until they feel crisp and completely dry. Store the hops in an airtight container, and use them within six months.

Uses
Try hops in these ways:
Beer production Hops flowers impart a bitter, tangy flavor to beer. Different varieties offer varied flavors. Check with your county extension service for the best varieties for your region.
Landscape use Choose an ornamental hops variety for its interesting foliage, if you prefer.
Dream pillow Stuff a small pillow with the dried flowers, and use it to inspire sweet dreams.

VARIETIES

1. **'AUREUS'** or golden hops vine is an ornamental vine with yellow-green lobed leaves. It bears small white flowers.

Horehound
Marrubium vulgare

Horehound is another hardy member of the mint family. It has fuzzy gray-green foliage and small white flowers. Like mint, this plant can become invasive. Horehound's longstanding claim to fame is its use as an ingredient in old-fashioned candies and cough medicines.

Championed as an ancient medicinal to treat coughs and upper-respiratory illnesses, horehound is still used in this way. It tastes bitter, however, and lots of sugar or honey is used to make it more palatable.

Best site
Horehound is not fussy about growing conditions, but it does prefer full sun. Almost any soil type will do as long as it is well-draining. The plant grows to 2–3 feet tall. Horehound can spread aggressively, so be sure to plant where it can be controlled.

Planting
Horehound can be started from seeds, divisions, or stem cuttings. The plant is drought-tolerant but needs supplemental water if rain is scarce for an extended period. Young plants will need regular watering to become established. Cultivate around young plants to eliminate competition from weeds.

Growing
There are few secrets to growing horehound. Basically, you can plant it and forget it. Trimming the plant periodically will encourage bushy growth. Horehound leaves have a minty fragrance when rubbed or brushed. The plant develops white flowers in mid- to late summer. Remove the seed heads before they mature to help keep horehound from spreading. Zones 3–9.

Harvest
Harvest leaves throughout the growing season by snipping off the stem tips, and then use the leaves as needed. In mid- to late summer, harvest the plant: Cut the stems a few inches above ground level, and hang them upside down in a cool, dry, airy location. Pull the dried leaves off the stems, compost the stems, and store the leaves in an airtight container.

Uses
Try horehound in these ways:
Deer-resistant gardens Neither deer nor rabbits will eat horehound unless they are extremely hungry. Plant the herb to deter these pests if they are a problem in your neighborhood.
Cough suppressants Dried or fresh leaves can be boiled with water and honey to make homemade cough syrups and lozenges.
Sweets The boiled leaves of horehound can be used to make flavorful candy and syrup. Old-fashioned confectioneries still stock horehound candy.

YOU SHOULD KNOW
As a member of the mint family, horehound can easily grow out of control. Plant it in a pot or confine it within a bed to prevent it from becoming weedy.

VARIETIES
1. VARIEGATED BLACK HOREHOUND (*Ballota nigra*) is a white-variegated plant with tiny purple flowers that appear in summer. It grows 2–3 feet tall, spreads aggressively, and has a strong odor. Zones 4–9.

Horseradish
Armoracia rusticana

This perennial herb has large green leaves, small white flowers, and large, tapered edible roots. Beware! Horseradish can become invasive. Plant it in a spot where you can control its spread. The sinus-clearing, pungent flavor of horseradish root adds zip to meat and potato dishes.

Best site
Plant in full sun and moist, well-draining soil.

Planting
Start horseradish plants in early spring from root cuttings. Plant the root cuttings horizontally, laying them in a 3-inch-deep trench. One or two plants will provide a generous harvest for horseradish lovers.

Growing
Water horseradish root cuttings well for about four weeks after planting. Once plants are established, they will withstand dry periods. Root cuttings planted in spring produce roots in 180–240 days. Zones 3–9.

Harvest
Dig up horseradish roots in fall. You may also harvest them in winter and spring. For best flavor, leave the roots in the ground until after a few frosts—this sweetens them.

YOU SHOULD KNOW
Harvested horseradish roots turn green quickly if exposed to light. To keep their white color, store them wrapped in black plastic in the refrigerator.

Hyssop
Hyssopus officinalis

An evergreen, bushy perennial, hyssop produces upright stems with small white, lavender, or blue flowers. It grows to 2 feet tall and makes a good plant for garden edging and containers. This plant is not related to anise hyssop, but both plants attract bees, butterflies, and hummingbirds.

Best site
Hyssop requires a sunny location that receives at least six to eight hours of sun a day.

Planting
Grow hyssop from seed. Sow seeds about ¼ inch deep in soil. As the seedlings grow, thin them to 1 foot apart.

Growing
Hyssop blooms in midsummer. Remove the flower spikes as they fade to keep the plants looking good. After a few years, you may need to replace older plants. Zones 4–9.

Harvest
Fresh leaves can be harvested at any time. Use hyssop in sachets and potpourris. Snip flower stalks just before they open, then hang them upside down in a dark, airy place until dry.

YOU SHOULD KNOW
At one time commonly used as both a medicinal and culinary herb, hyssop is not often seen in U.S. gardens but deserves much more appreciation.

Juniper
Juniperus communis

This large group of evergreen trees and shrubs bears round green fruits (small cones) that ripen to dark blue. Juniper berries are used as a flavoring similar to rosemary, with piney and citrusy notes. As the primary flavoring in gin, juniper berries are sometimes called gin berries.

Best site
Plant juniper in full sun and well-draining soil. Plants tolerate a wide range of growing conditions and become drought-tolerant once established.

Planting
Select container-grown, potted, or balled-and-burlapped nursery plants. Choose from upright, bushy, or low-growing junipers for versatile landscape plants.

Growing
Junipers fill space fast, adding color and texture whether used as a groundcover, privacy screen, vertical punctuation in a border, or topiary. They vary in color from green to gray to blue. Sizes range from 6-inch groundcover varieties to 60-foot trees. Zones 3–9.

Harvest
Harvest berried branches in fall and winter. Use them fresh in holiday wreaths and dried in fragrant potpourris.

YOU SHOULD KNOW
Junipers require little care. Most varieties tolerate hot, dry conditions and thrive in poor soil, making them ideal evergreens for hard-to-plant locations.

Lady's Mantle
Alchemilla mollis

Lady's mantle gets its name from its pretty scalloped and folded leaves, once thought to resemble the cape of the Virgin Mary. Lady's mantle continues to be appreciated for its gray-green, fuzzy foliage. When it catches dew and other water droplets, the foliage appears to be sprinkled with sparkly diamonds.

Best site
Lady's mantle prefers a rich, moist soil in a partially shady location. It can also be grown in containers along with hostas, ferns, and other shade dwellers.

Planting
Plant in early spring when the weather is still cool and damp. This herb can be grown from seed, but it is faster to start it from transplants.

Growing
Lady's mantle makes a great addition to an herb or a perennial border. It grows only 18 inches tall, so it's ideal at the edge of a border or along a garden path. Remove faded flower stalks to promote new growth and keep plants tidy. Zones 4–8.

Harvest
Snip the leaves and flowers throughout summer, and use them in bouquets.

YOU SHOULD KNOW
Historically, lady's mantle had many medicinal uses, and today it may be used to make hand lotions and facial creams.

> **YOU SHOULD KNOW**
> Lavender grows well in containers. Place it in a pot or window box of well-draining potting mix in a sunny location.

Lavender
Lavandula

One of the most beloved herbal fragrances, lavender evokes visions of neat rows of flower-packed fields in France's Provence region. The shrubby Mediterranean herb is usually topped with purple flowers. Some varieties of the perennial have blue, pink, or white flowers. The flowers bloom for a month or more in summer. The leaves and flowers emit fragrance.

Lavender's scent is so distinctive that references to it appear in ancient texts from many different cultures. It has been associated with washing clothes and bathing—lavender makes things smell fresh and clean. Today the sweet and ever-popular fragrance of lavender enhances soaps, shampoos, bath products, linen sprays, sachets, and air fresheners.

Best site
Plant lavender in full sun and well-draining soil. Lavender thrives in sandy loam, but not in heavy clay or wet soils. It grows best in moderately fertile, slightly alkaline soil and flourishes with added drainage (gravel or perlite). This shrubby perennial is a must-have in an herb garden but also mixes well with perennials, annuals, and roses in beds or borders.

Planting
Start lavender from seedlings or cuttings in spring, or in fall where winters are mild. Water fall-planted transplants regularly to encourage root growth. Space transplants 2–3 feet apart, depending on the variety.

Growing
Lavender tolerates drought, heat, and wind. Choose a variety best suited to conditions where you live. Although lavender is considered drought-tolerant, it requires regular watering during the first six weeks after transplanting to get a good start.

VARIETIES

1. 'MUNSTEAD' ENGLISH LAVENDER (*Lavandula angustifolia*) is a popular culinary variety with purple-blue flowers and green leaves. It reaches 2–3 feet tall. Zones 5–9.

2. 'JEAN DAVIS' (*L. angustifolia*) is a light pink flowering form with a fruity flavor. It is hardy in Zones 6–11 and grows to 2 feet tall.

3. SPANISH LAVENDER (*L. stoechas*) has dark purple flowers on short stems and is very fragrant. It grows 2–3 feet tall. Zones 7–10.

To promote dense plants and repeat blooms, shear plants by one-third after they bloom. In spring, wait until the new growth has begun before cutting back plants. Trim them, removing dead stems, but do not cut them down to the ground. To prune, trim out about one-third of the stem length. In cold-climate areas, mulch around and on top of a plant to protect it over winter.

Harvest

Lavender flowers are easy to harvest because they grow on long, stiff stems. Gather the flower stalks when about half of a plant's flowers open. Cut stems early in the morning when the oils are most concentrated. To dry flowers and stems, hang small bundles upside down in a dark, airy place.

Uses

Try lavender in these ways:

Herbes de Provence Make the classic culinary blend using the following herbs in amounts that taste best to you: oregano, thyme, basil, sage, savory, rosemary, and lavender flowers.

Baking Lavender flowers have a distinct flavor and can be used in baked goods such as shortbread, pound cake, and cookies.

Simple syrup Boil 1 cup water, 2 cups sugar, and 2–4 tablespoons fresh lavender to make a simple syrup to add to mixed drinks or lemonade.

Rosemary substitute Use the stems and leaves in place of rosemary in many recipes.

Crafting Make sachets, wreaths, and bouquets with dried lavender flowers. Place them in your bedrooms and closets. The scent helps you relax—and also repels insects.

VARIETIES

4. FRENCH LAVENDER (*L. dentata*) offers finely serrated leaves on 2- to 3-foot-tall plants. Winter indoors in cold climates. Zones 8–11.

5. 'HIDCOTE' (*L. angustifolia*) is a popular lavender for hedging. It grows 12–16 inches tall and attracts pollinators. Zones 5–9.

HERB ENCYCLOPEDIA

> **YOU SHOULD KNOW**
> Lemon balm spreads easily and can take over. Plant it in a contained bed or a spot where it can self-seed without becoming invasive.

Lemon Balm
Melissa officinalis

Where you cannot grow lemons, plant lemon balm. Use the pretty heart-shape leaves for their delicious mint-married-to-lemon scent and flavor. Add the fresh leaves to vegetable dishes, fruit salads, and drinks.

Lemon balm was used as far back as the Middle Ages to reduce anxiety and promote sleep, and it still is today. The herbal liqueurs Chartreuse and Benedictine include lemon balm.

Best site
For the largest, most flavorful plants, grow lemon balm in part shade. If the soil is moist and rich, the herb can grow in full sun. Lemon balm self-seeds readily, making it a good candidate for a container garden. Plant it in a well-draining potting mix.

Planting
Lemon balm grows easily from seeds. Sow seeds in early spring or fall. The seeds are tiny, so cover them with a fine layer of soilless potting mix and water gently. Keep the seed-starting medium damp until the seeds germinate. Avoid overwatering. When starting with nursery-grown seedlings or divisions, plant in early spring. Space plants 2 feet apart. For the most flavorful foliage, improve the soil by working in a 2-inch layer of compost before you plant.

Growing
Plants grown from seed may be a bit small the first year but will fill out eventually and grow to 2 feet tall. When plants mature, remove the flower heads before they form seeds to prevent plants from self-sowing and becoming weedy. In areas where the ground freezes in winter, mulch lemon balm plants with a 4- to 6-inch-thick layer of organic mulch. Zones 4–10.

Harvest
The best time to harvest lemon balm leaves is just before the plant blooms. Snip off the leaves to use them fresh or preserve by drying. Dried leaves lose much of their lemony scent. Keep the leaves from turning black by drying them quickly on a rack. Once they are dried, store them in an airtight container away from light and heat.

Uses
Try lemon balm in these ways:
Lemon balm tisane Make a calming cup of tisane using lemon balm leaves: Cut fresh leaves, and place them in a cup. Add hot water; cover and steep for 5 minutes. Sweeten with honey.
Mint substitute Use lemon balm any place you'd use mint. This member of the mint family imparts a lemony-minty flavor to beverages such as iced tea, lemonade, and fruit juice.
Lemon balm pesto Grind together 2 cups fresh lemon balm leaves with ½ cup olive oil and 3 cloves garlic in a food processor. Use the pesto on pasta or rice, or as a marinade for fish or chicken.
Pollinator attractor Lemon balm flowers attract bees and other pollinators.
Bath herb Use fresh or dried lemon balm to make a strong infusion, then add the tea to a bath for a relaxing effect.

VARIETIES
1. VARIEGATED (*Melissa officinalis* 'Variegata') offers yellow-tinged leaves. It reaches 1–2 feet tall. Zones 4–9.

Lemongrass
Cymbopogon citratus

An essential ingredient in Thai and Vietnamese cuisine, tropical lemongrass is a snap to grow in containers even in cold-climate gardens. Leaves of this tall, grassy, fast-growing plant can be harvested more than once a year where the climate allows.

A native of India, lemongrass was used throughout history as a medicinal and culinary herb. Prescribed as a digestive aid, lemongrass is still used in many countries as a folk remedy. It is also used in aromatherapy.

Best site
Lemongrass likes it hot. That's why it requires a sunny location, either in the ground or in a pot; and it thrives where summers are hot. It's not fussy about growing conditions, but lemongrass does best in rich, moist soil with a high nitrogen content.

Planting
It's easy to start lemongrass from young plants purchased at your local garden center or from an online source. Or take a division from an established clump. Lemongrass detests cold weather. Plant after any frost danger has passed and nighttime temperatures remain warm. If planting lemongrass in a container, use a commercial potting mix that includes slow-release fertilizer. This 4- to 6-foot-tall plant requires a large pot.

Growing
Once planted, lemongrass needs little assistance. Just keep the plant well watered during dry spells. The hotter the temperatures, the more your lemongrass will grow. This fast grower can be pruned or sheared to maintain a more manageable size. Zones 9–11.

Harvest
Cut leaves as needed throughout the growing season, clipping them off at the base of the plant. You can also cut and dry the leaves for future use. Or you can freeze them for up to a year.

Uses
Try lemongrass in these ways:
Marinade Lemongrass melds well with garlic and chiles. Place herbs in a food processor and make a paste. Use the paste to suit your taste on fish or poultry.
Lemongrass tisane Lemongrass requires liquids to disperse its essential oils. Steep leaves and stems in hot water, then flavor the tisane with honey.

> **YOU SHOULD KNOW**
> In late summer, take a small division of lemongrass, pot it in soil, and bring it indoors to spend the winter on a sunny windowsill.

HERB ENCYCLOPEDIA

> **YOU SHOULD KNOW**
> Finely chop lemon verbena leaves before using the fresh herb in recipes, because the leaves are somewhat tough.

Lemon Verbena
Aloysia triphylla

This herb grows 3–4 feet tall as an annual in most gardens. Raised in a frost-free climate, the tropical shrub reaches 15 feet tall. The plant's intense lemon fragrance and flavor make it a favorite herbal ingredient in beverages and desserts.

A native of Chile and Argentina, lemon verbena has a fresh scent and flavor that made it a favorite among Victorian women, who tucked the herb into clothing. It remains a favorite for making various lemony drinks, from lemonade to alcohol-infused beverages. The citrusy scent is also used in perfumes and other fragrant products.

Best site
Plant in full sun. Easy-to-grow lemon verbena adapts to many soil types—from wet clay to sandy loam—but prefers rich soil. In warm climates, lemon verbena grows as a perennial, but elsewhere it is treated as an annual. Growing the plant in a container makes it easy to move it outdoors in spring, and indoors to keep it going over winter.

Planting
Plant cuttings or container-grown plants in the garden after the soil has warmed and the threat of frost has passed. Lemon verbena plants may be difficult to find. Look for them at specialty nurseries and mail-order sources. Lemon verbena also grows well in a container of well-draining potting mix.

Growing
Give lemon verbena plants about 1 inch of water per week for the first six weeks after spring planting. Trim the stem ends regularly to keep lemon verbena growing lush and bushy. This cold-sensitive plant drops its leaves if exposed to chilly weather. Protect your potted plant by moving it indoors in late summer and placing it in a bright, sunny window. If whiteflies become a problem, spray the plant with a blast of water from the garden hose. Zones 9–10.

Harvest
The lemony leaves can be harvested anytime by cutting the stems' tips. Harvest the entire plant at season's end, and hang it upside down in a cool, well-ventilated place. Allow the leaves to dry thoroughly, then store them in a jar.

Uses
Try lemon verbena in these ways:
In the kitchen Get a lemony blast from lemon verbena by using the leaves to make salad dressings, marinades, jellies, cakes, and sorbets.
Fragrant blends Lemon verbena leaves hold their scent for months and provide a bright note in a sachet, dream pillow, or bath herb blend.
Lemon verbena simple syrup Add 1 cup sugar to 1 cup water in a saucepan; stir to dissolve. Add ½ cup whole lemon verbena leaves and bring to boiling. Remove the pan from heat; let the mixture cool. Strain the leaves; refrigerate.

Licorice Root
Glycyrrhiza glabra

This shrubby perennial is a member of the legume family. The plant has attractive leaves and develops an edible, sweet root. It is unrelated to the ornamental annual called licorice plant (*Helichrysum*).

The woody root of licorice has been used medicinally for a wide range of illnesses—from coughs to depression. On a sweeter note, it's also used to flavor candy. Glycyrrhizin, one of the compounds in the root, is 50 times sweeter than sugar and quenches thirst instead of increasing it.

Best site
Licorice requires a sunny spot with well-draining soil. Provide water during dry spells because this plant likes moist soil. You can also grow licorice in containers.

Planting
Start licorice by dividing the roots of established plants. You can also find licorice rhizomes available for sale from mail-order nurseries. Plants can occasionally be found at local garden centers.

Growing
Licorice is one of the taller herbs, often growing 3–6 feet tall. Plant it where it can reach mature height without getting in the way of other plants. Space the plants about 3 feet apart. Keep the planting area weeded to eliminate competition for nutrients and rooting space. Mulch plants heavily in the northern part of their range to help them survive winter. If you grow licorice in a pot, use a high-quality potting mix. Bring the plant indoors in early fall before frost occurs. Zones 7–10.

Harvest
Most plants will not produce harvestable roots until they are at least several years old. When the roots are large enough to harvest, dig up the plant and cut off the foliage. Rinse any soil off the roots, then set them in an airy place to dry.

Uses
Try licorice root in these ways:
Candy Licorice candies get much of their flavor from the addition of anise; the licorice root is mainly used as the sweetener.
Perennial border This shrubby plant has a branching form. The small blue-violet flowers appear in midsummer. It's an ideal back-of-the-border plant in warmer climates.

YOU SHOULD KNOW
This is a plant for patient gardeners. Only when licorice is three to four years old will the roots be ready for harvest.

> **YOU SHOULD KNOW**
> Give lovage plants plenty of room to grow. Leaving 2 feet between plants will help prevent diseases such as blight.

Lovage
Levisticum officinale

A relative of celery, lovage is a hardy perennial whose leaves can be used in soups and salads. The attractive leaves can even be used in bouquets. Although it dies back after frost, lovage produces a flush of new growth the following spring.

A European native, lovage was included in apothecary gardens to treat stomach upsets and diminish flatulence. It is similar in appearance to angelica.

Best site
Plant lovage in full sun and deep, compost-enriched, moist soil. Unlike most herbs, lovage thrives in wet soil. It also does well in clay and other slow-to-drain soils.

Planting
Start from seeds or divisions. Sow seeds directly in the garden in fall or early spring. If starting indoors, sow in late winter for transplanting in spring. Lovage can also be started by the division of established lovage plants in spring or fall. To give it a nutrient boost, mix a 2-inch layer of compost into the soil before planting. Water plants well after planting to help them establish strong root systems. This is necessary to keep plants over winter.

Growing
Lovage grows up to 5 feet tall and 2 feet wide. Place this herb in an area where it can spread and not compete with other plants. Its small yellow-green flowers attract beneficial insects. After planting, lovage grows vigorously for about four years and then slows. Lovage is a self-seeder. Clip off flowers as soon as they appear unless you want more plants. Removing flowers also promotes more leafstalks. To help retain moist soil, mulch around lovage plants, adding a 4- to 6-inch-thick layer of organic mulch for overwintering in cold climates. Zones 3–9.

Harvest
Start harvesting a few leaves about three months after sowing seeds. After the plants are a year old, harvest leaves and stalks throughout the growing season. Although this plant self-seeds, allowing some flowers to develop is a good idea because they attract beneficial insects to the garden. Lovage seeds are edible and have a flavor reminiscent of anise and celery. Collect seeds by cutting off the nearly mature seed heads and hanging a bunch of them upside down in a paper bag. When dried or frozen, lovage leaves hold their flavor for about one year.

Uses
Try lovage in these ways:
Salads Harvest young leaves, which have a celery flavor, and clip into spring salads.
Parsley substitute Cooks often use lovage in place of parsley or celery leaves, but in limited quantities because the flavor is stronger.
Perennial border Because of its shrubby habit and lush green leaves, lovage suits a mixed flower border as well as an herb bed.

Marigold
Tagetes

Among the most recognizable flowers in the world, marigolds have varied uses, from a colorful garden insect repellent to decorative flower garlands. These nonstop annual bloomers add cheery color to herb beds and flower gardens.

Marigolds were considered sacred flowers by the Aztecs. These long-blooming flowers are also used in Hindu ceremonies and can be made into beautiful wearable garlands.

Best site
Marigolds require a sunny location that receives at least six to eight hours of direct sun a day. They prefer a rich, well-draining soil and grow as well in containers as they do in a garden bed.

Planting
Start marigolds from seed or from seedlings purchased at your local garden center. If you use seeds, sow them ½ inch deep. Remember that marigolds are tender annuals; avoid planting them outdoors until all frost danger has passed. Eliminate weed competition by mulching marigolds after planting.

Growing
Marigolds are unfussy, and once established they will flourish even if unattended. They prefer damp—not wet—soil. During dry periods, water them once or twice a week. To keep weeds from competing, mulch between plants. For potted plantings, water as needed when the soil begins to feel dry to the touch—daily during hot weather. Pinch off faded blooms. When frost comes, marigolds die. Remove the plants and consign them to the compost pile.

Harvest
Marigold flowers can be harvested at any time for use fresh or dried. If you want to save seeds, hang plants upside down and allow the seed heads to dry. Crumble the dried seed heads, and sort out the needlelike seeds. Store the seeds in an airtight container to plant the following year.

Uses
Try marigolds in these ways:

Edging plants Dwarf varieties make a neat and colorful edging for beds and borders. Plant them around vegetable gardens to help deter insect pests from crops.

Dyes The flower petals can be used to make dye for fabric.

Kids' gardens Because marigolds are so easy to grow from seeds or seedlings, they are the perfect choice for children's gardens. If you have any budding gardeners at home, get them growing with bright marigolds.

YOU SHOULD KNOW
Most insects avoid marigolds, but slugs and snails will dine on the stems and leaves. Use an organic slug and snail bait to keep these pests from destroying your plants.

VARIETIES

1. SIGNET MARIGOLD (*Tagetes tenuifolia*) has finely divided lacy foliage topped with 1-inch-diameter flowers in bright orange, tangerine, and yellow. Signet marigolds grow 12–18 inches tall and are believed to be the most effective in repelling destructive nematodes that live in soil.

2. FRENCH MARIGOLD (*T. patula*) grows 8–12 inches tall and has frilly petals, often with a raised center.

3. AFRICAN MARIGOLD (*T. erecta*) is the giant of the family, growing up to 3 feet tall with large balllike blooms in orange, yellow, or white.

YOU SHOULD KNOW
Marjoram and oregano are both members of the mint family. Plants in the family have square stems and opposing sets of leaves. Marjoram is more tender than oregano.

Marjoram, Sweet Marjoram
Origanum majorana

This tender perennial, often called sweet marjoram, is related to oregano and a major player in Italian cuisine. The herb has a flavor that's milder and sweeter than oregano, offering fragrant notes of pine and citrus.

Marjoram was the symbol of happiness in Greek and Roman cultures. Because of this association, it was often included in bridal bouquets.

Best site
Plant in full sun and well-draining soil. Marjoram does well in most soils but grows best in average, sandy soil.

Planting
Marjoram is slow to germinate and challenging to start from seed. A better bet for quicker harvests is to start with nursery-grown plants. In spring, wait to set out plants until after the danger of frost has passed. Space plants 12 inches apart, and water them well after planting.

Growing
This tender perennial grows as an annual for most gardeners. Marjoram grows well in a container. Bring plants indoors over winter. The plants are low-growing and form attractive clumps. The leaves and flowers are edible; varieties produce white, pink, or red flowers in mid- to late summer. Because of its trailing habit, marjoram adds beautifully to hanging baskets. Cut off long, trailing stems to encourage bushier growth. Plantings dry out quickly. Water regularly to keep soil moist but not wet. When plants become woody, divide them. In mild regions where marjoram can overwinter in the garden, cover plants with a 4- to 6-inch blanket of mulch. Zones 8–10.

Harvest
Pick leaves and stems for use fresh or dried in cooking. Cut and bundle stems, and hang the bunch in a cool, dark, airy place. Strip the dried leaves from the stems and store them whole in airtight glass jars. Dried marjoram retains its flavor better than dried oregano, keeping well for about one year.

Uses
Try marjoram in these ways:
Oregano substitute Marjoram has a sweet, mild, slightly balsamic flavor that complements basil, bay, garlic, onion, and thyme in culinary herb blends.
Za'atar Make this Arabic herb blend with marjoram, sumac, thyme, sesame seeds, oregano, and salt.
Vegetable seasoning Snip fresh leaves directly into salads or on top of cooked dishes just before serving to enjoy the herb's full flavor. Cooking diminishes marjoram's flavor.
Knot gardens Marjoram has a more compact growth habit than its cousin oregano, making it the herb of choice for edging many English knot gardens.

VARIETIES
1. VARIEGATED (*Origanum majorana* 'Variegata') has yellow-and-green leaves and a low-growing, prostrate habit. Zones 6–9.

Milk Thistle
Silybum marianum

Milk thistle is a striking member of the daisy family, but its thorny demeanor makes it feel more like a true thistle. When cut, the plant produces a white, milky liquid, which is how it got its name.

Native to the Mediterranean, milk thistle has been cultivated for centuries as a treatment for diseases of the liver and gallbladder, and an antidote to poisoning by death cap mushrooms. The plants are grown primarily for their seeds. The leaves, flowers, and roots can be eaten.

Best site
Any sunny location is acceptable for this annual or biennial plant. It prefers rich, moist soil but will grow in almost any conditions and has escaped cultivation in the Eastern United States and elsewhere to become a weed.

Planting
Milk thistle grows quickly from seeds sown 1 inch deep in the soil. Thin the seedlings to stand about 2 feet apart. Water your plant as needed during drought to sustain it.

Growing
Once planted, milk thistle requires no assistance from you. The plants will eventually grow 2–4 feet tall, producing shiny, pointed green leaves with white streaks. The plant develops a bold purple, prickly thistle blossom. Remove the blossoms to prolong the plant's interesting appearance. Keep an eye on your planting to ensure it does not self-sow wildly and become a weed. Zones 5–9.

Harvest
Collect the seeds after the bright purple flowers have faded and begun to dry. Wear heavy-duty gloves to avoid being poked by the thistles, and carefully clip each blossom from the plant. Break open the thistle and remove the seeds. Set them in a protected place to air-dry thoroughly. Store the dried seeds in an airtight container.

Uses
Try milk thistle in these ways:

Tea Thistle seeds can be ground and brewed into a tea made tastier with the addition of mint leaves.
Physic gardens Milk thistle is a traditional plant for medicinal herb gardens.
Salad greens Tender young milk thistle leaves can be added to salads or eaten as cooked greens.
Dried flowers Cut and dry the thistles for decorative use in wreaths and other crafts.

YOU SHOULD KNOW
Check local regulations before you plant milk thistle. It may be considered a noxious weed in your region.

Mint
Mentha

Fragrant and flavorful, mint is a vigorous perennial herb with a host of culinary and cosmetic uses. There are more than 600 varieties of mint, with luscious fragrances and flavors ranging beyond peppermint's refreshing menthol and spearmint's surprising sweetness. This versatile herb is easy to grow. For some gardeners, it grows too easily, spreading wildly throughout the garden.

Native to the Mediterranean, mint is a symbol of hospitality. Reputedly, ancient Romans welcomed guests to banquets by littering the room with fragrant mint leaves.

Best site
Mint is adaptable to many soil types and light conditions. For best results, plant in full sun or part shade in rich, moist, well-draining soil. Amend soil with a 2-inch layer of compost before planting. Mint's hardiness depends on the variety. Use a creeping variety such as Corsican mint as a groundcover, tucking it between stepping-stones of a pathway. Other varieties grow more upright, reaching up to 2 feet, and work well in mixed beds.

Planting
Mint grows so easily that gardeners often look for ways to get rid of it. Start seeds in early spring. About six weeks before the last frost in your area, sow herb seeds indoors to get a head start on the outdoor growing season. Plant purchased plants in spring, after the threat of frost has passed. Or grow plants from root cuttings or divisions. Mint cross-pollinates easily; separate different varieties to prevent this. To limit mint's spreading tendencies, plant it in a container that is sunk directly into the soil. See *page 59* for details.

VARIETIES

1. PEPPERMINT (*Mentha × piperita*) produces the strongest mint flavor. There are many varieties of peppermint. Zones 3–9.

2. SPEARMINT (*M. spicata*) packs a distinctive sweet flavor. Zones 4–10.

3. 'HILLARY'S SWEET LEMON' (*M. dulcia citreus*) produces large, flavorful leaves. Grows 1½–2 feet tall. Zones 4–10.

4. PINEAPPLE MINT (*M. suaveolens* 'Variegata') offers white-edge leaves and a fruity taste. Zones 5–10.

Growing

Cutting mint regularly keeps it looking lush, bushy, and attractive. Snip off the flowers as they appear. To provide mint with the maximum nutrients and moisture, remove competing weeds and grasses. To keep plants in top producing shape, divide mint every few years. Shear stems to the ground in late fall, and then savor this end-of-summer mint crop.

Chase mites and aphids away by blasting them with a strong spray of water from a garden hose. If a soilborne disease such as verticillium wilt is a problem, plant mint in containers. When planting, leave room between plants to encourage air circulation. Zones 3–10.

Harvest

Mint leaves and flowers are edible. Freeze fresh leaves to retain their bright color. Cut off the flowers when they begin to form to promote more leafy growth. Use the flowers and leaves fresh, or air-dry them. Cut stems, gather them into bundles, and hang in a cool, dry place. Strip the leaves and flowers from the stems, and store them whole in airtight containers.

Uses

Try mint in these ways:

Drink flavoring The list of mint-inspired drinks is long. Start with mint julep, mojito, and iced tea.

Salad surprise Snip mint leaves into a green or fruit salad for a refreshing flavor blast.

Mint simple syrup Combine 1 cup sugar, 1 cup water, and ½ cup mint leaves in a saucepan. Bring to boiling, then allow to cool; strain.

Bath herb blend or tub tea Include your favorite mint in an herb blend for a relaxing and cooling bath. Try mixing equal parts dried mint, lavender, rose, lemon balm, and chamomile.

YOU SHOULD KNOW

Mint can be invasive. It grows fast and spreads rampantly. If you like the fresh flavor of its green leaves, grow mint in containers near your back door so you can clip leaves for recipes.

VARIETIES

5. CHOCOLATE MINT (*M.* × *piperita*) has a subtle chocolate fragrance and flavor. It has pretty dark stems and bright green foliage. Plants grow 2 feet tall. Zones 4–9.

6. ORANGE MINT (*M.* × *piperita citrata*) develops bright green leaves lightly tinged with red. Foliage bears a citrus fragrance and flavor. It grows 2 feet tall. Zones 4–9.

7. APPLE MINT (*M. suaveolens*) has a wintergreen flavor and fragrance. The fresh leaves can be used to make apple mint jelly or a stomach-soothing tea. It reaches 2 feet tall. Zones 4–9.

8. 'HIMALAYAN SILVER' MINT (*M. spicata*) bears silver-green, fuzzy leaves with pink flowers. This variety grows 12–18 inches tall. Zones 4–10.

HERB ENCYCLOPEDIA

Mugwort
Artemisia vulgaris

Mugwort is an herb that sounds like one of Harry Potter's alchemy ingredients. In fact, it was used by ancient herbalists for several purposes, but today its primary use is in aromatherapy. Mugwort has a sagelike scent with mint undertones and a bitter flavor.

Best site
Plant mugwort in sun or partial shade. Once established, mugwort can grow in dry soil.

Planting
Sow seeds indoors in late spring, and transplant into the garden once the threat of frost has passed. Or sow seeds directly on top of moist, sandy soil.

Growing
Mugwort grows 2–4 feet tall. It is a hardy perennial. Mugwort flowers from July through September. Plants can be reproduced by division. Zones 5–10.

Harvest
Harvest stems just after flowering in early summer and again in late fall. Bundle the stems and hang them in a cool, dry location to dry.

YOU SHOULD KNOW
Mugwort has a reputation for being invasive. Plant it in a place where it can spread out, contain it a pot, or harvest before it goes to seed.

Mullein
Verbascum thapsus

Mullein is a biennial often found growing wild in fields and ditches. It was used medicinally to guard against asthma and cure respiratory illnesses. Plants grow up to 6 feet tall, and the leaves are gray-green, fuzzy, large, and thick. Flowers are yellow and can be infused in olive oil to create a soothing oil for skin.

Best site
Plant mullein in full or partial sun. It does well in nearly any soil (hence its ability to grow wild).

Planting
Plant seeds indoors in early spring. Transplant plants into the garden after the threat of frost has passed. If growing outdoors from seed, sow directly in the garden in late spring or early fall. The plant also self-sows if allowed.

Growing
As a biennial, mullein will flower the second year. To protect plants over winter, mulch in autumn. Zones 3–9.

Harvest
Pick flowers throughout summer as they bloom, or harvest the entire plant when it is flowering.

YOU SHOULD KNOW
Mullein is a good choice for cottage gardens because of its tall stature, wandlike blooms, and soft, fuzzy leaves.

Mustard
Brassica juncea, B. nigra

Mustard is a multipurpose annual plant: The greens are used for food, and the seeds are used for spices and condiments. The seeds of different varieties yield the condiment's colors, such as yellow or brown. Black mustard is a pungent herb used externally in warming poultices and baths.

Best site
Plant mustard in a sunny spot in well-draining, compost-enriched soil.

Planting
Mustard prefers cool weather. Sow mustard seeds directly in the ground in early spring about ¼ inch deep. Sow a second crop in early fall.

Growing
Plant small crops in succession (about a week apart) to ensure a continuous supply of greens. Water plants during dry periods.

Harvest
Pick mustard greens as soon as they are tall enough to harvest. To harvest seeds, allow the plants to set seed. Then cut stalks below the branching stems. Bundle the stems and hang upside down to dry in a cool, dry place.

YOU SHOULD KNOW
If you allow mustard plants to develop seed heads, harvest the stalks and let them cure for one to two weeks before using the seeds.

Myrtle
Myrtus communis

An evergreen shrub from the Mediterranean and Middle East, myrtle is used as an emblem of love. It can grow 2–10 feet tall and has glossy, dark green leaves and small white blossoms. The leaves have a sweet fragrance when crushed. Avoid overwatering myrtle to prevent root rot.

Best site
Grow myrtle in full sun and well-draining soil.

Planting
In areas with mild winters, plant myrtle in the ground. In a cool-weather climate, plant myrtle in a container that can be moved indoors. Choose dwarf myrtle for hedges.

Growing
Lightly prune myrtle in spring to help retain its shape. Lightly fertilize while the plant is in flower. Water when the soil begins to feel dry to the touch. Zones 8–11.

Harvest
Gather and dry the leaves for use in potpourris or sachets. Add fresh sprigs to bouquets. The purple-black berries can be used in cooking as you would use juniper berries.

YOU SHOULD KNOW
The dwarf variety of myrtle (*Myrtus communis* 'Compacta') is a slow-growing evergreen plant that reaches 2–3 feet tall.

HERB ENCYCLOPEDIA

YOU SHOULD KNOW

If you are looking for the best oregano for culinary use, choose Greek oregano (*Origanum vulgare hirtum*).

Oregano
Origanum vulgare

This low-growing, sprawling perennial herb excels in gardens or containers. Clipped fresh into pasta sauces, sprinkled over stews, or used in marinades for meat, oregano adds a warm, aromatic flavor. For lovers of Mediterranean cuisine, fresh or dried oregano is essential.

Oregano has been used for medicinal and culinary purposes since ancient times. The pungent herb was associated with happiness, good luck, and health. For this reason, it was worn for weddings in ancient Greece and Rome.

Best site
Plant in full sun and well-draining soil. Like most herbs, oregano will not tolerate wet soil. If your soil is slow to drain, add organic matter (chopped leaves and compost) to your planting area. Otherwise, grow oregano in a raised bed or container.

Planting
Oregano is difficult to start from seed. Buy nursery-grown transplants instead, and ensure that you are getting a true culinary variety. Set out plants in spring after frost danger has passed. Because of oregano's rangy growth habit, space plants 18 inches apart.

Growing
Water only during dry periods; too much moisture can result in root rot. Divide plants every few years when they become woody or begin to lose their compact habit. Plants grow to 18 inches tall. In cold climates, mulch plants to provide protection. Zones 5–10.

Harvest
Oregano leaves are most flavorful when gathered just before the flower buds open. Cut stems as needed, using the fresh leaves and edible flowers for vegetable salads and other favorite recipes. To obtain two large harvests per season, shear back the entire plant to about 3 inches just before it flowers; after it regrows, shear it back again in late summer. Oregano has a somewhat strong flavor; use it sparingly. Oregano retains good flavor when dried. Clip stems, bundle them, and hang upside down to dry in a cool, dark location with good air circulation. When the stems are crisp-dry, pluck off the leaves and store them in an airtight jar. Fresh leaves can also be preserved by freezing.

Uses
Try oregano in these ways:
Landscape use Plant oregano as a low-grower in flowerbeds or between stones of a pathway or rock garden.
Pollinator attractor Allow your oregano to flower and it will attract bees and butterflies.
Rock gardens Dittany of Crete (*Origanum dictamnus*), a relative of oregano, is a beautiful choice for rock gardens because of its round, fuzzy gray leaves.

VARIETIES

1. GREEK OREGANO (*Origanum vulgare hirtum*) offers the best flavor for culinary use.

2. 'AUREUM' (*O. vulgare*) is sometimes sold as creeping golden marjoram. It has yellow-green leaves and white flowers. Zones 6–9.

3. 'HERRENHAUSEN' (*O. laevigatum*) has purple-tinted leaves and showy pink flowers. It grows 18 inches tall. Zones 5–10.

Parsley
Petroselinum

More than a tasty garnish, parsley is rich in vitamins and minerals. The green fronds of this herb are pretty enough to use in bouquets. Parsley's neat, mounding growth habit makes it an edible edging plant for ornamental and vegetable gardens. Choose from two types of parsley: curly and flat-leaf.

Parsley was used by the Greeks to adorn the winners of athletic contests. It has been cultivated for more than 2,000 years.

Best site
Plant in full sun and moist, well-draining soil.

Planting
Sow seeds or set out transplants in early spring. Parsley seeds are slow to germinate, so if planting directly in the ground, use a cold frame over the seeding site to warm the soil. Space plants 10–18 inches apart; parsley grows about as wide as it is tall—18–24 inches. If growing parsley from seed, thin plants to 10 inches apart. In warm climates you can sow seeds in spring and fall. To give newly planted parsley a boost, dig a 2-inch-thick layer of compost into the site before planting.

Growing
Spread a 2-inch-thick layer of mulch between plants to prevent soil from splashing onto the leaves when watering. Snap off flower stalks as they form. Although parsley is a biennial grown as an annual, it can overwinter in a cold frame or under a thick layer of straw in all but the coldest climates.

Harvest
Harvest parsley as soon as the plants are large enough—and as often as needed. Consistent harvests encourage new growth. Snip the full stem when harvesting. The entire plant may be harvested before winter or mulched heavily to protect it over winter. Stand fresh-picked parsley stems in a glass of water, and keep it on the kitchen counter or in the refrigerator for several days. Dry or freeze parsley for later use.

Uses
Try parsley in these ways:

French herb blends Parsley is a key ingredient in bouquet garni and fines herbes.

Basil substitute for pesto Use parsley instead of basil to make a mild pesto.

Butterfly gardening Swallowtail butterflies use parsley as a host plant for their larvae (caterpillars with black, green, and yellow stripes). Although these caterpillars will eat some parsley leaves, it won't be enough to damage the plant. Let them dine, and enjoy the beautiful butterflies that ensue.

YOU SHOULD KNOW
Harvest fresh parsley in winter by growing it in a cold frame or on a sunny windowsill. The plant will continue to produce new leaves until spring.

VARIETIES

1. FLAT-LEAF ITALIAN (*Petroselinum neapolitanum*) makes an attractive garnish or addition to salads. Zones 5–9.

2. CURLY LEAF (*P. crispum*) contains vitamin C and iron, like other varieties. Nibbling on the leaves is an effective breath-freshener.

> **YOU SHOULD KNOW**
> Patchouli requires moist soil. Keep the plant well watered, especially when growing it in a container. Mulch around the plant to help conserve soil moisture.

Patchouli
Pogostemon cablin

The scent of patchouli is cryptic: Its spicy fragrance is used extensively in perfume production and is considered an aphrodisiac, yet it also repels insects. A member of the mint family, this tender perennial produces fragrant leaves that release their distinctive scent when rubbed.

Used in China to cure headaches and in India to treat snakebites, patchouli is known to Western herb fans as a sweet woodsy scent in perfumes, lotions, soaps, and incenses.

Best site
Plant patchouli in partial shade in rich, moist soil.

Planting
Sow seeds indoors about six to eight weeks before the last frost date in your area. Transplant seedlings outdoors once the threat of frost has passed. Plant transplants 2 feet apart. Patchouli also grows well in containers and makes an interesting conversation piece.

Growing
Patchouli is a bushy plant that grows 2–3 feet tall, with subtly scented leaves and small white flowers. This native plant of India thrives and grows quickly in hot, humid weather. Bring your plant indoors before frost if you want to overwinter it; frost will kill patchouli. Aphids and spider mites can be controlled with insecticidal soap. If you have slugs in your area, apply a layer of diatomaceous earth around plants. Patchouli is a perennial in Zone 11; elsewhere it is considered an annual.

Harvest
Clip the flowers, which are small but more aromatic than the leaves. Harvest leaves throughout summer. Bundle stems and hang in a warm, dry location. Remove dried leaves and store in an airtight container. You can keep a potted patchouli in your bedroom to scent the air while you sleep. If the fragrance is overpowering, move the plant to a shaded location.

Uses
Try patchouli in these ways:
Insect repellent Store clothing with sprigs of patchouli to repel moths. Or soak cotton balls with patchouli oil and place them in drawers and armoires to release the long-lasting scent.
Aromatherapy Add the flowers to potpourri. Release the seductive scent of patchouli in your home by simmering a few fresh leaves in water.

Pennyroyal
Mentha pulegium

This perennial grows 4–16 inches tall and features fluffy lavender flowers along the stems. The plant has a creeping habit, and as a member of the mint family, pennyroyal tends to spread and become invasive.

Pennyroyal is native to south and central Europe. Used in ancient times to repel pests, it is used today in natural insect repellents.

Best site
Grow pennyroyal in full sun to partial shade. It does best in moist, well-draining soil and is often found growing near streams.

Planting
Sow seeds directly in the garden about ¼ inch deep in early spring after the threat of frost has passed. In warm climates you can plant seeds in fall.

Growing
To prevent it from spreading throughout the garden, plant pennyroyal in containers or a confined bed. This herb grows up to 16 inches tall and produces lavender, pink, or bluish-purple flowers in mid- to late summer. It can become weedy by spreading via underground runners or horizontal roots. When pulling gregarious plants, make sure to pull out the entire root to prevent the plants from regrowing. Zones 6–9.

Harvest
Pick leaves to use fresh when the plant is in full bloom—in early summer—when the leaves bear the strongest scent. To dry, bundle stems and hang upside down in a cool, dry place.

Uses
Try pennyroyal in these ways:

Insect repellent Use fresh leaves and stems to repel insects such as fleas. Rub leaves directly on skin; but first test for an allergic reaction by rubbing a leaf on a small area of skin. Do not apply the essential oil to pets or ingest pennyroyal oil—it is toxic. Pregnant women should avoid any use of pennyroyal.

Groundcover This vigorous grower makes an ideal groundcover in areas that don't receive direct foot traffic. When brushed, it releases a pleasant minty fragrance.

> **YOU SHOULD KNOW**
> Like many members of the mint family, pennyroyal can be invasive. Plant it prudently in a place where it can spread without taking over.

HERB ENCYCLOPEDIA

YOU SHOULD KNOW
Because edible poppy seeds are from the same poppy used to make opium, they contain small amounts of opiate alkaloids, which can be detected in drug tests.

Poppy
Papaver somniferum

Breadseed poppies' crepe-paperlike blooms are as welcome in the flower garden as they are in the herb garden. Poppies have another claim to fame: Opium can be extracted from the dried heads. However, you're more likely to encounter the talents of this plant on top of a bagel in the form of poppy seeds.

Poppies were commonly cultivated by ancient cultures, including Sumerians, Assyrians, Babylonians, Egyptians, Romans, and Greeks.

Best site
Plant poppies in full sun and rich, moist soil.

Planting
It's best to grow poppies from seeds planted directly in the ground, as plants do not transplant well. Sow seeds ¼ inch deep and water well.

Growing
These annuals are easy to grow and often self-seed, so they appear year after year. They grow about 3 feet tall. In late spring, plants bear gorgeous flowers in shades of pink, lilac, mauve, red, or white. The seedpods form in autumn. Zones 3–9.

Harvest
Allow the seed heads to dry on the plant. Cut the stems of the dried seedpods, and use them in floral arrangements and wreaths. To harvest the seeds, place the seed heads in a paper bag and allow them to dry for several weeks. Break open the dried seedpods, and shake the seeds into a bowl. Separate any nonseed plant material. Store the seeds in an airtight container away from light and heat. Use them in recipes or for planting in the next year's garden.

Uses
Try poppies in these ways:
Cottage gardens Poppy blooms are a cottage garden standard and look stunning scattered among late-spring-blooming perennials.
Baking The common name for *Papaver somniferum* is breadseed poppy. The small, round bluish-black seeds get top billing in lots of recipes: poppy seed bagels, poppy seed sweet breads, and poppy seed rolls.
Dried arrangements The sculptural seedpods from poppy flowers are beautiful used in dried arrangements or tucked into wreaths.

Rose
Rosa selections

One of the most revered plants in the flower garden and landscape, roses are also an asset to herb gardens. They produce edible petals. And the hips, which are the fruit of the plant, are packed with vitamin C; they're consumed in a variety of ways, including in tea, jam, jelly, and syrup.

In ancient times, *Rosa* species were used to remedy a wide range of ailments, from the common cold to problems of the skin, heart, and circulation.

Best site
Roses excel in a sunny spot where they will receive at least six hours of sun daily. Plant in well-draining soil enriched with compost and rotted manure.

Planting
Roses are sold in two forms: bare root and in containers. Bare-root roses are dormant. They come to life quickly once planted. Container roses are typically leafed out and may also be blooming. Plant roses 2–3 feet apart. Roses need plenty of air circulating around them to prevent fungal diseases.

Growing
Roses need consistent watering. Water slowly at the base of a plant, allowing the soil to be thoroughly soaked. Avoid wetting the leaves, which can promote disease. Feed the shrubs with an organic fertilizer formulated for roses. Fertilize in spring when the bush leafs out. Feed again in midsummer when roses have finished their flush of bloom. Mulch around the base of the plants to help retain soil moisture and discourage weeds. Grow roses organically if you plan to use them in culinary or cosmetic recipes.

Harvest
To harvest rose petals, cut off the entire flower. Handle petals as little as possible, and store in the refrigerator until you are ready to use them. Pull the petal from the flower and remove the white end, which tastes bitter. To harvest rose hips, allow the summer's last flowers to remain on the plant. As the flowers fade, the fruits will form. Cut off the hips when they are plump and ripe. Use them fresh or dried. Freeze the hips to preserve them, if you prefer.

Uses
Try roses in these ways:

Rose-hip tea Crushed rose hips steeped in hot water are a good source of vitamin C. Chop fresh rose hips, cover them with water, and simmer for 15 minutes. Strain the liquid and refrigerate it.
Astringent Used in lotions and facial products, rose water is made from rose petals.
Edible flowers Mince rose petals and sprinkle them on salads or desserts just before serving for a colorful, delicately flavored touch. Rose petals can also be used to make jelly, jam, syrup, and other sweet treats.

YOU SHOULD KNOW
Roses benefit from growing near a structure for shelter and support. Plant tall or climbing varieties of the shrub against a sturdy trellis, arbor, wall, or fence.

VARIETIES
1. *ROSA GALLICA* 'VERISCOLOR', also called the Apothecary rose, has flowers that are carmine-pink, cupped, and semidouble. They appear in spring to early summer and are followed by orange-red hips at the end of the season. Zones 3–9.

2. *ROSA RUGOSA* 'ALBA' offers large hips, prickly thorns, and wavy leaves. Its white flowers open from pink-tinged buds and are sweetly tea-rose scented. It grows 8 feet tall and wide. Zones 2–9.

HERB ENCYCLOPEDIA

Rosemary
Rosmarinus officinalis

Fragrant and delicious, rosemary is also a beauty. Pruned into topiaries or allowed to grow into shrubby plants, rosemary is a favorite of gardeners and cooks alike. In warm climates, this plant is an evergreen shrub that has scaly bark and multitudes of narrow dark green leaves. The flavor of the leaves is distinctive; the scent is pungent and piney. It's a signature herb in Mediterranean dishes.

This Mediterranean native was reputed in ancient folklore to improve memory and safeguard against witches. A necklace made of rosemary was said to keep people young—and attract elves. Rosemary was also used to flavor wine.

Best site
Plant in full sun and well-draining soil. Rosemary needs quick-draining soil; it does not tolerate wet sites. If your soil is slow-draining or clay, plant rosemary in a raised bed or grow it in a pot.

Planting
In spring after the danger of frost has passed, set out transplants or plants that spent the winter indoors. Start new plants from cuttings in spring or summer. Grow rosemary in a container indoors and outdoors. In warm climates, use plants as evergreen shrubs or groundcovers.

Growing
This herb comes in various forms, from stiff and upright (ideal for a hedge) to mounded and spreading (perfect for scrambling along a slope or wall). The secret to beautiful rosemary is to give plants warm, dry conditions. Grow plants in well-draining soil or a raised bed, and surround them with gravel mulch. In warm-winter areas, protect rosemary from cold winter winds that may dry it out by wrapping the plant with burlap. In cold climates, grow rosemary

in containers and bring plants indoors in late summer. To succeed indoors over winter, rosemary needs consistent watering to keep the potted plant's soil damp. Zones 6–10; elsewhere an annual.

Harvest

Cut stems above the woody growth as needed throughout the growing season. Regular harvests encourage bushy growth. Strip off the resinous leaves from the stems and chop or grind them. To dry rosemary, bundle stems and hang them upside down in a cool, airy place. Dried rosemary leaves provide good flavor for culinary use, but fresh leaves pack more robust flavor and offer a softer, more edible texture.

Uses

Try rosemary in these ways:

Kabob skewers The woody stems provide flavorful skewers for kabobs or satay recipes. Strip off most of the leaves, and put the stems to work as you would bamboo skewers.

Topiary Rosemary's woody stems make the herb an ideal candidate for tree-form topiaries.

YOU SHOULD KNOW

Enjoy rosemary throughout the seasons. The leaves are tender in spring but have fewer aromatic oils. By late summer, the foliage packs a more potent flavor.

VARIETIES

1. TRAILING ROSEMARY (*Rosmarinus officinalis* 'Prostratus') has a low-growing, creeping habit that makes it excellent as an evergreen groundcover. It grows 3 feet tall and spreads 4–8 feet in Zones 8–10. In midsummer, this shrubby tender perennial is covered with light blue flowers.

2. 'BARBEQUE' is a selection of common rosemary developed for its excellent flavor and aroma. It grows 4 feet tall and develops beautiful blue blooms. Annual except in Zones 8–10.

3. 'ROMAN BEAUTY' is a dwarf rosemary that grows about 2 feet tall and is topped with lavender blooms. It's an ideal choice for containers because of its compact and mounded growth habit. Annual except in Zones 8–10.

4. 'TUSCAN BLUE' is one of the best rosemary varieties for topiaries. Plants develop dense, blue-green foliage that's easily sheared to any shape. It's also a highly fragrant variety that has many uses in the kitchen. It can grow 4 feet tall. Annual except in Zones 8–10.

5. VARIEGATED ROSEMARY features deep green leaves with yellow mottling. Variegated rosemaries include 'Gold Dust' and 'Aureus'. Plants have small blue flowers and an upright growth habit. Annual except in Zones 8–10.

HERB ENCYCLOPEDIA

YOU SHOULD KNOW
Rue has a bitter flavor and a strong scent, as indicated by its species name: *graveolens*, meaning "heavy smell" in Latin.

Rue
Ruta graveolens

This aromatic shrubby herb has been used for medicinal and culinary purposes for centuries. Although rarely eaten in the United States (because it has a bitter flavor and not-so-pleasant scent), rue is used in small quantities to flavor cheese and egg dishes in some Mediterranean countries.

In ancient times rue was ingested to remedy a host of problems, such as poor eyesight and gastrointestinal ills. Rue was also applied topically to ward off insect pests.

Best site
Grow rue in full sun or light shade. Although the plant can grow in poor soil, it must be well-draining for rue to survive. Once established, this perennial herb grows well in hot, dry locations.

Planting
Sow seeds indoors four to six weeks before the last average spring frost date. Or you can sow seeds directly in garden soil once it has warmed in spring. The seeds usually germinate easily. Keep the soil consistently damp until the seeds sprout and the seedlings develop. Set out transplants after the threat of frost has passed. Water regularly until the plants become well-established—well into their first growing season. Rue can also be grown in container gardens. Lift the plant from a pot in early fall and transplant it into the garden, giving it time to root before winter arrives. You can enjoy the plant in the next year's garden, or transplant it again into a container.

Growing
In spring, clean up the plant by pruning away any of the prior year's spent foliage. Divide plants in spring. After summer flowering, cut the faded blooms to encourage new growth. Rue self-seeds, so remove flower heads if you don't want more plants. In Northern areas, mulch the plant in late fall to help protect it from damage due to winter's freeze-thaw cycles. Rue grows 1–2 feet tall. Zones 4–9.

Harvest
Wear gloves when harvesting rue leaves because their essential oil can cause a skin rash and blistering on hot days.

Uses
Try rue in these ways:
Knot gardens This woody shrub can be clipped into a neat hedge, making it an ideal herb for knot gardens.
Floral arrangements Use the attractive bluish gray-green leaves and yellow flowers in fresh flower arrangements.

Saffron
Crocus sativus

Whether you call it an herb or a spice, saffron is the dried stigmata of one crocus species, *Crocus sativus*. If you love paella, curry, or other dishes that include saffron in their ingredients, you probably know about its costliness. This precious herb can be worth thousands of dollars per pound. Grow your own crop to gain significant savings.

Saffron has been in cultivation for more than 3,500 years. During the Renaissance, saffron was worth its weight in gold.

Best site
Plant in full sun to light shade in well-draining soil. If the soil is heavy with clay or drains poorly, the bulbs may rot. Improve the soil by digging in loads of organic amendments, such as compost and chopped leaves, before planting.

Planting
Plant *Crocus sativus* bulbs in early autumn. They will flower four to six weeks later. This perennial bulb will bloom year after year if planted in conducive conditions in Zones 6–8. Plant the bulbs 3–4 inches deep and about 2 inches apart. After planting, water well and spread a 2-inch-deep layer of mulch over the planting area.

Growing
C. sativus grows just 2–4 inches tall, so make sure it's planted in an area where you'll notice the flowers and gather their stigmatas in time to use them. Water the plantings unless nature takes care of that for you.

Harvest
When the crocuses bloom, harvest the stigmatas by carefully plucking each one, using your fingertips or small scissors. Each flower produces three stigmatas. Harvest them on a sunny day when the flowers are fully open. Dry the stigmatas in a warm, well-ventilated place. When dried, store them in an airtight jar. Many recipes call for saffron by the strand or thread, which amounts to one stigma.

Uses
Try *C. sativus* in these ways:

Recipes that call for saffron The fine stigmatas are typically used sparingly in recipes. For example, most paella recipes call for a generous pinch of saffron. But those threads impart rich flavor and color to the classical Spanish dish.

YOU SHOULD KNOW
Each *Crocus sativus* flower produces only three stigmatas. To grow 1 ounce of saffron, you need about 14,000 stigmatas, or about 4,667 flowers.

HERB ENCYCLOPEDIA

YOU SHOULD KNOW
Nonculinary varieties of sage make excellent ornamental edging plants in gardens. Colorful variegated types offer leaves striated with purple, chartreuse, and white.

Sage
Salvia officinalis

For poultry-stuffing fans, sage is a traditional ingredient. This savory herb is also a favorite addition to breads, soups, and herb mixes used for vegetables (particularly squash and potatoes) and meat. But sage also has a sweeter and wilder side, showing up in cookies, sorbets, and even martinis. Besides sage's talents as a culinary herb, it's a popular fragrance used in perfumes, soaps, and hair products.

Native to the Mediterranean, sage was believed by ancient Romans and Greeks to impart wisdom. It has been used for centuries as a way to scent and purify the air.

Best site
Plant sage in full sun. The perennial grows best in rich soil that drains well, although the plant adapts to a range of soil conditions. Sage also grows well in containers—grouped with other herbs or mixed amid flowers. The ornamental varieties add color to the garden, too. Once established, common sage blooms in late spring.

Planting
Seeds are difficult to germinate. Transplant container-grown plants or divisions in spring. Space plants 2–3 feet apart. Improve the soil by adding a 2-inch-thick layer of compost before planting. Sage grows 2–3 feet tall and wide.

Growing
Sage is a low-maintenance, drought-tolerant herb. Trim sage plants as needed to maintain their shape and to promote dense new growth. In autumn, protect sage by spreading a 4- to 6-inch-thick layer of mulch at the plant's base to prolong the harvest season. To enjoy fresh leaves through winter, dig up a garden plant in late summer or early fall and transplant it into a container of well-drained potting mix. Place the pot in a sunny window indoors. Zones 4–10.

Harvest
Cut 6- to 8-inch lengths of leafy growth above the woody stems in summer before the plant blooms. For the best flavor, snip stems in the morning after dew has dried. Cut flowering stems for bouquets. Trim off spent flowers. To dry sage, bundle stems and hang them upside down in a dark, airy space, or strip leaves from the stems and spread the foliage on a screen to air-dry. When completely dried, remove leaves from stems and store them in a jar away from light and heat for up to one year.

Uses

Try sage in these ways:

Insect repellents Some naturalists swear by the insect-deterring qualities of sage leaves. To use, rub fresh leaves on skin. The distinctive scent also deters moths from damaging stored woolen clothing; dried sage smells much better than mothballs.

Dry rubs Make your own dry rubs for preparing poultry or pork for cooking. Blend dried sage with oregano, thyme, and rosemary for a flavorful seasoning.

Smudge sticks Bundles of smoldering desert or white sage stems and leaves played a part in Native American cultural traditions. To make a smudge stick, cut a handful of any variety of sage stems in 6- to 8-inch lengths, and allow them to dry for about a week. Bundle the dried sage stems, add lavender or another fragrant herb if desired, and tightly wrap the bunch from top to bottom with heavy thread. To burn, light one end of the bundle, blow out the flame, and allow the herbs to smolder and smoke. The smudge stick will release the fragrance of the sage and any other herbs included in the bundle.

VARIETIES

1. COMMON SAGE produces textural oval gray-green leaves and purple flowers. The ornamental and edible plant grows 2 feet tall and should be replaced every five years or so. Zones 4–9.

2. 'ICTERINA' or golden sage is a variegated green-and-gold variety and a colorful alternative to common sage. Plant it in beds, borders, and containers. It reaches 2 feet tall. Zones 5–11.

3. 'TRICOLOR' SAGE leaves are variegated green, cream, and purple. Zones 6–9.

HERB ENCYCLOPEDIA

> **YOU SHOULD KNOW**
> Salad burnet makes a lovely container planting for outdoor dining areas. The serrated leaves are pretty and can be snipped into salads, soups, and stews served alfresco.

Salad Burnet
Sanguisorba minor

Cultivated in medieval gardens, salad burnet is a perennial herb native to western Asia and Europe. It was brought to North America by the Pilgrims and has naturalized here. Because it does well in poor soil, Thomas Jefferson used salad burnet to curb erosion. It was also used as food for livestock.

Salad burnet was once erroneously thought to be a cure for the bubonic plague. The herb has been adapted in European cuisine. It is added to salads for its refreshing cucumberlike flavor.

Best site
Plant salad burnet in partial to full sun. The herb is adaptable and grows well in a variety of soil conditions. Although it grows best in a well-draining site, it will tolerate poor soil.

Planting
Start from seeds or transplants. If planting from seeds, sow indoors in early spring and transplant outdoors after the danger of frost is over. In areas with a long growing season, sow seeds directly in the garden after the threat of frost has passed. Salad burnet makes a textural addition to kitchen gardens as well as containers.

Growing
Pretty salad burnet has small, serrated leaves; green-and-magenta flowers; and a mounded growth habit. Salad burnet does not need fertilizer—average garden soil provides the plant's needed nutrients. Keep the soil free of weeds for best results when growing salad burnet. The plant does not need much water, but it should have adequate drainage to prevent root rot. Cut back blossoms to encourage growth of new, tender leaves. Plants grow 1½ feet tall. Zones 4–10.

Harvest
Pick the leaves when they are young and tender; salad burnet gets bitter with age. Use this herb fresh or frozen; the leaves lose their flavor when dried. Pick the flowers for use as garnishes; they are pretty but have only mild flavor.

Uses
Try salad burnet in these ways:
Herb substitute Use salad burnet leaves in recipes that call for dill, oregano, basil, or mint.
Herb blends The mild flavor of salad burnet blends well with other culinary herbs, including tarragon, thyme, and marjoram.
Spicy salad greens Harvest whole leaves to sprinkle onto salads; they impart a fresh taste amid other greens.

Santolina
Santolina

Also called lavender cotton, santolina is grown mainly for its textural and aromatic foliage. It displays gray or green leaves and small yellowish flowers, which are pretty in passing but not the main event. It's all about the foliage, which mixes well in flowerbeds and borders—as well as in herb gardens.

Santolina is a popular plant used in knot gardens. There are two types—one that offers beautiful gray-blue foliage and one that is bright green. Both have woody stems and dense foliage.

Best site
Plant santolina in a sunny location and well-draining soil. Santolina is drought-tolerant and can grow in poor, sandy soil. The plant does best in warm regions with low humidity.

Planting
Raise santolina from seeds or nursery-grown plants. Start seeds indoors in early spring. Transplant outdoors after the last frost date. To use this herb in a hedge or knot garden, start with transplants. Santolina grows 1–2 feet tall, depending on the variety. Space plants 1–2 feet apart, and closer for a clippable hedge.

Growing
In cold climates, plant santolina in a container and bring it indoors over winter. The plant blooms in mid- to late summer; the yellow flowers are small and can be removed to keep the neatness of the plant intact. Zones 6–9.

Harvest
Cut santolina flowers for fresh bouquets or dried-flower arrangements. To dry the stems of flowers or foliage, cut and bundle them, and hang the bunch upside down in a cool, dry place.

Uses
Try santolina in these ways:
Knot gardens Santolina's contrasting foliage and shrubby growth habit make it an ideal plant for a knot garden. Avoid heavy pruning when the plant is flowering; it may not recover.
Topiaries Santolina makes a lovely topiary. The woody stem forms a trunk for a tree-form standard that can be shaped into a sphere or square, for instance.
Low hedge This textural plant makes an excellent low hedge or edging plant in flower or herb gardens.
Drought-tolerant gardens Santolina can star in a low-water-use garden. It requires little supplemental water to flourish.
Moth repellent Add dried santolina leaves to aromatic sachet blends, made to help repel moths from clothing and linens in closets and drawers.
Soup/sauce flavoring Although not well-known in culinary circles, gray santolina leaves can be used in sauces and soups. Add a tiny amount at first to determine whether you like the flavor; it may be an acquired taste.

YOU SHOULD KNOW
Cut or bruised santolina leaves can irritate skin or cause a rash. So beware while cutting or handling this herb.

VARIETIES
1. GRAY SANTOLINA (*Santolina chamaecyparissus*) is used for containers, topiary, edging, rock gardens, and knot gardens. Zones 6–9.

2. GREEN SANTOLINA (*S. virens*) is used for its lacy foliage in much the same way as the gray variety. Zones 7–9.

HERB ENCYCLOPEDIA

USDA Plant Hardiness Zone Map

Each plant has an ability to withstand low temperatures. This range of temperatures is expressed as a Zone—and a Zone map shows where you can grow a plant.

Planting for your Zone
The U.S. Department of Agriculture designates 11 Zones from Canada to Mexico, and each represents the lowest expected winter temperature in that area. Each Zone is based on a 10°F difference in minimum temperatures. Once you know your hardiness Zone, you can choose plants for your garden that will flourish. Look for the hardiness Zone on the plant tags of the perennials, trees, and shrubs you buy.

Microclimates in your yard
Not all areas in your yard are the same. Depending on your geography, trees, and structures, some spots may receive different sunlight and wind, and consequently experience temperature differences. Take a look around your yard, and you may notice that the same plant comes up sooner in one place than another. This is the microclimate concept in action. A microclimate is an area in your yard that is slightly different (cooler or warmer) than the other areas of your yard.

Create a microclimate
Once you're aware of your yard's microclimates, use them to your advantage. For example, you may be able to grow plants in a sheltered, south-facing garden bed that you can't grow elsewhere in your yard. You can create a microclimate by planting evergreens on the north side of a property to block prevailing winds. Or plant deciduous trees on the south side to provide shade in summer.

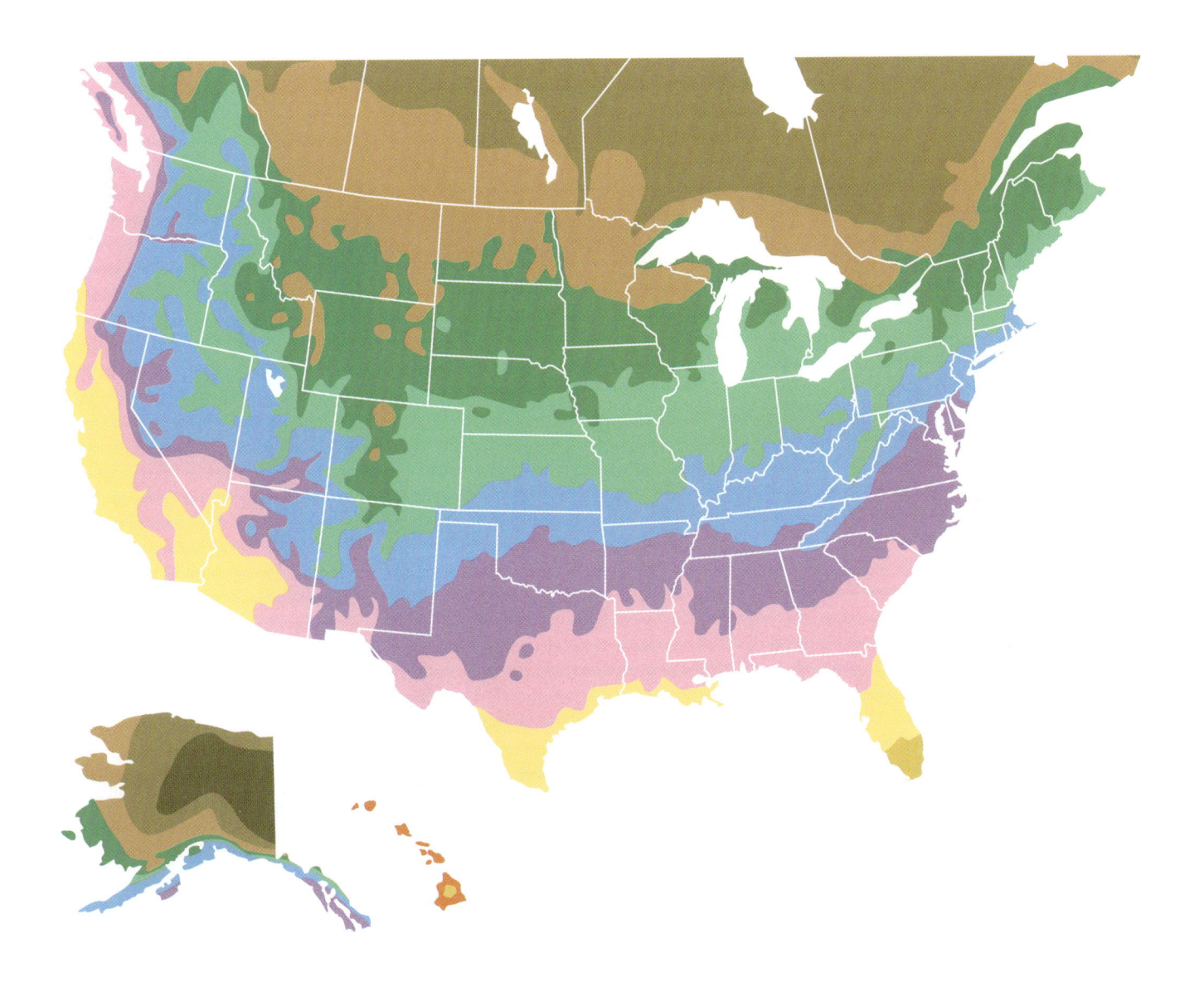

Range of Average Annual Minimum Temperatures for Each Zone

- Zone 1: below -50°F (below -45.6°C)
- Zone 2: -50 to -40°F (-45 to -40°C)
- Zone 3: -40 to -30°F (-40 to -35°C)
- Zone 4: -30 to -20°F (-34 to -29°C)
- Zone 5: -20 to -10°F (-29 to -23°C)
- Zone 6: -10 to 0°F (-23 to -18°C)
- Zone 7: 0 to 10°F (-18 to -12°C)
- Zone 8: 10 to 20°F (-12 to -7°C)
- Zone 9: 20 to 30°F (-7 to -1°C)
- Zone 10: 30 to 40°F (-1 to 4°C)
- Zone 11: 40°F and above (4.5°C and above)

Source: U.S. Department of Agriculture

opposite Some perennial varieties, such as lavender, come in a range of Zones. Check plant tags to verify that the Zone is appropriate before you plant.

USDA PLANT HARDINESS ZONE MAP

Resources

Use these trusted herbal resources when selecting herbs and products for your herb garden.

Plants and Seeds

BONNIE PLANTS
1727 Hwy. 223, Union Springs, AL 36089
334/738-3104, bonnieplants.com

NICHOLS GARDEN NURSERY
1190 Old Salem Rd., NE, Albany, OR 97321
800/422-3985, nicholsgardennursery.com

RENEE'S GARDEN SEEDS
6060 Graham Hill Rd., Felton, CA 95018
888/880-7228, reneesgarden.com

RICHTERS HERBS
357 Hwy. 47, Goodwood, ON, L0C 1A0 Canada
800/668-4372, richters.com

SANDY MUSH HERB NURSERY
316 Surrett Cove Rd., Leicester, NC 28748
828/683-2014, sandymushherbs.com

Index

A

Acclimating herbs, 87
Achillea (yarrow), 25, **209**
Agastache foeniculum. See Anise hyssop
Agastache rupestris (sunset hyssop), *39*
Alchemilla mollis (lady's mantle), **163**
Allium cepa var. *viviparum.* See Egyptian onion
Allium sativum. See Garlic
Allium schoenoprasum (chives), *21*
Allium tuberosum. See Garlic chives
Aloe vera (*Aloe vera*), *10*, **130**
Aloysia triphylla. See Lemon verbena
American ginseng (*Panax quinquefolius*), *12*
Anethum graveolens. See Dill
Angelica (*Angelica archangelica*), *71*, **131**
Anise hyssop (*Agastache foeniculum*), *15, 25, 58*, **132**
Annual herbs, 7
 cutting back, 62
 easy, *21*
 invasive, 58
 leaving outside, 87
 soil for, 20
Aphids, 87, 91
Archangelica gigas (purple angelica), *131*
Armoracia rusticana (horseradish), **162**
Aromatherapy, 9
Artemisia abrotanum (southernwood), **199**
Artemisia (*Artemisia*), *71*, **133**
Artemisia dracunculus ('Sativa'), See Tarragon
Artemisia vulgaris (mugwort), **176**
Artful uses of herbs, 29
Asthma, mullein for, 9
Ayurveda, 11

B

Bartram's Garden, 12, *13*
Basil (*Ocimum*), 6, *21*, **134–135**
 Basil/Chai Punch, 113
 'Boxwood', 70
 edging, 27
 height, *71*
 in herb blends, 104
 in knot garden, *15*
 Lemon-Basil Pasta, 114, *114*
 mint as flavor substitution, 109
 for nausea, 9
 pairing with tomato, 66
 'Red Rubin', 25, 135
 Sparkling Basil Lemonade, 117, *117*
 'Spicy Globe', *27*, 70, *71*, 135
 taste, 92
 for topiary, 29
 uses of, 76, 135
 as walkway edger, 71
Bath oils, herb-infused, 126, *127*
Bayberry (*Myrica pensylvanica*), **137**
Bay laurel (*Laurus nobilis*), 79, 104, **136**
Bee balm (*Monarda didyma*), 12, *13*, **138**
 for bee attraction, 73
 flowers, *25*
 invasive nature of, 58
 pruning, 68
 in tea garden, 38, *39*
 uses of, 77
Bees, attracting, *72*, 73
Bee skep, 61
Bench, covered in herbs, 29
Benedictine (liqueur), 14
Bergamot. See Bee balm (*Monarda didyma*)
Betony (*Stachys officinalis*), **139**
Beverages, 113
Biennial herbs, 7
Birdbath, 61
Black snakeroot (*Cimicifuga racemosa*), 12
Black walnut trees, 41
Borage (*Borago officinalis*), *25*, **140**
 for bee attraction, 73
 height, *71*
 self-seeding by, 58
Botanical garden, 12, *13*

Bouquets
 bouquet garni, 104
 freezing, 125
 spring herbs, 99
 summer herbs, 74
Boxwood, in knot gardens, *16, 17*, 34–35
Brassica (mustard), **177**
Broccoli, pairing sage with, *57*
Bug-repelling garden plan, 49
Bulbs, pairing perennial herbs with, *57*
Bundles, herb, 84
Butter, herb, 99
Butterflies, attracting, *72*, 73
Buying plants, 54

C

Cabbage, pairing hyssop with, *57*
Calamint (*Calamintha nepeta*), **141**
Calendula (*Calendula officinalis*), *25, 99*, 113, **142**
Capsicum annuum (pepper), **182**
Caraway (*Carum carvi*), 77, **143**
Carrots, pairing chives with, *57*
Cast-stone planter, 44
Caterpillars, attracting, *72*, 73
Catharanthus roseus (Madagascar periwinkle), 14
Catmint (*Nepeta* x *faassenii*), *25*, **144**
 for bee attraction, 73
 height, *71*
 pruning, 68
 self-seeding by, 58
Catnip (*Nepeta cataria*), 68, 92, **145**
Celery (*Apium graveolens dulce*), **145**
Celtic Cross garden plan, 32–37
Centerpiece
 fragrant herb bouquet, 99
 herb bowl, 118, *119*
 rosemary, **95**
 savory herb, 48
Chamaemelum nobile (Roman chamomile), 24, 38, *39*

212 GARDENING MADE EASY **HERB GARDENING**

Chamomile (*Chamaemelum nobile, Matricaria recutita*), **146**
  for covering benches, 29
  creeping varieties, 23
  flowers, *25*
  for fragrant path, 23
  for herbal lawn, 24
  for insomnia, 9
Chartreuse (liqueur), 14
Checkerboard garden, 26, *27*
Cheese, herb, 99, 100
Chelsea Physic Garden, 14
Chervil (*Cerefolium crispum*), *57*, *125*, **147**
  in herb blends, 104
  mild flavor of, 125
  seeding in containers, 62
  tarragon as flavor substitution, 109
Chicory (*Cichorium intybus*), **148**
Children, engaging, 92
Chinese medicine, traditional, 11
Chives (*Allium schoenoprasum*), *21*, *56*, **149**
  cool period for, 88
  edible flowers, 99
  flowers, *25*
  in herb blends, 104
  pairing with carrots, *57*
  spring harvesting, 62
  transplanting indoors, 87
Choosing herbs, 52–53
Chopped leaves, 65
Cilantro (*Coriandrum sativum*), *21*, **150**
  Hearty Boys Cilantro-Garlic Ribs, *102*, 103
  parsley as flavor substitution, 109
  pesto, 107
  seeding in containers, 62
  sowing in autumn, 62
Cimicifuga racemosa (black snakeroot), 12
Citronella, 9
Citrus (*Citrus*), **151**
Clary sage (*Salvia sclarea*), 77, **152**
Classic gardens, 17
Clay soil, 20, *20*, 53

Cleanup, fall, 84
Climate
  indoor, 88
  microclimates, 210
  USDA plant hardiness Zone map, 53, 210–211
Climbing plants, 26
Cloche, 61
Cloister gardens, 14
Closing up the garden, 84
Clothing dyes, herb use in, 8
Cocoa hulls, 65
Color
  herb flowers, 25, *25*
  herb use in dyes, 8
Comfrey (*Symphytum officinale*), 58, 67, 68, **153**
Compost, 20
  fertilizing with, 67
  in fragrant pathway, 23
  mulching with, 65
  new bed preparation, 61
  prepping beds for winter, 84
  sources of, 53
Concrete planter, 44
Containers
  for bee attraction, 73
  garden plans, 42–49
    bug-repelling, 49
    cast-stone or concrete, 44
    cluster of containers, 42–43
    mint, 47
    savory centerpiece, 48
    shade, 45
    window box, 46
  grouping, 42
  hanging baskets, 26, *27*
  invasive species in, 59
  materials, 26
  moving indoors, 87
  mulching indoor, 91
  planting herbs from, 54
  spring herbs in, 62
  tender plants in, 26, *27*
  windowsill herb garden, 89
Cooldowns, herbal, *112*, 113
Coriander (*Coriandrum sativum*), 77, **150**. *See also* Cilantro
Crafting, herb use in, 8
Creeping mint, for herbal lawn, 24

Crocus sativus (saffron), **191**
Culinary herbs, 8, 19, 76–77
  decorating with, 95
  experimenting with, 74
  flowering herbs, 77
  leafy herbs, 76
  planning next year's garden, 92, *93*
  seedy herbs, 77
Cultivars, 12
Cuttings, 79
Cymbopogon citratus. See Lemongrass

D

Deadheading, 68
Decorating with herbs, *94*, 95
Decorative elements in the garden, 61
Depth, planting, 54
Desiccants, 83
Dill (*Anethum graveolens*), *21*, *125*, **154**
  flowers, *25*
  insects and, 21
  Lemon Dill Sauce, 107
  Lemon-Dill Shrimp & Pasta, *116*, 117
  mild flavor of, 125
  reseeding by, 58
  seeding in containers, 62
  seed saving, 80, *81*
  uses of, 77
Dividing plants, 55
Drainage, 20, *20*, 53, 55
Drawing a garden plan, 60
Dressings, 107
Drip irrigation, 64–65
Drying herbs, 74, *82*, 83
Dyes, herb use in, 8
Dysphania ambrosioides (epazote), **156**

E

Edging, 17, *27*, 70
Edible landscaping, 24–25
Egyptian onion (*Allium cepa aggregatum*), **155**
Elderberry (*Sambucus*), **155**
Encyclopedia, 129–209
Entertainment ideas, spring, *98*, 99

Epazote (*Dysphania ambrosioides*), **156**
Essences, 9
Essential oils, 9, 21, 62
Eucalyptus (*Eucalyptus*), **156**
Exfoliating scrub, 126

F

Fall, 78–87, 118–123
  bringing herbs indoors, *86*, 87
  drying and storing herbs, *82*, 83
  planting for spring herbs, 62
  prepping beds for winter, 84
  propagating herbs, 78–79
  recipes, 118–123
  saving seeds, 80–81
  watering, 84
Fennel (*Foeniculum vulgare*), **157**
  in five-spice powder, 124
  height, 71
  in herb blends, 104
  as insect host plant, 21
  in Orange Fennel Marinade, 124
  staking, 71
  uses of, 77
Fertilizing herbs, 66–67
Feverfew (*Tanacetum parthenium*), 9, 12, 21, **157**
Fines herbs, 104
Flavor
  herb substitutions, 109
  strong and mild herbs, 125
Flowers
  bouquets, 74, 99
  colorful herbs, 25, *25*
  edible spring, 99
  flowering culinary herbs, 77
  mixing herbs with, 25
  seeds from, 80
Foeniculum vulgare. See Fennel
Food. *See also* **Culinary herbs; Recipes**
  fresh/dry herb ratio, 109
  herb butter or cheese, 99
  herb flavor substitutions, 109
  meat brushes, *106*, 107
Foot soak, peppermint, 113
Formal gardens, 17, 19
Fragaria vesca (alpine strawberry), 38, *39*

Fragrance, 8, 9, *18*, 19, 84
  burning bundles, 84
  fragrant path, 23
  groundcover, 24
  May basket, 99
  theme garden for smell, 92
Freezing herbs, 74, *110*, 111, 125
French tarragon, cool period for, 88
Frost, protecting from, *85*
Fungal disease, 91

G

Galium odoratum (sweet woodruff), **203**
Garden design
  artistic herb use, 29
  checkerboard, 26, *27*
  classical, 16–17
  containers, 26, *27*
  covered benches, 29
  decorative and utilitarian elements, 61
  drawing a plan, 60
  green roofs, 26
  hanging baskets, 26, *27*
  modern, 18–19
  pathway plantings, 23
  planning a new bed, 60–61
  rock gardens, *22*, 23
  siting your garden, 20
  size, 19, 60
  topiary, 29, *29*
  traditional, 14–15
  walls, *22*, 23
Garden plans
  Celtic Cross, 32–37
  container, 42–49
    bug-repelling, 49
    cast-stone or concrete, 44
    cluster of containers, 42–43
    mint, 47
    savory centerpiece, 48
    shade, 45
    window box, 46
  drawing a plan, 60
  knot garden, 34–35
  raised bed, 40–41
  tea garden, 38–39
  wagon wheel, 36–37
  welcome home, 42–43

INDEX **213**

Gardens
  botanical, 12, *13*
  casual, 19
  classic, 17
  cloister, 14
  formal, 17, 19
  indoor kitchen, 95
  knot, *15*, *16*, *17*, 17, 34–35
  modern, 18–19
  physic, 14
  potager, 14, *15*
  rock, *22*, 23
  tabletop, 29
  theme, 92
  traditional, 14–15
  vertical, 23
  weeds in, 14
  windowsill, 88
Garland, 95
Garlic (*Allium sativum*), **158**
  Chicken Breasts with Herbs, 114, *115*
  edible flowers, 99
  Hearty Boys Cilantro-Garlic Ribs, *102*, 103
  Lemon-Dill Shrimp & Pasta, *116*, 117
  pairing with rose, 57
Garlic chives (*Allium tuberosum*), 58, 69, 87
Genus name, 12
Geography of herbs, 11
Geranium. *See* Scented geranium
Germander (*Teucrium chamaedrys*), *16*, 17, **159**
Gifts, 126, *127*
Ginger (*Zingiber officinale*), **159**
Glycyrrhiza glabra (licorice root), **169**
Greenhouse, mini, 126
Green roofs, 26
Grooming herbs, 68–69
Groundcover, 24, 26
Grow-lights, 88

H
Hair rinse, 113
Hanging baskets, herbs in, 26, *27*
Hardiness Zone, 53, 210–211

Harvesting
  in hot weather, 74
  in morning, 62, 74, *75*
  spring herbs, 62
  summer herbs, 74–75
Hedge, 71
Herbal tea, 38–39, 118
Herb blends, 104, *104*
Herbes de Provence, 104
Hierochloe odorata (sweetgrass), **203**
High-intensity discharge (HID) lights, 88
Hippocrates (Greek physician), 11
History of herbs, 12
Hops (*Humulus lupulus*), 26, **160**
Horehound (*Marrubium vulgare*), **161**
Horseradish (*Armoracia rusticana*), **162**
Humidifying, *90*, 91
Hummingbirds, attracting, *72*, 73
Humulus lupulus (hops), **160**
Hypericum perforatum (St. John's Wort), **200**
Hyssop (*Hyssopus officinalis*), 57, 73, 77, **162**

I
Indoor herbs
  bringing herbs indoors, *86*, 87
  decorating with, *94*, 95
  leaf drop, 88
  lighting, 87, 88–89
  pests and diseases, 91
  watering and humidifying, *90*, 91
Insects
  attracting butterflies, bees, and caterpillars, *72*, 73
  checking for, 87
  indoors, 91
  repelled by herbs, 21, 49
Insomnia, chamomile for, 9
Invasive herbs, controlling, 58–59
Irrigation, drip, 64–65
Italian seasoning, 104

J–K
Juniper (*Juniperus communis*), **163**
Kabobs, lemongrass, 107
Kids, engaging, 92
Kitchen gardens, 14, 19, 62, 95
Knot gardens, *15*, *16*, *17*, 17, 34–35

L
Lady's mantle (*Alchemilla mollis*), **163**
Landscaping with herbs, 24–25, 70
Laurus nobilis (bay laurel), 79, 104, **136**
Lavender (*Lavendula*), *6*, *13*, *18*, *76*, **164–165**, *210*
  for bee attraction, 73
  decorating rosemary tree with, 95
  drainage, 55
  flowers, 25
  Grilled Apricot Appetizer, 107
  height, 71
  in knot garden, *16*
  Lavendula x *intermedia* 'Provence', *13*, 165
  pruning, 53, 68
  sachets, 126
  in tea garden, 38, *39*
  for topiary, 29
  transplanting indoors, 87
  uses of, 77
  whipped cream, 109
Lawn, herbal, 24
Leaf drop, 88
Leaves, chopped, 65
Lemon balm (*Melissa officinalis*), 38, *39*, 58, 92, **166**
Lemongrass (*Cymbopogon citratus*), 92, 107, **167**
Lemon thyme, 38, *39*, 92
Lemon verbena (*Aloysia triphylla*), 92, 108, 113, **168**
Levisticum officinale (lovage), **170**
Licorice root (*Glycyrrhiza glabra*), **169**
Life cycles, herb plant, 7
Lighting, indoor, 87, 88–89

Light requirements, 20, 53
Liniment, 113
Linnaeus, Carl (Swedish botanist), 12
Lovage (*Levisticum officinale*), **170**
Lungwort, 12

M
Madagascar periwinkle (*Catharanthus roseus*), 14
Marigold (*Tagetes*), *25*, *57*, **171**
Marinades, 107, 124
Marjorum (*Origanum majorana*), 104, **172**
Markers, plant, 57
Marrubium vulgare (horehound), **161**
Matricaria recutita. *See* Chamomile
May basket, 99
Meat brushes, *106*, 107
Medicine, herbal, 8, 9, 11, 12, 14
Melissa officinalis. *See* Lemon balm
Mentha. *See* Mint
Mentha pulegium (pennyroyal), 23, 58, **181**
Microclimates, 210
Migraine headaches, feverfew for, 9
Milk thistle (*Silybum marianum*), **173**
Mint garden plan, 47
Mint juleps, 99
Mint (*Mentha*), *18*, *21*, **174–175**
  basil as flavor substitution, 109
  in containers, 26, *59*
  controlling spread of, 59
  for fragrant path, 23
  for herbal lawn, 24
  invasiveness of, 58–59
  lemon-mint water, 124
  mint juleps, 99
  peppermint foot soak, 113
  Stevia-Sweetened Mint Syrup, 109
  taste, 92
  transplanting indoors, 87
  uses of, 76

Misting plants, 91
Monarda didyma (bee balm), **138**
Mugwort (*Artemisia vulgaris*), **176**
Mulching herbs, 54, 61, 65, 84, 91
Mullein (*Verbascum thapsus*), *9*, *71*, **176**
Mustard (*Brassica juncea*, *B. nigra*), **177**
Myrica pensylvanica (bayberry), **137**
Myrrhis odorata (sweet cicely), **202**
Myrtle (*Myrtus communis*), 29, **177**

N–O
Names of herbs, 12
Naphthalene, 9
Native Americans, herb use by, 12
Nausea, basil for, 9
Nepeta cataria. *See* Catnip
Nepeta x *faassenii*. *See* Catmint
Ocimum. *See* Basil
Oregano (*Origanum vulgare hirtum*), **178**
  Chicken Breasts with Herbs, 114, *115*
  creeping varieties, 23
  in herb blends, 104
  thyme as flavor substitution, 109
  for topiary, 29
Origanum majorana (marjorum, sweet marjoram), 104, **172**
Origanum vulgare hirtum (oregano). *See* Oregano
Ornamental herbs, 70–71
Overplanting, 61
Overwatering, avoiding, 65, 91

P
Pairing herbs, 57
Panax quinquefolius (American ginseng), 12
Papaver somniferum (poppy), **186**

Parsley (*Petroselinum*), 21, *125*, **179**
   Chicken Breasts with Herbs, 114, *115*
   cilantro as flavor substitution, 109
   edging, *27*
   in herb blends, 104
   as insect host plant, 21
   mild flavor of, 125
   protecting from frost, *85*
   sowing in autumn, 62
   uses of, 76
   as walkway edger, 70
Patchouli (*Pogostemon cablin*), **180**
Pathways, 23, *28*, 61, 70
Pelargonium. See Scented geranium
Pennyroyal (*Mentha pulegium*), 23, 58, **181**
Pepper (*Capsicum annuum*), **182**
Peppermint foot soak, 113
Perennial herbs, 7
   bringing indoors, 87
   easy, *21*
   fall watering, 84
   invasive species, 58
   landscaping with, 70
   pairing with bulbs, 57
   planting, 54
   tender, 54
Perilla (*Perilla frutescens*), **183**
Pesto, 103, *103*, 107
Pest-repelling herbs, 9, 49
Pests, indoors, 91
Petroselinum. See Parsley
pH, soil, 53
Phenols, 9
Physic gardens, 14
Phytotherapy, 8
Pinching back, 68
Pineapple sage (*Salvia elegans*), **184**
Pine straw, 65
Place settings, 74
Planning. See also Garden plans
   a new bed, 60–61
      drawing a plan, 60
      marking your bed, 60
      number of plants, 61
      plant list, 60

      soil preparation, 61
      watering and mulching, 61
   next year's garden, 92, *93*
Planter, cast-stone or concrete, 44
Plant hardiness Zone map, 210–211
Planting
   depth of, 54
   fall, 62, 84
   herbs, 54–55
   knot garden, 17
   spring herbs, 62
Plant list, 60
Plectranthus (*Plectranthus*), **185**
Pogostemon cablin (patchouli), **180**
Pollinators, attracting, *72*, 73
Poppy (*Papaver somniferum*), **186**
Potager gardens, 14, *15*
Potting mix, 54
Powdery mildew, 91
Propagation, 78–79
Pruning, 68–69
   annual herbs, 62
   deadheading, 68
   pinching back, 68
   rosemary standard creation, 69
   shearing back, 68, *69*
   tools, 69
   topiary, 29
   woody herbs, 53
Purple angelica (*Archangelica gigas*), *131*
Pyrethrum, 9

R

Radish, pairing chervil with, *57*
Raised beds, *20*, 36–37, 40–41
Recipes
   Basil/Chai Punch, 113
   Chicken Breasts with Herbs, 114, *115*
   Cilantro Pesto, 107
   Cranberry-Sage Rolls, 121, *121*
   fall, 118–123
   Five-Spice Powder, 124
   Grilled Apricot Appetizer, 107
   Hearty Boys Cilantro-Garlic Ribs, *102*, 103

   Herb-Baked Olives, 118, *119*
   herb blends, 104
   Jamaican jerk seasoning, 125
   Lavender Whipped Cream, 109
   Lemon-Basil Pasta, 114, *114*
   Lemon Dill Sauce, 107
   Lemon-Dill Shrimp & Pasta, *116*, 117
   Lemongrass Kabobs, 107
   Lemon-Mint Water, 124
   Lemon Verbena Tisane, 113
   Orange-Fennel Marinade, 124
   Pumpkin, Barley, and Sage Soup, 122, *123*
   Rosemary Marinade, 107
   Rosemary Potato Frittata, 122, *122*
   Sage Stuffing, 118, *119*
   Sparkling Basil Lemonade, 117, *117*
   Spinach, Sorrel, and Orange Pesto, 103, *103*
   spring, 100–103
   Stevia-Sweetened Mint Syrup, 109
   Sugared Herb Flowers and Leaves, 108, *108*
   summer, 114–117
   Tarragon Dressing, 107
   Tarragon Yogurt Cheese, 100, *100*
   Thyme-Garlic Chicken Breasts, 100, *101*
   Thyme Potatoes Au Gratin, *120*, 121
   Verbena-Vanilla Sugar, 108
   winter, 124–125
Red barberry, *16*
Rhizomes, 58
Rhus coriaria (sumac), **202**
Rock gardens, *22*, 23
Roman chamomile (*Chamaemelum nobile*), 24, 38, *39*
Roofs, green, 26
Rooting cuttings, 79
Roots, health assessment, 54
Rosemary (*Rosmarinus officinalis*), 70, 76, *125*, **188–189**
   centerpiece, 95
   in containers, *27*
   decorating with lavender, 95

   drainage, 55
   hair rinse, 113
   for herbal lawn, 24
   herb-baked olives, 118, *119*
   in herb blends, 104
   indoors, 87, *124*
   marinade, 107
   prostrate, 23, 24
   Rosemary-Potato Frittata, 122, *122*
   standard, 69
   strong flavor of, 125
   topiary, 29, *29*
Rose (*Rosa*), *18*, *38*, *39*, *99*, **187**
Row covers, *85*
Rue (*Ruta graveolens*), 9, **190**
Rumex. See Sorrel
Runners, 58

S

Sachets, 8, 9, 126
Saffron (*Crocus sativus*), **191**
Sage (*Salvia officinalis*), *15*, *18*, *21*, *125*, **192–193**
   Cranberry-Sage Rolls, 121, *121*
   height, *71*
   'Icterina', 70, 193
   pairing with broccoli, *57*
   pruning, 53, 68
   Pumpkin, Barley, and Sage Soup, 122, *123*
   savory as flavor substitution, 109
   strong flavor of, 125
   stuffing, 118, *119*
   'Tricolor', 70, *71*, **193**
   as walkway edger, 70
Salad burnet (*Sanguisorba minor*), **194**
Salvia elegans (pineapple sage), **184**
Salvia officinalis. See Sage
Salvia sclarea (clary sage), 77
Sambucus (elderberry), **155**
Sandy soil, 20, *20*, 53
Sanguisorba minor (salad burnet), **194**
Santolina (*Santolina*), 29, *71*, **195**
Saponaria officinalis (soapwort), **198**

Satureja (savory), 104, 109, **196**
Sauces, 107
Savory centerpiece, 48
Savory (*Satureja*), 104, 109, **196**
Scent. See Fragrance
Scented geranium (*Pelargonium*), *21*, **197**
   in bouquets, 99
   in tea garden, 38, *39*
   for topiary, 29
   touch sense, appeal to, 92
Scrub, exfoliating, 126
Seasons
   fall, 78–87, 118–123
   spring, 52–65, 98–103
   summer, 66–77, 104–117
   winter, 88–95, 124–127
Seeding, self, 58
Seeds
   collecting, 68, 80
   growing herbs from, 52
   saving, 80–81
   seedy culinary herbs, 77
   sowing, 54
   storing, 80
Seed-saver organizations, 11
Selecting herbs, 52–53
Senses, herbs that appeal to, 92
Shade
   garden plan, 45
   ornamental herbs for, 71
   part shade/full shade, 53
Shearing back herbs, 68, *69*
Silybum marianum (milk thistle), **173**
Slopes, 23
Smell, theme garden for, 92
Soaker hose, 64–65
Soap, insecticidal, 91
Soapwort (*Saponaria officinalis*), **198**
Society garlic (*Tulbaghia violacea*), **198**
Soil
   amending, *20*, 21, 53
   for annual herbs, 20
   pH, 53
   potting mix, 54
   preparing new bed, 61
   in raised beds, 40, 41
   rooting in, 79

Sorrel (*Rumex*), 62, 103, *103*, **199**
Southernwood (*Artemisia abrotanum*), **199**
Spacing of plants, 61
Specialty herbs, 11
Species name, 12
Spice trade, 11
Spring, 52–65, 98–103
  controlling invasive herbs, 58–59
  dividing plants, 55
  entertainment ideas, *98, 99*
  harvesting spring herbs, 62
  pairing herbs, 57
  planning a new bed, 60–61
  planting herbs, 54–55
  recipes, 100–103
  selecting herbs, 52–53
  watering herbs, 64–65
Spritz, herbal, 113
St. John's Wort (*Hypericum perforatum*), **200**
Stachys officinalis (betony), **139**
Stairway planting, *28*
Staking, 71
Standard, rosemary, 69
Stevia (*Stevia rebaudiana*), 109, **201**
Stone planters, 44
Storing herbs
  dried herbs, 83
  seeds, 80
Strawberry, alpine (*Fragaria vesca*), 38, *39*
Stuffing, sage, 118
Sumac (*Rhus coriaria*), **202**
Summer, 66–77, 104–117
  culinary herbs, 76–77
  fertilizing herbs, 66–67
  flowering herbs, 77
  freezing herbs, *110,* 111
  harvesting herbs, 74–75
  herbal cooldowns for, *112,* 113
  herb blends, 104, *104*
  leafy herbs, 76
  ornamental herbs, 70–71
  pruning and deadheading, 68–69
  recipes, 114–117
  savory selections for, 107
  seedy herbs, 77
  sweetening with herbs, 108–109
  wildlife attraction, 72–73

Summer savory (*Satureja hortensis*), **196**
Sundial, 61
Sunlight, requirements for, 20, 53, 88
Sunset hyssop (*Agastache rupestris*), *39*
Sweet cicely (*Myrrhis odorata*), **202**
Sweetening with herbs, 108–109
Sweetgrass (*Hierochloe odorata*), **203**
Sweet marjoram (*Origanum majorana*), **172**
Sweet woodruff (*Galium odoratum*), **203**
Symphytum officinale (comfrey), **153**

T

Tabletop garden, 29
Tagetes (marigold), *25, 57,* **171**
Tanacetum parthenium (feverfew), 9, 12, *21,* **157**
Tanacetum vulgare. See Tansy
Tansy (*Tanacetum vulgare*), 9, *25, 71,* **204**
Tarragon (*Artemisia dracunculus* 'Sativa'), **205**
  chervil as flavor substitution, 109
  dressing, 107
  in herb blends, 104
  Tarragon Yogurt Cheese, 100, *100*
Taste, theme garden for, 92
Taste basket, 126, *127*
Tea, herbal, 38–39, 118
Tea garden plan, 38–39
Tender herbs, planting, 54
Tender perennials, 7
Teucrium chamaedrys (germander), *16,* 17, **159**
Theme gardens, 92
Thyme (*Thymus*), *18, 21, 76,* **206–207**
  for bee attraction, 73
  in checkerboard garden, *27*
  for covering benches, 29
  creeping varieties, 23
  for fragrant path, 23, *28*
  for herbal lawn, 24
  in herb blends, 104

  Jamaican jerk seasoning, 125
  oregano as flavor substitution, 109
  Thyme-Garlic Chicken Breasts, 100, *101*
  Thyme Potatoes Au Gratin, *120,* 121
  for topiary, 29
  transplanting indoors, 87
  uses of, 76
  wreath, 118, *119*
Tomato, *57, 66*
Tools, 69
Topiary, 29, *29, 94, 95*
Touch, theme garden for, 92
Transplanting herbs, 87
Tulbaghia violacea (society garlic), **198**

U–V

USDA plant hardiness Zone map, 210–211
Valerian (*Valeriana officinalis*), **208**
Varieties, 12
Vegetables, pairing herbs with, *56,* 57
Verbascum thapsus (mullein), 9, *71,* **176**
Vertical gardens, 23
Viola, pruning, 68

W–Z

Wagon wheel garden plan, 36–37
Walls, planting in, *22,* 23
Watering
  fall, 84
  grouping plants for, 64
  hand-watering options, 65
  indoor, *90,* 91
  low-maintenance options, 64–65
  new bed preparation, 61
  overwatering, avoiding, 65, 91
  spring, 64–65
Watering can, 65
Watering wand, 65
Weeds, 14, 58
Welcome home garden plan, 42–43
Wildlife attraction, 72–73
Window box garden plan, 46

Windowsill herb garden, 89
Wine-bottle bundles, 84
Winter, 88–95, 124–127
  decorating with herbs, *94, 95*
  garden gifts, 126, *127*
  lighting, 88–89
  pests and diseases, 91
  planning next year's garden, *92, 93*
  recipes, 124–125
  watering and humidifying, *90,* 91
Winter savory (*Satureja montana*), 125, *125,* **196**
Wood mulch, 65
Wormwood, 9
Wreath, 74, 118, *119*
Yarrow (*Achillea*), *25,* **209**
Zingiber officinale (ginger), **159**